Vertical Margins

Vertical Margins

MOUNTAINEERING AND THE LANDSCAPES OF NEOIMPERIALISM

Reuben Ellis

The University of Wisconsin Press

The University of Wisconsin Press
1930 Monroe Street
Madison, Wisconsin 53711

www.wisc.edu/wisconsinpress/

3 Henrietta Street
London WC2E 8LU, England

1   3   5   4   2

Printed in the United States of America

Library of Congress Cataloging-in-Publication Data
Ellis, Reuben J., 1955–
Vertical margins : mountaineering and the landscapes of
neoimperialism / Reuben Ellis.
240 pp.   cm.
Includes bibliographical references (p.   ) and index.
ISBN 0-299-17000-4 (cloth: alk. paper)
ISBN 0-299-17004-7 (pbk.: alk. paper)
1. Mountaineering — History.
2. Mountaineering expeditions — History.
3. Mountaineering in literature. I. Title.
GV199.89 .E44   2001
796.52'2 — dc21   2001000712

Contents

Dedicatory Preface

Hey boys — what kind of a time is this for a story? First, picture your mom driving up Highway 95 from Moscow, Idaho, flat out for Bonners Ferry. Mount St. Helens had blown up only a couple of hours before, and some guy who sure sounded like Orson Welles was on the radio saying that breathing volcanic ash may or may not mean certain death.

Two hundred miles to the north, I was having my own problems. Jerry Pavia and I and a bunch of Canadians were on the east ridge of Canada's Mount Loki in the Purcells. By sunset, two of us were late down-climbing the route. After a half hour of fumbling around in the dark, we finally admitted that either we were going to spend the night in the open on the ridge or die stupidly stepping off into space. It was a strange and lonely decision. This was supposed to be a one-day "alpine" gig — we had no real clothes, no food at all. It was cold. But there was more than that. Once we made up our minds to stay the night in the open, everything familiar suddenly seemed gone. We were truly *out there* in a place infinitely bigger, more dangerous, and more mysterious than we were.

Anyway, your mom was blasting along the extravagant distance of a western highway, through the close falling ash of the volcano. I was freezing in the infinite night of the bivouac. Mountains were shaping our lives. We were having second thoughts. But it really didn't matter — things were out of our hands.

This Canadian guy and I dropped off the crest of the ridge to get out of the wind, planted our ice axes in the snow, and tied ourselves in. For the next twelve hours we huddled in our rucksacks or stood jumping up and down. We talked — I don't remember about what. Time was the weird alchemy of physical exposure and the deep aloneness and personal *disper-*

sion that happens in the wilderness. When the eastern horizon finally showed up against the sky, it was rich and pure beauty. I found myself remembering the words of the Navajo *Night Chant?*

Beautifully my young men are restored to me
With beauty all around me, may I walk

I even think I heard them. By midmorning we were walking into camp, backslapping the friends who had pretty much assumed some disaster or another.

"I'm glad you're not dead," Jerry said. It was a nice thing to say.

Your mom made it too, heading for a streak of light on the horizon, the day as dark as night. But she can tell you about that. Anyway, by early afternoon both of us were racing home, from the north and from the south, each with our own proud new stories of adventure to blurt out. The ash kept coming down, no one went to work, and we played dominoes. Everybody listened to the radio, pretty sure the world was not coming to an end.

I wish for you boys wild places, aloneness, sunrises, survival, and stories. I dedicate this thing to my sons, Isaac and Daniel.

Acknowledgments

I would like to express my appreciation to David Simpson at Columbia University, whose friendly guidance and sense of quality inspired my work by example and direction. I would also like to thank, especially, my faithful friend George Moore and also Steve Swords, Anita Menking, Mike Preston, John Stevenson, Lee Krauth, and Skip Hamilton at the University of Colorado for a variety of cheering remarks at key moments. I would also like to acknowledge the English Department and the Graduate School at the University of Colorado at Boulder for their award of the invaluable George F. Reynolds Fellowship. I appreciatively remember the life and work of George F. Reynolds, whose emphasis on teaching as the hallmark of academic excellence has given me an important model. I also would like to thank the University of Colorado Center for British Studies, whose sponsorship supported my archive studies in Britain, contributing significantly to the success of this project. In this connection let me say thanks to Miss Buxton of the School of Geography, Oxford, Christine Kelly and the entire staff of the Royal Geographical Society Library, London, as well as the staff of the Alpine Club, London, for their help with my manuscript studies. I would also like to thank Hope College for the award of a Summer Research Grant, which allowed me to revise the manuscript, and my colleagues at Prescott College for their interest in my work. Thanks too to Mary Braun for her kind encouragement and to Polly Kummel for her detailed work on the manuscript. Finally, let me take this opportunity to express special gratitude to my dear friend Leslie Workman who so persistently told me, "Write the book, dear boy."

Vertical Margins

Introduction

The Cheerful Denial of Empire

I remain possessed by stories and obsessed with their complex uses.
— Stephen Greenblatt

THE ACCIDENT CAME SWIFTLY AND UNEXPECTEDLY ON A high Himalayan col on an afternoon in 1906. The British climber Tom Longstaff and his team were descending a 45-degree ice slope at high elevation. Longstaff was in the lead, facing down the precipitous ice, painstakingly carving steps with the adze of his ice axe, pausing between careful moves to fight for breath in the thin air. Suddenly, behind him, one member of the party slipped. Still roped together, the three climbers were one after another pulled off their feet. Within seconds they had been tossed to the ice and were sliding hopelessly out of control toward the glacier a thousand feet below. At the last possible moment, with the sheer ice cliff of the open bergschrund just below them, the picks of their ice axes finally found purchase and began to slow their fall. They came to rest, battered, breathless, and cut, in the last thin band of rocks before the edge. As Longstaff described it in an *Alpine Journal* essay a few months later, "The sensation was a very curious one" (221).

Curious indeed. When I came across Longstaff's story, although I was sitting in the comfortable reading room of the University of Colorado's Special Collections a safe distance from the mountains, my own memories raced back. I recalled a winter climb of Copper Creek Falls in northern Idaho when my partner peeled off an unprotected lead on the second pitch, his crampon points whistling past my head, and disappeared in a bloody streak over a bulge in the ice below. When the rope caught him and he hung there upside down with compound fractures in his legs, I know from talking to him later that the sensation of the fall was something significantly more than curious. I remembered too a particularly bad day on the upper reaches of Mount Rainier's Liberty Ridge when the wind, gusting to ninety miles an hour, blew me off my feet as I was planting my ice axe for the next step. Like Longstaff, with blinding suddenness I found myself sliding spread-eagle down a five-hundred-foot ice slope. *Shock* and *sheer terror* are the words I use to describe the experience. I'm not at all curious about it.

Of course, I am being too hard on Tom Longstaff, a genuine pioneer of early twentieth-century mountaineering. In reality, in the decades since 1906 we have come to expect from mountaineers the kind of cheerful denial of danger and risk that we read in the yellowed pages of his *Alpine Journal* essay. It is part of the image of the stiff-lipped climber. It reinforces the stereotype. It maybe even suggests the existence a highly coded and specific language for acknowledging and validating the danger and adventure of high altitude. The tribal lexicon of climbers. The history of mountaineering, from its "golden age" in the nineteenth century, as British gentlemen climbers followed guides into the Alps and then went on alone to explore the highest mountain ranges in the world, through its technology-driven expansion in the twentieth century, when sometimes all the limits and all the high routes seemed ready to fall, is laced with remarks like Longstaff's, extraordinarily understated or ruggedly stoic descriptions of adventure and desperation — events we all *know* are more exciting and frightening than the writer lets on.

Even when mountaineers occasionally become more effusive and expressive about their exploits, the result can be a comparable tendency toward obfuscation. Because something about it sounds so startlingly irrational, many people who don't even care much about mountaineering seem to remember George Mallory's cryptic explanation of why climbers take on Mount Everest — "Because it's there." Today, although we recognize that mountaineering has produced a great and extensive literature of its own, the way that the language can break down, constrict, or become cryptically loaded with implied meaning as climbers describe mountaineering and its philosophy continues in some ways to epitomize the climbing experience. So prevalent, in fact, is the tendency to play down the risk, the rewards, and, perhaps especially, the occasional horror of climbing that the laconic or sometimes mystifying voice of the climber has probably come to characterize for the general public the way that mountain climbers think about what they do and, as a result, probably makes them seem even more bizarre in their motivations than they might otherwise be. The public voice of the climber often seems eager to quickly dismiss irritating questions like "Why climb at all?" or "What does it feel like to hurtle head first down a sixty-degree ice field at fifty miles an hour?"

Today this public voice may be changing. Readers now respond to very different kinds of writing about travel and adventure. The era of what Paul Fussell calls "post-tourism" is now upon us. As the title of John Krich's 1984 travel narrative, *Around the World in a Bad Mood,* might suggest, post-tourism has produced a literature of ecotourism and *Lonely Planet* narratives that often distinguish travel and adventure travel by what a genuinely bad time the author is having. This, according to Fussell, represents "the tendency in contemporary travel writing toward annoyance, boredom, disillusionment, even anger" (755). Because of the unique challenges and hardships inherent in climbing, mountaineering narratives have from time to time put their own specific stamp on post-tourism, with the perhaps increasing tendency to freeze the heroic to emphasize the negative, mundane, or horrifying. Chris Jones's wonderfully useful and readable 1976 *Climbing in North America* enlivens the history of American climbing with anecdotes that often emphasize the all-too-human experiences of climbers. As Jones tells it, in 1967 Denny Eberl, Gray Thompson, Roman Laba, and Dave Seidman were confined to a high camp during a fourteen-day storm on the south face of Denali. Barely able to move farther than a few feet from the door of their tent, the climbers realized that they had been shitting in the same place where they scooped snow for meltwater when toilet paper showed up floating in the soup (342). Paul Theroux on a mountain ledge. Arguably, the depiction of the horrific side of climbing can be dated to Maurice Herzog's 1952 *Annapurna* and more recently in the work of David Roberts in, for example, *The Mountain of My Fear*. Both authors, in different ways, take on the issue of whether the great price that climbers pay, in human life and peace of mind, is worth the achievement of the summit.

Since the mid-1990s mountaineering literature has dramatically and pointedly taken aboard the aesthetics of post-tourism in the accounts of the brutal tragedies that have beset guided climbing on Mount Everest. The year 1996 was a bad one on Everest, with twelve climbers dying in the attempt to reach the summit. In May 1996 the shocking news came that on one day alone eight members of two professionally guided climbing parties on Mount Everest had died on the summit ridge and on the

South Col. We learned that one of the world's most respected climbing guides, New Zealander Rob Hall, stranded with a dying client on the upper reaches of the mountain, had calmly tried to reassure his wife, patched through by radio, even while he was already slipping away in hypothermia. An outpouring of commentary, personal narrative, and news coverage of the tragedy has shaped the events of May 1996 into a very public fable of risk and loss. Books by survivors, Jon Kraukaur's remarkable *Into Thin Air* and Anatoli Boukreev's *The Climb: Tragic Ambitions on Everest,* have elaborated the nightmare on the summit ridge and on the col from different perspectives and continue to find an eager reading audience. Boukreev's death on another climb only months after the publication of his book extends the sense of barely understood ruin and waste that emerges from the narrative. Hall's haunting radio call stays with me above all—laconic grace in the midst of high-altitude disaster. It resides uneasily alongside Kraukaur's conclusion that, finally, climbing "is life itself" (59). Climbers nod their heads perhaps. To others the remark sounds cryptic, inadequate, absurd. The television news ends and cuts to a Mountain Dew commercial. Actors playing bored and tight-lipped extreme athletes mutter "Climbed that . . . skied that." Although the highly publicized 1996 Everest death toll dropped to a more modest eight in 1997, and has stayed lower since, the armchair climbing world continues to sense that mountaineers are concealing some Great Unspoken. The laconic register has changed, but it has not disappeared.

Don't get me wrong. Despite my partial acceptance of the 1990s fetish for dialogue and communication-as-therapy, I'm not immune to the old tendency to expect climbing writers to be wonderfully suggestive inarticulates. I continue to find a certain beauty in the terse aesthetic of mountaintop register-book writing—brief, scrawled entries that say things like "7/95—Had good weather to the summit up the East Ridge" or "J. Browne, Kamloops B.C.—great views above the clouds." Sometimes saying too much can be simply frightful—as in the climbers' hut at the base of Mount Shasta when I found a register book polluted with a five-page, illustrated, spiritual narrative about some guy's encounter near the summit with bearded, robed patriarchs, exiles from the lost continent of Mu. The standards for New Age freakoids, I told myself, must certainly be different than those for *real* climbers.

But as I thought about all this—the relationship between actual mountain experience, its motivations, and the language used to express it—a couple of questions arose and would not go away. If mountaineering stories tend to mute the character of adventure, exploit, and sometimes appalling risk inherent in the experience, what else are they not telling us? What else resides within the Great Unspoken at the apparent spiritual heart of this modern sport? I dug deeper into the archives, and this book emerged as one answer to these persistent questions. The search took me back to Longstaff's era, an exciting and complex period in the history of mountaineering. Although climbing was originally associated with the spiritual and aesthetic transport of romantic poets, by the 1860s it had become the leisure sport of gentlemen and had been tugged in the direction of scientific investigation. By the 1890s, as British and other European climbers began to push their expeditions beyond the Alps into the Caucasus Mountains and deeper into Asia, North America, and Africa, climbing became more intricately interwoven with the motivations of genuine exploration — a simultaneously geophysical and political project.

What I present here cannot be said to be a thorough literary history of mountaineering from the late 1890s to the 1930s, but its focus is within that history, based on the premise that what mountaineers actually say about climbing suggests a much broader historical context than the immediacy of rock, ice, and individual and group endeavor. Looking closely at three books written about climbing, Halford Mackinder's 1899 manuscript, "Mount Kenya" (finally published in 1991 as *The First Ascent of Mount Kenya*), Annie Smith Peck's 1911 *A Search for the Apex of America,* and John Noel's 1927 *Through Tibet to Everest,* I am suggesting that, behind the lingering romantic ideals of the spirituality of individual adventure in the mountains, we can find a somewhat less pure side to climbing and, in the case of early twentieth-century mountaineering, sometimes an intriguing complicity with what has been called the neoimperialism of the era. My purpose is not a cynical one. As a climber myself, I have no reason to debunk the exploits and achievements of the men and women who head up the trail. What I think this history demonstrates is something that many climbers already take seriously — that climbing mountains is a complex mixture of individual motivations and cultural contexts, that it is far more than the antics of driven adrenalin junkies. It has its place in history. Today, as the climbing community debates the future of what we have come to think of again as purely a sport, a look back to an earlier period in the history of mountaineering might provide some perspective. We might better understand the increasing commercialization of mountaineering, the marketing of its technology and fashion, the sale of packaged summit experiences, and the realization that climbers are sometimes a special interest group in competition with other interests for the political disposition of public lands. The freedom of the hills always has a context.

Even through the understated voice of Longstaff, we might recognize that mountaineering in the early twentieth century was more than simply sensation, curious or otherwise. It was instead a topic for debate, an endeavor in which meaning, motivation, and end were often contested and in need of definition. In a playful 1925 *Alpine Journal* essay exploring the current status of British mountaineering, Alfred Denis Godley, a mountaineer and a poet, suggested a great deal about how his contemporaries thought about mountains. Godley observed that the dean of St. Paul's Cathedral, responding to the energy and popularity of mountaineering, had recently lamented that for most climbers, a mountain is merely "a sort of greased pole to be swarmed up" (quoted in Irwin, 377). In fact, the dean had taken it a step further, calling for what he regarded as a return to the roots of the climbing experience in a more philosophical, spiritual, or "meditational" attitude about climbing mountains.[1] The thoughtful clergyman's criticism, which appeared in the 1920s, was clearly reactionary. Godley quickly responded: "In this matter of meditation I cannot help thinking that the Dean demands too much of human nature — which is, after all, in its blind groping fashion, pursuing the Ultimate Good, but even in the mountains finds itself hampered by mortal weaknesses" (quoted in Irwin, 377).

Godley's tongue-in-cheek tolerance of human spiritual frailty goes a long way to suggest important aspects of the status of mountaineering during the early decades of the twentieth century. Implicit in Godley's remarks, in fact, is a recognition of how mountains, by 1925, were often understood in a context very different from the more traditional symbolic and literary associations that had defined mountains in terms of spiritual quest, the summits of John Milton's high places, Edmund Burke's icons of fear, or Percy Bysshe Shelley's infinite silences. As had its issues since 1863, the issue of the *Alpine Journal* in which Godley's essay appeared gave testimony that the nonfiction first-person climbing narrative had significantly replaced the romantic poem as an accepted and authoritative literary vehicle for recording and making sense of mountain geography and experience. Furthermore, it implicitly defined an audience of mountaineers and other more sedentary mountain enthusiasts cognizant of this specific kind of writing as, in its own way, a conventional and appropriate form.

The dean of St. Paul's may have had a difficult time, for example, imagining Tom Longstaff's laconic "curious sensation" coming from the mouth of Moses, high on Sinai. An important and persistent motif within Western cultural traditions, after all, encourages a somewhat more profound association between mountains and spiritual experience. Linked by story and symbolism to divinity and inspiration, such mountains as Ararat, Sinai, Pisgah, Olympus, and Parnassus figure prominently in Western notions of the sacred and tend to associate mountains with significantly more than simply geographical landscapes. It is no coincidence that Martin Luther King Jr. galvanized the civil rights movement of the 1960s by having "been to the mountain top" of idealized racial equality nor that in the 1980s Ronald Reagan sought again to breathe rhetorical life into the Puritan John Winthrop's 1630 vision of America as a "City on a Hill."

Although Godley didn't say so, the dean of Saint Paul's also might have had something of the romantic in him. Readers of literature who have enjoyed their romanticism from Wordsworth to Ruskin are particularly conditioned to regard mountains, when they appear in a literary context, as geographical touchstones to abstraction and epiphany. The dean's remarks suggest not only the biblical and Greco-Roman associations of mountains with the divine but the newer "spilled religion," to use T. E. Hulme's famous phrase, of romanticism. Edmund Burke's 1757 *Philosophical Enquiry into the Origins of Our Ideas of the Sublime and Beautiful* associates mountainscapes with an intensity of psychological effect a bit stronger than the "curious." Specifically, for Burke it is the kind of sublime *terror* prompted by the strange vertical environment of the Alps that is most capable of producing what the first-century Greek philosopher Longinus had called *hypsos*, ecstasy or "transport."[2] This became the foundation of an entire aesthetic of mountains. As romantic writers elaborated, interpreted, and transformed this notion of the sublime, it developed into a literature that represented mountains in the palette of immaterial spirituality. Marjorie Hope Nicolson's important 1959 study, *Mountain Gloom and Mountain Glory,* a discussion of how romantic aesthetics incorporated the imagery of mountains, argues that mountains are "not only central to descriptive poetry but almost as sacred as Sinai" (viii).

True enough. Wordsworth's description of Simplon Pass remains one of the central moments in English romanticism, and the crags of Coleridge and Shelley are cast in even more exuberant language.[3] In "Hymn before Sunrise" Coleridge imagines a mountain in the somewhat conventional intermediate position between heaven and earth but, in a vertiginous gesture at the end of the poem, goes further, giving the mountain actual voice to bridge the gap, to speak on behalf of the world below:

Rise like a cloud of incense from the Earth!
Thou kingly Spirit throned among the hills,
Thou dread ambassador from Earth to Heaven,
Great Hierarch! tell thou the silent sky,
And tell the stars, and tell yon rising sun
Earth, with her thousand voices, praises God. (Perkins, 435)

Significantly less reassuring are the final lines of Shelley's "Mont Blanc," which conclude with the poet's inability to be sure that he can read meaning into the unfamiliar mountain wilderness:

And what were thou, and earth, and stars, and sea,
If to the human mind's imaginings
Silence and solitude were vacancy? (Perkins, 970)

Shelley fashions a distant and silent mountainscape into an unsettling geography of indeterminacy and sublimely ultimate uncertainty. What if the mountain, in all its awe-inspiring majesty, finally means nothing? What if it just *is*?

A handful of writers in the American nature-writing tradition have embraced Shelley's stunning speculation, and philosophers of deep ecology have warned us against our anthropocentric perspective on the natural world. Edward Abbey, the novelist and essayist of the American West, for example, looks out over the high mesas and canyons of Arizona and insists "there is nothing out there. Nothing at all. Nothing but the desert. Nothing but the silent world" (22). Despite these relatively isolated voices, Western culture has largely rejected the idea that physical geography is devoid of philosophical or other kinds of meanings and has been persistent in enthusiastically, even exuberantly, investing nature with meanings, often conflicting and overlapping. Modern industrial and global society takes multiple courses with the natural world, of course, on one hand riding roughshod over it, reducing it to mere resource, sometimes constructing it as a political symbol, even within the politics and rhetoric of environmentalism. All the while society uses the natural world metaphorically in association with other ideas in the full range of popular culture constructed by advertising and market development. The television image of an emission-spewing sports utility vehicle, for example, wheeling easily up that mountain road, splashing lightly through the desert creek, drives to the heart of America's vision of itself.

But long before Henry Ford began selling cars or Mount Shasta began lighting up movie screens for Paramount, the investment of mountains with meaning had taken thoroughgoing shape in our tradition of celebrating nature in visionary poetry. Whether mountains are cast as Coleridge's ambassadors to God, or Shelley's rocky, snow-clad mutes, it would be shortsighted to discount their significance and vitality as symbolic landscapes. Given the tendency of modern industrial society to minimize the importance of the natural world, associating mountains with the sacred or with their own intrinsic value can help affirm healthy relationships between humans and place, relationships that need, now more than ever, to be nurtured. Mountaineers, by the very nature of their craft, have often been regarded with the same sort of awe and sometimes suspicion that we afford our poets and visionaries. The title of Laurence Mikel Vause's study of mountaineering narratives, "Voices of Madmen," suggests how romantic conceptions of the mountains as a spiritual landscape, conventionalized as they may be today in cartoon images of gurus perched on summit crags, continue to shape the way that many readers expect to see mountains depicted in literature and condition our attitudes about the mountaineers who write it.[4]

There is no mistake, however, that the dean of Saint Paul's was correct in noticing that modern writers, in addition to bringing with them a lingering heritage of romantic mountains evocative of the sublime, had in the 1920s taken to very different ways of representing mountains. Alongside the nineteenth-century romantic tradition grew another tradition of representing mountains in terms of sport, science, and, finally, exploration.[5] The Caucasus Mountains were the first region beyond the Alps extensively penetrated by European mountaineers. Douglas Freshfield in his 1900 *Exploration of the Caucasus* reveals the conjunction of sport, science, and exploration that animated mountaineering:

Caucasian explorers, if they desire to obtain any general sympathy, must revert to the practice and methods of our founders — of men like Mr. John Ball, who has left in the *Alpine Guide* an invaluable example of how much one traveler can see and do for his own pleasure and the profit of his fellows, and Mr. Adams Reilly, who did so much for mountain cartography. (quoted in Irving, 53–54)

From the time that the Alpine Club began publishing its *Alpine Journal* in 1863, a body of narratives began to grow that portrayed mountain space in conspicuously concrete and strenuously nonmetaphysical terms.

At first these were primarily accounts of the leisure pastimes of men of independent means and — largely as a result of the early Alpine fieldwork of scientists like Jean Louis Rodolphe Agassiz, Pierre Jean Edouard Desor, and James David Forbes — occasions for reporting experimental investigation.[6] Mountaineering thus developed its own literature, very distinct in its concerns from the philosophical, aesthetic, and poetic concerns of Burke, Wordsworth, Shelley, Coleridge, Turner, Ruskin, or any of the other figures whom we conventionally associate with the artistic representation of mountains. In Wordsworth's *The Prelude,* Simplon Pass in the Alps is a point of entrance to the "types and symbols of Eternity" (218). Writing in the first issue of the *Alpine Journal,* thirteen years after the 1850 edition of *The Prelude,* H. B. George, however, saw a radically different Simplon Pass. At the height of *his* version of enthusiasm, George merely referred to the pass as "this greatest of Alpine roads" (207) and, with not a trace of what would conventionally be regarded as aesthetic evaluation, went on to point out empirical and geographical information, specifically, that, as not previously reported, he could see Monte Rosa (then a popular focus of mountaineering interest) from Simplon. The sublime was fading within the ascendancy of sport and recreation.

By the beginning of the twentieth century, mountains as a subject to be written about had already been recognized as not merely the province of the poet and novelist, the sportsman, and the scientist but also, increasingly, of that rather ambiguously defined figure of Western history and ideology, the explorer. Casual references to mountaineering as a form of exploration appeared in the literature of the Alpine Club and Royal Geographical Society from the 1850s, but only with the extensive expansion of climbing out of the European Alps later in the century did the term *exploration,* as applied to mountaineering, take on the same meaning that it has when applied to other types of exploration. Whereas exploration had formerly tended to be associated with other geographical regions and phenomena — rivers, coastlines, basins, deserts, the Arctic — by the 1890s mountains were more noticeably and categorically being added to the list of open questions pursued by exploration.

This shift has implications for the way that mountains were represented to the reading public. Exploration writing, as full of adventure or muted by understatement as it might be, is inherently representational, empirical, technological, statistical, and often political in its controlling assumptions and style. Explorers simply spend more time writing about food supplies, frozen toes, and compass bearings along the margins of the empire than they do celebrating the sublimity of the eternal. As mountaineering became exploration in the modern period and increasingly found its way into technical and scientific journals that published exploration literature, the ideology associated with exploration came to life within narrative accounts of climbing, just as the romantic sublime of wild geography and imagination did in romantic literature more than a century before. What Fussell in his *Abroad: British Literary Traveling between the Wars* calls "the athletic, paramilitary activity of exploration" that "ends in knighthoods for Sir Francis Drake and Sir Aurel Stein and Sir Edmund Hillary" (39) came to supplant the reflections of the poet among the crags of the Lake District or the glaciers of Mont Blanc. The sociologist Judith Adler calls travel and exploration a means of "worldmaking" (quoted in Stowe, 1). They are tools for defining, delimiting, and understanding geographical space from the perspective of the traveler or explorer, and the meaning that travelers or explorers construct for individuals inevitably participates in larger, cultural constructs of ideology. Nature is converted to culture; world making mythologizes the landscape. In particular, the stories that explorers tell were empowered during the late nineteenth and early twentieth centuries to recreate the world through the assumptions of priority, superiority, and destiny at play in the empire building then occurring around the globe. The thorough adoption of mountaineering narratives into the larger canon of exploration writing during the 1890s, and thence into the realm of politics and empire, represents the transition of mountaineering narratives to their own modern period. Postcolonial theorists and writers, Edward Said most notable among them, have challenged us in the early twenty-first century to look at history by connecting culture and empire, geography and literature.[7] Bringing mountaineering into this larger network of relationships is the task that I pursue in this book.

As a background to the mountaineering ventures of Mackinder, Peck, and Noel, chapter 1 first describes the state of geographical knowledge and the extent of exploration as this modern era began. It suggests how European and Euro-American geographical theory, previous exploration, and cartography set the stage for modern exploration, and it highlights the principal remaining geographical problems. Second, chapter 1 describes in more detail the paradigm shift that I just suggested — how, beginning in the 1890s, mountains and mountaineering were increasingly associated not merely with spiritual symbolism, literary and romantic settings, the sporting lives of English gentlemen, and the field investigations of pure science but with modern geographical exploration, including the economic and political contexts that exploration assumed during the later stages of European empire building and the onset of the "American Century." Third, chapter 1 suggests how the so-called Royal Geographical Society style became a conventional format for describing mountaineering in the geographical journals of the day and how the society's published manual for explorers, *Hints to Travellers,* edited by Back, Collinson, and Galton, encouraged, codified, and enforced a style of mountaineering writing that implicitly addressed the strategic concerns of Britain and the United States during the late nineteenth and early twentieth centuries as these nations pursued international policies of consolidating and maintaining both economic and political empire — the phenomenon that historians have labeled neoimperialism.

Chapter 2 focuses on "Mount Kenya: Being the Narrative of a Vacation Journey in Equatorial Africa," Sir Halford Mackinder's account of his 1899 climb of Africa's second-highest peak, a climb that was not repeated for more than thirty years. Much more commonly known as a geographer than as a mountaineer, Mackinder continues to be recognized for the germinal role he went on to play in the foundation of geography as an academic discipline and as one of the most influential geopolitical theorists of the early twentieth century. The young Mackinder likely conceived of his Mount Kenya climb as a way of establishing a reputation, and his expedition is sometimes referred to as the only climbing party in history that literally had to fight its way to a mountain. Regardless of whether this claim is borne out in fact, Mackinder's narrative engages a broad range of issues revolving around individual ambitions within evolving academic institutions, British colonial politics in East Africa, and racial and cultural difference. Interestingly, Mackinder's book was not published when it was written and until 1991 existed only in manuscript form in the archives of the School of Geography at Oxford.

Chapter 3 shifts emphasis from the already established British colonial empire to the era of the emergence of the United States as a world power following its brief war with Spain. This chapter examines Annie Smith Peck's 1911 *A Search for the Apex of America,* a narrative account of her several climbing expeditions to Peru and Bolivia shortly after the turn of the century, including her first ascent of 22,200-foot Huascarán. An enthusiastic feminist, Peck was one of a number of female mountaineers during the suffrage period who unfurled banners reading VOTES FOR WOMEN on mountain summits. Her narrative effects a fascinating conjunction of mountaineering with gender and property relations while using the occasion of her exploration to promote Yankee investment in South America.

Chapter 4 moves the discussion forward to the period between the world wars and to John Baptist Noel's 1927 *Through Tibet to Everest,* his account of the first three British expeditions to Mount Everest in the early 1920s. As official cameraman and filmmaker to the 1922 and 1924 expeditions, Noel had a unique perspective on mountaineering, wishing not so much to reach the summit as to film someone doing so. His narrative suggests how the evolving documentary film movement, and perhaps Western technology in general, interacted with the British imperial posture in central Asia in the closing days of the Raj, with some very unexpected results in the case of Noel's film work.

Finally, a brief epilogue suggests closure for the association of mountain exploration and empire that influenced mountaineering during the early twentieth century by focusing on the contrasting perspectives of two twentieth-century dramas that depict mountaineering, W. H. Auden and Christopher Isherwood's 1937 allegorical tragedy, *The Ascent of F6,* and Patrick Meyer's 1982 one-act play, *K2.* Although more clearly identifiable as "literature" than as "exploration narratives" per se, these two plays, as works reflective of their times, illustrate how mountaineering has now largely abandoned the imperial implications it flirted with during the early decades of the twentieth century for the more traditional aims and ideology of personal achievement, more specifically, for the uneasy relationship between the challenge of sport, the commercialization of mountaineering, and the single-minded goal — and hefty price tag — of bagging the trophy ascent.

From the context of class distinction as a gentleman's sport and a venue for individual achievement, mountaineering in the early twentieth century fashioned for itself a degree of collective and imperial symbolism and sometimes found itself in often inadvertent partnership with international affairs. Today it has largely set this role aside to reimmerse itself in a peculiar late twentieth-century mixture of its original links to sport, romanticism, and spirituality, perhaps even a commercial, and, perhaps, I am tempted to suggest, even as a "mainstreamed" parody of its original roots. Whether this will prove to be a one-time shift shaped by specific historical factors or will come to represent a stage in a cycle to be repeated with the development of new circumstances yet unforeseen remains an enticingly open question. Perhaps contemporary mountaineering is indeed a function of today's market-driven internationalism, increasingly a creature of a global economy and consumer adventure. In any case, by reading about mountaineering within the context of history and literature, we have an occasion to better understand that the writings of our mountain climbers, often relegated to dusty volumes of arcane journals or exhibited as the occasional and short-lived best-seller, have a justifiable place within broader discussions of those ideas that shaped the twentieth century, for better or worse.

1

Where the Map Is Still Blank

It is permitted to the geographer, no doubt, to have
hypotheses; it is the task of the explorer to go and see.
—J. C. Beaglehole

THE INSCRIPTION CARVED IN THE TRUNK OF THE ANCIENT
tree was only barely legible. The letters had become so indistinct, so
overgrown with bark, that Robert Codrington had to bend closer
to read them:

Dr. Livingstone
May 4, 1873
. . . za mniasere
. . . chopere

The tree itself seemed to be in no better condition. One whole side of the
trunk had rotted, and borers were well at work near the ground. The
populous town that had once surrounded the tree was largely deserted. "It
is not all pleasure, this exploration," David Livingstone had written a few
days before his death. As Codrington, deputy administrator of the British
South Africa Company's Fort Jameson in Northern Rhodesia, viewed the
scene, it was not even all *apparent*.

This had not always been so. Nineteenth-century England and Amer-
ica had been captivated by accounts of the journeys of Livingstone in the
Zambezi basin and around Lake Mweru. When rumors had come from
Africa in 1871 that the missionary-explorer had died, and Henry Morton

Stanley found him for the *New York Herald* at Ujiji on Lake Tanganyika, Stanley's famous question — "Dr. Livingstone, I presume?" — became a motto to conjure by in the public imagination, a point of transport to a penny press world of the exotic, the heroic, the faraway. When Livingstone died of dysentery at the thriving village of Old Chitambo near the Lake Bangweulu swamp in 1873, his heart was buried beneath the huge tree in the center of the village, even as his embalmed body was carried to the coast at Zanzibar and on to interment at Westminster Abbey. The burial scene in Old Chitambo — the anguish on the faces of the loyal followers, the suitably exotic throng of Africans, the menacing forest backdrop — became the stuff of engravings and lithographs, a living and contemporary moment so frequently reproduced that it became for a time the latest icon of the British Dying Well Abroad.

On May 10, 1900, however, when Codrington visited Old Chitambo about twenty-six years after Livingstone's death, his comments about Livingstone's burial tree suggest a somewhat different view. For the practical Codrington the tree had become a valuable historical artifact of a recently bygone epoch of exploration and adventure, now in danger of being lost to the elements. "There was also a risk of the inscription being carried away by private persons for the sake of speculation," Codrington wrote in a paper to the Royal Geographical Society, so "having taken steps to preserve the inscription from damage," he continued, "I immediately cut down the tree, and sawed it off above and below the inscription" (229). As his porters used adzes to hollow out the trunk section that included the inscription for transport to England, Codrington directed others to raise an iron telegraph pole where the tree had once stood. As he remembered it later: "The lonely spot where Livingstone died twenty-six years ago appears to me to be appropriately marked by this symbol of European occupation, bringing with it the blessings of peace and the safety of life and property to the wretched people amongst which his last days were spent" (230).

Codrington's telegraph pole was indeed an appropriate symbol of the European presence in the colonies. Postcolonial scholars have successfully established, of course, that behind Codrington's optimistic, self-congratulatory, and ethnocentric rhetoric of imperial progress lay a much more complex and disturbing sequence of historical events. But for those of us who read the history of geographical exploration and the narratives of those who conducted that exploration, the iron pole serves as a symbol of another, more limited, sort. In May 1900 the tide of war was beginning to shift against the Boers in favor of the British. Codrington was in Old

Chitambo to solidify the control of Cecil Rhodes's British South Africa Company over the area. The grid of European colonies established after the Berlin West Africa Conference of 1884 lay over Africa like a net, and the contest between Germany, Portugal, and Belgium for south-central Africa complicated Rhodes's dream of spanning Africa by rail and telegraph line. Somehow the mystery of Livingstone and his sanctification as a lost imperial saint in the wilderness already was beginning to seem like something from an earlier era, a heroic age rapidly being replaced by the world-shrinking power of communication, the technological grip of empire solidifying the unknown. The telegraph pole suggests a historical fault line between two ages. It defines European and Euro-American exploration in the twentieth century as different from that which had gone before, even as it situates the exploration in ongoing events.

Codrington's story, of course, finds its setting in the forests, not the mountains, of Africa. Yet it suggests how, at the turn of the century, the modern exploration narrative, traversing a variety of geographies, often found itself inevitably involved in the solidification of empire. Twelve hundred miles to the northeast of Old Chitambo, Mount Kenya and the Ruwenzori range also fell, plotted on the map of imperial political space, within British East Africa, Uganda, and the Belgian Congo. As the notion of mountain exploration and its narration developed during the modern period, it took aboard exploration literature's clear reflection of its location at the nexus of contemporary imperial events. More than most literatures, therefore, these narratives are crucially and primarily defined by their historical moment, that is to say, the era of what has been called the new imperialism. During this era both the well-seasoned imperial powers like Britain and France, as well as the more novice United States, gradually shifted from acquiring new territories to consolidating control of the overseas conquests that they had already made, increasingly through economic means.

Accompanying these developments were a renewed sense of rivalry between imperial powers and an increasingly abstract political symbolism, often expressed in terms of and embodying attitudes about geography.[1] The transition made by modern mountaineering exploration literature into its own identity, distinct from both earlier exploration literature and earlier mountain literature, was signaled in a peculiar way in a 1938 *Alpine Journal* narrative by J. R. Jenkins in which he described the first British expedition to the Caucasus after the Russian Revolution. Jenkins's climbing narrative is richly laced with political content as its asides describe Soviet life and as it suggests political "barriers" (12) to mountaineering that sometimes were as formidable as topographical ones. This political commentary attains an interesting historical focus when Jenkins offhandedly mentions the seemingly rather unimportant arrival of one of his climbing partners in camp "with a Doctor-Livingstone-I-Presume gesture" (18). This once-famous moment in the literature of nineteenth-century exploration as the romantic missionary-explorer and the intrepid journalist meet can be amusingly trivialized as a twentieth-century mountaineer-explorer acknowledges a changing geopolitical globe as the backdrop to his climbing. In these terms Jenkins's narrative is clearly the literature of Codrington's telegraph pole.

During the 1890s the exploration of the physical world by Europeans and Euro-Americans continued apace with the sense of newness and progress that characterized the era. One real challenge of writing about exploration narratives comes in not forgetting that the entire notion of exploration and discovery is a very artificial, naturalized cultural construct rather than something we can take at face value. Henry David Thoreau noted in his account of his ascent of Maine's Mount Ktaadn in *The Maine Woods* that the "simple races" do not explore and that Europeans have conspicuously regarded places that they have not visited as "unexplored" (quoted in Irwin, 327). So although great tracts of land were thoroughly known by their indigenous inhabitants during the period, to Westerners knowledge of terrain was authentic only when it came into the possession of the Royal Geographical Society and other explorers who defined progress and expansion as their own.

Certainly, the broad outlines of geographical knowledge had already been established; no continents were left to discover, and even some of the most persistent mysteries and objectives of European curiosity, some dating to Ptolemy and Pliny, had been recently satisfied. The sources of the Nile and the Niger had been located. The Sahara, the interior of Australia, and Greenland had been traversed. A. E. Nordenskiöld had forced his way through the Northeast Passage, and the feasibility of the Northwest Passage had become largely a mute point. Mount Everest had been triangulated as Earth's highest point.

Yet as the twentieth century began, extensive areas of earth's surface remained "unexplored" in the minds of Europeans and Americans. Westerners still had not visited or mapped huge interior tracts of all continents except Europe. They only partially understood the configuration of the Arctic, and no one had reached the North Pole. The Antarctic, beyond a few scattered landfalls, remained almost a complete mystery. No one had climbed any of the earth's eight-thousand-meter peaks. Even the Alps, which Sir Leslie Stephen (Virginia Woolf's father) had labeled "the playground of Europe" as early as 1870, belied this tame sobriquet with the looming and ostensibly "unclimbable" Eigernordwand and Grandes Jorasses.

Unquestionably, the world of the modern era was geographically incomplete. The expansionist exploration that had served the cause of European colonialism and commerce throughout the nineteenth century was gradually shifting toward geographical investigation rather than discovery. But exploration still carried with it — in its ideology, organization, and even terminology — the impetus of imperial conquest, which in many ways reached its peak during the early years of the twentieth century. The first International Polar Year, 1882, seemed to signal the beginning of cooperative scientific exploration, but as late as 1935 Lincoln Ellsworth claimed more than 400,000 square miles of Antarctica for the United States with the iconic flag-planting bravado of a fifteenth-century explorer. The airplane, goose-down clothing, and bottled oxygen extended the range of explorers as the twentieth century added expanding technology to the well-tested mixture of national interests and field research developed by their predecessors.

In 1895 the well-known British mountaineer whose name has become almost synonymous with late nineteenth-century mountaineering, Albert Frederick Mummery, published *My Climbs in the Alps and the Caucasus*.[2] In it he observed: "Though the faithful climber is, in his essence, a thoroughly domesticated man and rarely strays from his own home, the Alps, a spirit of unrest occasionally takes hold upon him and drives him forth to more distant regions" (quoted in Irwin, 153). It is ironic, of course, that later in the same year Mummery would disappear off Nanga Parbat in the Himalayas while following that spirit, but of equal interest is that Mummery conveys in this remark a sense of the ambiguity regarding the status of mountaineering as a form of exploration that predominated as the twentieth century began.

Usually considered more sport than exploration before the 1890s, generally represented in literature in terms of abstract philosophical or aesthetic principles rather than scientific investigation or geopolitical aims, mountaineering before the modern period was not often associated with the notion of exploration. Gradually, however, as Europeans extended the margins of both their exploration and their cultural hegemony during the nineteenth century, a once conceptually limitless terra incognita shrank to mere "blank spaces on the map," as Clements Markham, president of the Royal Geographical Society, put it in 1893 ("Present Standpoint," 481). Many of those blanks were mountains. The alpine environment proved the most resistant of all the globe's regions to exploration, frustrating what Thoreau saw (in *The Maine Woods*) as the peculiarly European insistence that you have to get to the summit in order to understand the significance of the mountain. Thus mountains increasingly came to embody a sense of "lateness," representing the last places left for Western explorers to discover and traffic. In modern mountaineering narratives we can read an almost nostalgic residue of explorations past. Beginning in the late 1880s, the traveler and writer George Kennan roused American concern about the exile and imprisonment of political opponents of the Russian czar in a series of *Century* articles, "Siberia and the Exile System," based on his travels in Russian east Asia. Kennan also had a soft spot in his heart for untrammeled open spaces. As early as 1883, Kennan made this baleful lament in his narrative called "A Journey through Southeastern Russia":

It is becoming more and more difficult every year for the adventurous traveler and the enterprising student of geography to find a new field for exploration and study — or even a field about which anything new can be said. The blank spaces in the old maps of the world, which used to excite curiosity and stimulate the imagination with their inscription "unexplored" have one by one been filled up with prosaic topographical details. The civilized and semi-civilized parts of the globe from North Cape to the Cape of Good Hope, and from Alaska to the Strait of Magellan, have been overrun by an army of tourists, and described in a multitude of books; and even the "antres vast and deserts idle" of Asia and Africa, which served so long as hunting grounds for the poetic imagination, have lost their mystery, and their inhabitants, the Anthropophagi, instead of devouring the unwary traveler and leaving his bones to bleach on the sands as in the good old days, now recognize him as "cookie," welcome him with mercenary smiles and take coupon meal-tickets for board. The world has grown small and familiar even since the beginning of the present century, and the traveler of these days, unless he is prepared to attempt the North Pole, or plunge into the wildest and least accessible recesses of the great Asiatic mountain ranges, must be content to glean in fields where all the high geographical honors have already been reaped. (289)

Although Kennan's view of closing world frontiers is a bit clouded by sentimentality, it does serve to point out how mountains were coming to be seen as some of the "last best places" left to explore. The perception that undiscovered regions were increasingly rare, coupled with a tradition of climbing bred in the Alps, fueled the desire to transgress the vertical margins of the unknown.

At the same time, however, the exploration of the poles consistently provided the standard of challenge and significance by which all exploration was measured. Both before and after the Cook–Peary controversy of 1909 about the discovery of the North Pole, as well as Roald Amundsen's historic journey to the South Pole in late 1911 and Robert Falcon Scott's tragic death on the return from the Pole in early 1912, the poles were an index by which mountaineers evaluated the high altitude "arctic" conditions they encountered. Writing in 1911 on the assumption that the North Pole had already been reached and that Scott's and Amundsen's race for the South Pole would soon end in success, the mountaineers Herschel Parker and Belmore Browne, however, hinted at the growing significance of mountaineering as they shifted the standard of achievement beyond polar exploration. Mount McKinley, Parker and Browne insisted, "presents a geographical and mountaineering problem second only in difficulty if not in importance to the attainment of the summit of Mount Everest or the conquest of the South Pole" (57).

Many explorers turned the comparison back on itself, asserting that mountaineering presented the grander, more important, endeavor. John Noel, whose narrative about climbing and filming Mount Everest I will examine in some detail in chapter 4, described the state of mountain exploration in the early twentieth century this way: "When the North and South Poles had been reached, the ambitions of explorers centered more than ever on Everest. Here was a last task perhaps even more stupendous than the others. Here was a challenge to man's skill and courage, the alluring fascinating challenge of Nature's last secret stronghold" (*Through Tibet*, 29).

Annie Peck, whose account of her exploration of Huascarán and Illampu in South America I will discuss in chapter 3, went so far as to argue strenuously that mountaineering was in fact far more, to use her term, *practical* than polar exploration because it promoted commercial development and investment in the regions surrounding the mountains that she climbed. Only the Canadian ethnologist and explorer Vilhjamur Stefansson found practical value in the Arctic in any sense comparable to what Peck found in the mountains of South America. For Stefansson, however, as he described it in his *My Life with the Eskimo* (1913) and *The Friendly Arctic* (1921), the value lay in learning from the lifeways of its indigenous inhabitants and in adapting to the environment, not in capital development.

As mountain exploration and ascent gained a firm place alongside other activities more traditionally thought of as exploration, mountaineering narratives came to occupy a more prominent place in the journals, magazines, and publishing houses that published the nineteenth-century exploits at lower elevations of such explorers as Henry Morton Stanley, Richard Burton, and John Speke.

Consequently, mountains came to have meaning in an entirely different literary venue; they were understood in a context significantly different from that of Ruskin's description of them as "the beginning and the end of all natural scenery" (quoted in Irving, *Mountain,* 14) or Wordsworth's "black drizzling crags" overshadowing Simplon Pass. Mountains came to be increasingly readable in the language of modern exploration, an idiom that, as I will soon explain, brings together a perplexing complex of science, popular adventure, economics, and geopolitics. By the late 1930s, in the wake of the extensive and elaborate publicity garnered by the several British expeditions to Mount Everest and the ominous stories filtering out of the Alps and the Andes of German climbers who were planting (or sometimes dying in the attempt to plant) Nazi flags on previously unclimbed summits, mountaineering was widely recognized as a thoroughly modern form of exploration.

In part, this transition to geopolitical statement can be traced through the meeting rooms of the British Royal Geographical Society, the great clearinghouse of nineteenth-century British imperial exploration. Founded in 1830, the society absorbed the older African Association and the Raleigh Travellers Club and promoted the near-legendary explorations of David Livingstone, Sir Richard Burton, and John Speke in Africa, as well as the Arctic expeditions of Sir John Franklin and Sir George Nare. On November 13, 1893, Clements Markham stood up to speak to the assembled members of the Royal Geographical Society as their new president. He delivered an address later reprinted in the *Geographical Journal* under the title "The Present Standpoint of Geography." Markham described the status of exploration early in the modern period this way:

The work of geographical discovery, during living memory, has proceeded with such rapidity that many of us have been half inclined to think that there is little left to be done. Brilliantly successful expeditions have traversed the unknown parts of the great continents, blank spaces on our maps have been filled up year after year, entrancing narratives of perilous adventure have held us in rapt attention during each succeeding session, until we are tempted to believe that the glorious tale is nearly told. But this is very far indeed from being the case. There are still wide tracts, in all the great divisions of the Earth, which are unknown to us, and which will furnish work to explorers for many years to come. (481)

Making an argument at odds with Kennan's sad nostalgia from a few years before, Markham went on to detail, continent by continent, the precise character of this work that showed so much promise in keeping explorers occupied. He called it an "imperfect survey of our geographical *desiderata*" (504). Markham's address is important because it gives us an extremely accurate picture of what the world known to Europeans *looked* like in 1893. It is more instructive in what it does not say about earth's mountains.

In the midst of his exhaustive survey of what still remained to be done in geographical exploration, Markham made several, although still very marginal, references to mountaineering. Markham pointed out that in New Zealand "a glorious field is open for the mountaineer" (495) and commented on exploration in the Cordilleras of the Andes and on Edward Whymper's "delightful book" (497) about Ecuador (*Travels among the Great Andes of the Equator*).[3] Markham's comments about exploration in central Asia, however, reveal the extent to which mountaineering in the 1890s was still only ambiguously thought of as exploration. While Markham applauded the travels of Martin Conway "among the glaciers and higher passes of the Mustagh-Himalayas" (491), he did not directly recognize that climbing to the summits of the region's peaks deserved a place on his extended list of "geographical problems that remain to be solved" (482). He emphasized the importance of surveying Nepal and the "vast and wholly unexplored region of Tibet" (492) and outlined the uncertainty regarding the courses of some of the major rivers of Tibet. Above all, he expressed particular interest in the mountain passes between Nepal and Tibet. These, he said, "have a special interest for us, because the only great army that has invaded India since the commencement of British rule in Bengal marched through one of them" (491).[4] With this manner of discussion Markham *endorsed* the status of mountainous regions as "blank spots" on the map but largely only as intervening white space between strategically significant passes and river valleys. Markham made no mention at all in this address of Mount Everest, then already known to be earth's highest point, let alone the possibility or importance of climbing it.

Although Markham swept mountaineering under the rug during his 1893 inaugural address to the society, by 1896 he had apparently changed his thinking. Previous to Markham's tenure as president of the society, the annual addresses by the society's presidents were for the most part simply surveys of the past year's accomplishments in geography and exploration. In 1896 Markham initiated the practice of focusing the annual address on a specific topic, in addition to outlining the current status of geographical knowledge. Markham chose the Himalayas as the subject of that first topic-oriented address. Instead of making only passing reference to mountains as merely those geographical spaces between passes, as he had in 1893, in 1896 Markham focused on the mountains themselves, their exploration and ascent.

By the end of the modern period of exploration, on the eve of what would turn out to be World War II, the shift predicted by Markham's 1896 address was complete. Among the many popular histories of exploration that emerged from what amounted to a small boom in publishing on the topic between the wars, Charles Key's 1937 *The Story of Twentieth-Century Exploration* offers a useful sample of opinion and perspective concerning the status of mountaineering as bonafide exploration. Key plainly conceived of mountaineering as a kind of exploration. He described the duca d'Abruzzi's expedition to the Ruwenzori in 1906 and Staniforth Smith's 1910 climb of Mount Murray in New Guinea. Unlike the rhetorical circumvention of the Himalayas that made them conspicuous in their absence in Markham's first address, Key devoted substantial print to discussing mountaineering in Asia. While discussing the early expeditions to Kamet and Nanda Devi, Key focused on the six expeditions that the British made to Mount Everest between 1921 and 1936.[5] He concluded his history of exploration, in fact, with Hugh Ruttledge's failed 1936 expedition to the mountain, a narrative strategy that leaves a powerful and enticing impression of incompleteness in mountain geography and exploration even as it seems to imply that mountaineering in 1938 may represent the cutting edge of exploration in general.

For those of us who look for history in the record of what has been written in sometimes unlikely places, the development of mountaineering as a form of exploration is suggested by the aging tables of contents in the *Alpine Journal,* the prestigious organ of the British Alpine Club founded in London in 1857. Narratives recounting climbs in the Alps, many of them clearly sporting events and some merely casual excursions from Swiss hotels, dominated the first issue of the *Journal,* published in 1863. The thirteenth and fourteenth issues of the *Journal,* published in 1889, were still preoccupied with the Alps, although they also contained articles on mountaineering in Africa, Norway, Alaska, and on the frontier of British

India, as well as Francis Younghusband's narrative of his trip through the Mustagh Pass in Kashmir and several articles on climbing in the Caucasus. The sixteenth issue, published during the year of Markham's address, strongly reverted to Alpine articles, although it did contain one article on the Caucasus and Martin Conway's account of the mountaineering he self-consciously regarded as pure exploration in the Karakorum.[6] After 1896 the trend soon overwhelmingly moved away from Europe, never to return. By 1938 the fiftieth issue of the *Journal* included articles from all over the globe, with narratives on mountaineering in Lapland, the Caucasus, the Garhwal Himalayas, and the Sikkim Himalayas.

The medals and awards presented by the Royal Geographical Society substantiate the gradual acceptance of mountaineering as a bonafide form of exploration. The society first presented its gold medal for achievement in geographical exploration in 1831. In 1839 it split this award into the Founder's Medal and the Patron's Medal. Before 1892 the society had awarded only one medal for mountaineering, the 1864 Patron's Medal awarded to Karl Klaus von der Decken "for his Geographical Surveys of the lofty mountains of Kilimandjaro" (*sic*) (quoted in Cameron, 264). Between 1892 and 1938, however, the society presented eleven medals to mountaineers, including Edward Whymper, the duca d'Abruzzi, Douglas Freshfield, Martin Conway, Charles Bruce, Tom Longstaff, and Eric Shipton. After 1938 a full fourteen years would pass before the society recognized another mountaineer — Bill Tilman "for his exploratory work among the mountains of East Africa and Central Asia" (quoted in Cameron, 270).

Tilman himself, incidentally, seems to have had a clear sense that behind all these great achievements were some pretty good stories and that they all contributed to the greater tale that was mountaineering. In his 1938 *Mount Everest* (he had led an unsuccessful 1938 British expedition to the mountain) Tilman surveyed the literature on Everest:

The last book written about Mount Everest by Mr. Ruttledge, the leader of the 1933 and 1936 expeditions, was aptly named *The Unfinished Adventure*. This present account should be read merely as yet another chapter in this adventure story. . . . Someday, no doubt, someone will have the enviable task of adding the last chapter, in which the mountain is climbed, and writing "*finis*." (1)

Tilman's rather conventional metaphor, that the history of climbing can be likened to a single great book in which individual narratives like Ruttledge's are only individual chapters, suggests in a rather overt way that mountains are more than rock and ice, that they exist as stories, and that the way the stories are told makes the mountains, to an important degree. For Tilman, Shelley was clearly wrong.

It should be no surprise, then, that climbers back in Tilman's day (and before and since) published accounts of high-profile climbs and gave some significant thought to themselves as storytellers. Mountaineering is closely linked to narrative. The doing becomes quickly translated into the telling. Among climbers themselves, the telling of the climb afterward becomes the folklore of the sport. The climbing hotels and pubs of Wales are redolent in stories, as are those in Jackson Hole, Wyoming, and Camp Four in Yosemite. We know a good story when we hear it, but even individualist climbers have attempted to define how stories should be told. Sometimes institutionalized answers have emerged. What was the proper, that is to say, most effective and useful way to recount an expedition to the Karakorum, a first ascent in the Ruwenzori? In the nineteenth century the Royal Geographical Society attempted to provide answers to questions like these. Clements Markham, "turning once more to the qualifications of an explorer" in his 1893 address, had this to say concerning the literary component of exploration:

> It is seldom that a country resembles what the visitor has been led to expect from reading recent descriptions of it. It is not the so called "word painting," now so elaborately employed, that conveys the most correct picture; but rather pithy epithets and sharp clear touches. The old writers were often excellent in doing this, with their forcible homely language; and they should be read until some echo of their pure vigorous style has been caught. The necessity for cultivating the described faculty, and for studying the general principles underlying all good description should be inculcated by those who train men as geographical explorers; for a traveler is of no use if, when he comes back, he fails to convey to others a correct idea of what he has seen. ("Present Standpoint," 503)

As Markham suggested in these comments, during the modern period geographers recognized the reporting of exploration as vital and complementary to the actual physical process of approaching a peak through a jungle or cutting steps up glacier ice. The act of "going there" was in a sense not fully realized, or perhaps acculturated, until it had been rendered in words — whether as a lecture before the Alpine Club, an article in the *Geographical Journal,* or a slide presentation in a rented theater. The historical geographer J. D. Overton points out that "it was the chronicling of exploration and discovery that gave geography much of its early *raison d'être*" (53), a mission that continued well into the twentieth century. What Overton labels the "chronicling approach" (54) gained momentum as European influence and political control spread dramatically during the nineteenth century, so that narratives of exploration accompanied imperial expansion. Exploration narratives describing a self-proclaimed widening of European geographical knowledge and understanding took science and other Western modes of analysis and perception along on the same ideological mission with the expansion of territorial claims and economic hegemony. The journalist Bailey Millard illustrated the conjoining of narrative, exploration, and imperialism in many minds in a 1913 article in *Technical World Magazine,* "Where the Map Is a Blank." As if echoing Joseph Conrad's *Heart of Darkness,* Millard concluded this survey of contemporary exploration and the state of geographical knowledge with a self-consciously stirring encomium to European expansion: "And now, with our projective fancy, we have peered into nearly all the great blank spaces upon the map. What a world remains for man to explore, subdue, and exploit!" (944).

Responding to both the economic, and therefore often publicity-conscious, motives of expedition sponsors and the tastes of European readers, narratives of geographical discovery from the time of Henry the Navigator had exhibited a pronounced reportorial impulse. In the nineteenth century this impulse thrived through its engagement with the growing empirical orientation of geographical exploration that was perhaps best, and surely most influentially, illustrated by the work of Alexander von Humbolt in South and Central America.[7] By the late nineteenth century the work of Auguste Comte and John Stuart Mill had solidified into a philosophical rationale for empirical detail in exploration writing. And during the modern period various philosophies of science and the general thrust of logical positivism continued this tendency, philosophically underwriting all forms of direct investigation, including geophysical exploration of the blank spots. Working from the strong empirical orientation that by the closing years of the nineteenth century presided over geographical writing (as Clements Markham's address illustrates), mountaineering narratives worked through rhetoric that attempted at all times to be empirical, rational, sane, and understated.[8]

The era during which geography developed as a formal category of academic investigation in Britain is also the era of Europe's most pronounced imperial expansion.[9] From British geography's status in the early ninetenth century as a subject for dinner conversation at the Raleigh Travellers Club to the rapid and influential development of geography as a formal intellectual discipline early in the twentieth century, the percentage of the earth's land surface occupied, or otherwise politically controlled by, Europeans rose from about 35 percent to more than 84 percent (Field-house, *Economics,* 3). This conjunction of events, it can be argued, suggests that the geographical cataloging associated with exploration narratives is in fact descriptive of political and economic aims beyond the literal concerns of discovery and scientific analysis. Exploration, in other words, cannot be separated from the whole cloth of its historical moment. We recognize the truth of this proposition with regard to fifteenth-century discoveries of the New World. We see the stamp of empire in Lewis and Clark's 1804 cross-continental trek. We are less accustomed to seeing the overlap between politics and geographical exploration as we move into the twentieth century — Sputnik, Neil Armstrong, and Star Wars technology notwithstanding.

Like any other cultural practice, writing about exploration quickly became codified by convention, and much of this institutionalization traces to the central role played by the Royal Geographical Society in promoting and publicizing exploration from the early nineteenth century on. As Alan Edwin Day writes in his *Discovery and Exploration:* "It has been claimed, with some justification, that the history of the Royal Geographical Society is in fact the history of British geographical exploration in the nineteenth and twentieth centuries" (232). From its founding in 1830 the RGS defined itself in large part in terms of a literary reportorial role. As originally proposed, the objective of the society was "to collect, digest, and publish interesting and useful geographical facts and discoveries," a goal that superseded even its intention "to afford assistance, instruction, and advice to explorers" (quoted in Day, 232). The literary aims of the society quickly took the form of an official publication, the *Journal of the Royal Geographical Society* (later changed to the *Proceedings of the Royal Geographical Society* and finally shortened to the *Geographical Journal*), which almost immediately came to set the standard for a select group of periodicals publishing the results of geographical exploration.

The *Journal* came to embody the range of formal and acceptable ways in which explorers could report their accomplishments, that is to say, in what Overton calls "the narrow style of the RGS tradition" (54). Although there is some variance, of course, especially in booklength narratives — the somewhat eccentric works of Charles Montague Doughty, for example, or later the works of Apsley Cherry-Gerrard or Vilhjamur Stefansson — the *Journal* style generally became the model to either adopt or react against in exploration writing. Overton describes the conventions growing out of the editorial practice and authorial inclination of the *Geographical Journal* and its competitors as encouraging a "narrative-descriptive perspective, usually concerned with a small number of so-called 'important' journeys," and showing "a penchant for outstanding feats" (54). He goes on to maintain that this perspective involves a "frequent emphasis on the role of the individual and the predisposition for the heroic" (55). Walt Unsworth adds in his *Everest: A Mountaineering History* that many mountaineering narratives available during the modern period preserved what he calls the "lingering manner of Victorian England" in that they were "inclined to describe any difficulties with proper restraint" (242). Ian Cameron describes many of the early *Journal* articles as " 'and-so-we-climbed-to-the-top-of-the-hill' reminiscences" (203).

As early as 1870, however, members of the Royal Geographical Society heard rumblings concerning the society's official publication. Markham, along with the mountaineer Douglas Freshfield and others, objected that the *Journal* was too formal and, well, stuffy; they made two proposals — a format and style oriented more toward a popular audience (meaning illustrations and livelier writing) and more sound, concrete, scientific content. When Markham took up the presidency in 1893, he made this editorial shift official — it had been gradually occurring for some time — by adopting the more streamlined *Geographical Journal* as a title. So when Markham spoke in his address that year of the importance of conveying the "correct idea," he was actually referring to what he considered something of a novel and even still somewhat controversial "style" of narrative writing, the conjunction of popular appeal and empirical exactitude that ever since has characterized exploration writing.

The point is not so much that this idea of grafting the popular with the scientific was new. The *Alpine Journal,* first published by the Alpine Club in 1863, had in many ways anticipated the reorientation effected by Markham in the *Geographical Journal* in 1893. Its original subtitle, after all, was "a record of mountain adventure and scientific observation." Throughout the nineteenth century, as T. S. Blakeney suggests in a short history of the *Alpine Journal,* "picturesque detail," over and above mere topographical specificity, had been a hallmark of successful *Journal* essays (171). What is significant is that the RGS exerted immense influence and authority over the publication of exploration narratives. Although the *Journal* did not come close to enjoying a monopoly on exploration publishing — many competing journals and magazines and a market for book-length narratives existed beyond the RGS — it was simply *the* prestigious place to publish. When the RGS style officially changed, as it did in 1893, the formula for exploration writing changed as well.

Markham's attempt to popularize exploration writing clearly rode the current of the times. By the 1880s the *Journal* had already been joined by the *Scottish Geographical Magazine* and the *American Geographical Society Bulletin*. The twentieth century, particularly the period between the two world wars, witnessed a real burgeoning of periodicals devoted to geographical exploration as a hybrid of scientific description and adventure, especially in its *Journal* incarnation. By 1938 *Geographical Magazine, Geographical Review, National Geographic, Geography, Journal of Geography,* and the *Canadian Geographical Journal* had also begun publication. The popularity of geographical writing was reaching previously unheard-of proportions.

The "golden age" of mountaineering in the Alps in the 1850s had resulted in the publication of John Ball's 1860 anthology, *Peaks, Passes, and Glaciers,* a collection of narratives by early Alpine Club members and, according to its preface, "suitable for carrying in the knapsack" (viii). The publication of three collections of mountaineering narratives on the eve of World War I, however, suggests the even greater demand for this type of writing early in the twentieth century. Joseph McSpadden's *The Alps as Seen by the Poets,* Harold Spender's *In Praise of Switzerland,* both published in 1912, and Arnold Lunn's *The Englishman in the Alps* (1913) freely mixed conventional literary texts with climbing narratives while still allowing for distinction between the two. Spender insisted in his preface, for example, that the prose literature associated with the *Alpine Journal* was fundamentally different from poetry of the romantic tradition. The year 1938 saw publication of Graham Irving's *The Mountain Way: An Anthology in Prose and Verse,* one of the first collections to include contemporary twentieth-century narratives and thus extend the setting of the sport beyond Sir Leslie Stephen's playground of Europe to the more distant and remote regions where climbing mountains was a form of exploration.

Even if we do not today recognize exploration literature, including mountaineering narratives, as an important category of modern literature, earlier readers may have been a bit more inclined to do so. In the late nineteenth and early twentieth centuries Literature, that is to say, the accepted academic canon of literature, did not extend to contemporary writing. An educated person would just naturally keep abreast of recent writing; it did not require formal study. Exploration literature had the status of what we have recently come to call popular culture, before popular culture was an object of study. At the turn of the twentieth century it might have been called modern. Still, from the highly publicized disappearance of Sir John Franklin in the Northwest Passage in 1845, in fact, public interest in polar exploration, both in Britain and in the United States, never significantly waned until World War II. Along the way it prompted the formation of such groups as the Arctic Club of America and the Explorers Club. The narratives of Richard Burton, the sensational journalism of Henry Morton Stanley, and the publicity given such controversial events of colonial acquisition as the "Fashoda incident" produced a similarly extensive public response to exploration in Africa.[10] In reaction to this a vast popular and juvenile literature of exploration and adventure stories grew up during the late nineteenth and early twentieth centuries. The Great War further fanned public interest in exotic lands appealingly far from the western front.[11] Consequently, Peter Fleming's 1933 *Brazilian Adventure,* for example, was one of the most popular books in Britain between the wars, and Richard Byrd had no trouble securing donations to fund his second expedition to the Antarctic, even in one of the darkest years of the depression. The 1920s and 1930s, in fact, began a minor renaissance in the compilation and republication of exploration narratives, represented by such collections as Milton Waldman's *Golden Hind Series, The Broadway Travellers,* and *Classics of Travel and Exploration,* among many others, as well as by the founding of the highly influential Scott Polar Research Institute in 1920.[12]

"A modern Hakluyt or Purchas would be a superfluity," Frederick A. Blossom wrote in the foreword to his 1931 collection of exploration narratives, *Told at the Explorers Club.* According to Blossom, the promotional work of Richard Hakluyt and Samuel Purchas, the great seventeenth-century publicists of exploration, as well as the most dedicated compilers of its literature during the age of discovery, had been replaced in the modern period by what he calls "the current newspaper ballyhoo and motion-picture sensationalism" (v). As Blossom saw it, the promulgation of exploration by the increasingly diverse and persistent voices of twentieth-century mass media actually distinguish modern from earlier exploration in a way that other modes of distinction cannot. "On all sides," Blossom wrote, "there are publishers and film producers eager to record and distribute the home-coming traveler's tale. His book is on the stalls and his picture on the screen almost before his luggage is at the hotel" (v).

Clearly, Blossom was correct in distinguishing exploration narratives as an extremely popular body of literature during the early twentieth century. That Blossom may have been understating the popular appeal of earlier narratives was probably also the case. The search for Franklin in the Northwest Passage and the journeys of Livingstone and Stanley in Africa fascinated an earlier public and hurried the typesetters of the nineteenth century. But when exploration literature is measured by sheer gross volume and extent, we cannot entirely discount Blossom's assertion of special status for the new century's accounts. Furthermore, Blossom made an important point when he looked at modern exploration through its literature and how that literature was received at home. The translation of exploration into consumable media is the second life of the expedition.

Modern explorers often energetically put their projects before the public. Robert Peary, for example, was able to parlay his popularity in the public imagination into clear financial gain. The remarkable fund-raising success he enjoyed reflected not only a wide general interest in his exploratory work but also the extremely high profile he maintained to foster and then reinforce that interest. Cyrus C. Adams reported in the *Geographical Journal* in 1893 that Peary had spent nine months the year before lecturing and writing to earn money for his next expedition. Sometimes speaking twice a day and nearly every day of the week and supplementing this income with frequent, and as Adams asserted, well-paid, journal articles, Peary raised £6,000 (305). Or consider the elaborate publicity that surrounded the 1924 British expedition to Mount Everest. John Noel, the group's designated "photographic historian," began to promote the expedition more than a year before it left London. A scale model of Mount Everest appeared in the India Section of the highly wrought British Empire Exhibition at Wembley early in 1924. Noel saw to it that a pictorial postage stamp commemorating the expedition was designed and printed, and he sold more than forty thousand stamps by mail to British schoolchildren. Using then-experimental equipment and techniques, he had filmed portions of the 1922 expedition, the first serious attempt on the mountain, and at home had begun to use the film to marshal public support for the 1924 effort, circulating it throughout the country and the Continent. As a result, he wrote happily in his 1927 *Through Tibet to Everest*, "funds were plentiful" (203). Throughout his stay at Everest, Noel sent off to Europe clips of film showing the expedition's progress. Distributed in the Pathé Pictorial News, these releases played literally throughout the world, designed so that, as Noel put it, the man in the street could follow the expedition (214). How could Noel have anticipated what he began—that today Internet users can surf to "virtual on-line climbs" of the world's tallest mountain?

Whatever else the 1924 expedition was, it was a publicity success. When Europe learned of the tragic disappearance of George Mallory and Andrew Irvine six hundred feet below the summit, the expedition returned to instant notoriety. Several expedition members quickly produced books. Noel in particular stoked in colorful ways his countrymen's fascination with the "roof of the world." He promoted the film that resulted from the expedition, his *The Epic of Everest,* as it toured England, Scotland, Ireland, France, and Germany by sending along seven Tibetan lamas and his porter, Lakra, whom he had brought back with him from the Himalayas. This is a somewhat long and involved story, which I will discuss in greater detail in chapter 4.

In addition to publishing widely in the technical and professional journals of the prominent geographical societies of the day, many explorers wrote for newspapers and popular magazines. Annie Peck, for example, frequently contributed to *Harper's* and *Outing* in the 1900s and 1910s and in fact raised considerable money for her South American expeditions in doing so.

In the United States modern geographical writing is best represented by the dominant position of the *National Geographic Magazine.* The *Geographic* released its first issue in 1888, grew up with the modern period, and soon became the flagship of all American geographical publications, reaching a circulation of well more than one million by the end of the period. In a 1938 *Scribner's* article, "Geography, Inc.," Ishbel Ross provided a useful retrospective look at the *Geographic.* Although the *Geographic* was the official organ of a major research organization, the National Geographic Society, and thus roughly the American equivalent of the British *Geographical Journal,* the most salient feature of the magazine, in Ross's view, was its immense popularity. Ross put it this way: "Wherever the tom-tom beats, the Moslem kneels in prayer, or two or three persons speaking the English language are gathered together, may be found the *National Geographic Magazine,* an American product which in fifty years has taken on the familiar aspect of the map of the world itself" (23). Serving up what Ross called "a diet of adventure, exploration, and self-education—a touch of the Rover Boys teamed up with the staid professor" (23), the *Geographic* succeeded by satisfying a market.[13] Ross was correct in linking the magazine's quick and persistent popularity with the role that exploration and geography played in the complex events of modern world affairs: "Its timing was good. Science was entering a golden age, exploration was in bud, international complications of the most sensational sort were soon to fasten attention on boundary lines" (23).

Between 1893 and 1938 articles on travel and exploration were a standard feature in *Scribner's, Harper's,* the *Saturday Review,* and many other magazines on both sides of the Atlantic, and major events of exploration always claimed newspaper and magazine space. The Peary–Cook controversy about the North Pole, the deaths of Scott in Antarctica and Mallory and Irvine on Mount Everest were press-stopping news. The popular press followed a predilection for representing explorers in the grandiose terms of heroism, the exotic, the faraway, and the adventurous. The Royal Geographical Society Library in London, for example, maintains fascinating and extensive scrapbooks of newspaper clippings on the early 1921, 1922, and 1924 British Mount Everest expeditions. Press agencies and newspapers had clamored for the rights to cover the expedition before the *Times of London* was given a monopoly on press releases. Film producers were outraged when the Royal Geographical Society refused to put film rights on the market. Geoffrey Malins, who produced the famous *Battle of the Somme* and other documentary films during World War I, was among those sent away disappointed. When articles began to appear about the expeditions, even months before their departure from London, the tone was laudatory, even breathless. The *Evening Standard* of January 10, 1921, excitedly predicted that the 1921 expedition would "pass through uncharted regions; through vast white spaces where men have never trod before." On January 12, 1924, the *Cornish Post* enthused that the 1924 expedition marked "a thrilling new era of romance and adventure which will add new and vivid chapters to the story of British grit and enterprise in the field of exploration and research." The *Glasgow Herald* of January 10 of that year extended this sense of patriotic zeal, labeling the expedition a demonstration of "the indomitable spirit that has won for the British race its place in the world."[14] The language of warfare and conquest slides easily within the rhetoric of exploration.

That the heroics of exploration could be understood in the metaphorical conjunction of war and exploration was readily illustrated during this era. Ernest Shackleton, apologetic in the preface to his 1919 *South* for being dispatched to traverse Antarctica in 1914, just as Britain went to war in Europe, dedicated the narrative to

My comrades
who fell in the white warfare
of the south and on the
red fields of France
and Flanders

Similarly, in a 1913 article for *Technical World Magazine* F. R. Moulton concluded by wondering whether the scientific benefits of polar exploration are worth the cost in human life. Moulton answered this question by comparing exploration to the "religious freedom" won in Europe after "generations of bloody and barbaric war" (186). Moulton's editors made this comparison more clearly contemporary for a war era readership by immediately following the article with George H. Boker's poem, "Dirge for a Soldier." Boker's poem clearly caught the spirit of its time, equating the distant frontier of the poles with the western front: "Lay him low, lay him low, / In the clover or the snow!" (186).

And, of course, the explorers themselves had a sharp sense of the role they played on the sometimes yellow pages of the newspapers of the day. Sounding a little like a Hollywood star disgruntled by the latest issue of the *National Enquirer,* the mountaineer and feminist Fanny Workman described in 1917 how somewhat distorted news items about her 1911 expedition to Kashmir had leaked out of the wilderness. In *Two Summers in the Ice-Wilds of the Karakoram,* she and her husband, William Hunter Workman, wrote:

Most garbled reports of these accidents were carried by natives to Skardo, and thence by wire to Simla and throughout Europe and America. The coolie who carried the news of a Sahib's death to Skardo, which had been passed on to him by various other natives, did not know that Sahib was killed or how, and thus the report of Dr. Workman's death by avalanche first made the rounds of the Press, and later my demise was announced, so that when our mail reached us in the Kondus nala weeks later, we were treated to much delectable literature in the form of varied accounts of the fatal accident, of letters of condolence from friends, and some three hundred obituary notices. According to one of these accounts Dr. Workman had been killed while motoring over a Himalayan snow-pass. (141)

Although neither Workman had been even injured, and although the Himalayan passes were open only to yak travel for part of the year and never to automobile traffic, the expedition gained a fictional life of its own in the world's newspapers.

An awareness of the increasing commercial value of exploration as a kind of mass-market product may have even invaded the Royal Geographical Society. Sometime around 1904 Clements Markham began keeping a notebook about his years as president of the RGS. The result, the handwritten, still unpublished manuscript, "Royal Geographical Society," provides an informative and often entertaining look into the life and business of the society, from the point of view of one of its most lastingly influential leaders, the man whose image decorates the front entrance of the society's headquarters in Kensington Gore even today. At one point in "Royal Geographical Society" Markham summarized in his own way the history of the society's official journal, which by 1893 had gone through two different names and editorial formats.[15] As I have already noted, in 1893 the older *Proceedings of the Royal Geographical Society,* in Markham's view a "cumbrous, unwieldy volume, in dark green cloth" that "failed to meet the requirements of the Society" ("Royal Geographical Society," 207), was given its modern name of the *Geographical Journal* and updated in accordance with the wishes of Markham and others in the society. They favored a more modern, and marketable, format and editorial scheme. In Markham's mind the change succeeded. Of this new third format Markham wrote that a "satisfactory feature of the new series is the increasing income from sales and *advertisements*" ("Royal Geographical Society," 207), which he said amounted to almost £1,300 in 1894.

In the United States the style of geographical writing followed a comparable pattern. The pillar of American geographical magazines from 1888 on, *National Geographic Magazine,* spoke of the world's distant places in its distinctive voice. Although, as Ishbel Ross wrote in 1938, the *Geographic* had all along invited "frequent howls about its literary style" (25), it had featured the travel writing of such proven writers as Joseph Conrad and Donn Byrne. The *Geographic* served up an American version of the RGS style. Ross characterized the typical *Geographic* narrative as having "the chatty quality of a letter to the folks at home" (25). We probably still want to believe in explorers as natural heroes, born and not made, but let's take a closer look.

Let's say it is 1912 and you, like thousands of other British schoolchildren, have been inspired and galvanized by newspaper accounts of Robert Falcon Scott's tragic death near the South Pole. They even renamed your school after him. You decide that you too want to become a famous and courageous explorer and equal the deeds of Scott. Where do you turn? In

1854 the Royal Geographical Society began publishing its *Hints to Travellers,* at first a thin thirty-one-page volume of "how-to" advice about exploration for would-be explorers to take with them into the wilderness. Besides assisting explorers, the volume was designed to provide, as the editors of the 1865 edition wrote, "instructions by which they may make their labours useful to geography" (2).[16] As would all later editions, the 1854 *Hints* included lists of provisions and equipment but placed a special emphasis on scientific measurement equipment and techniques and materials for recording observations.[17] Francis Galton's extensive remarks concerning the kind of stationery and writing materials that explorers should pack along on their expeditions make very plain the society's long-professed interest in encouraging written records of exploration (Back, Collinson, and Galton).[18]

Hints also offered explorers clear guidelines about what kind of information should fill that stationery. Under the heading "Hints for Collecting Geographical Information," lists of questions were arranged in the categories: "Aspect, Surface, Physical Divisions, Mountains, Rivers, Lakes Sea Coast and Ports, Volcanoes and Mineral Springs etc., Maps, Charts, and etc., Astronomical Observations, Instruments, Meteorology, Natural History, Ethnography." The first of these categories, called "Aspect," enumerated a series of questions designed to define a primary scheme of spatial orientation describing an area undergoing exploration. The first question, "What is the general aspect of the country?" is sufficient to suggest how the questions guiding explorers' accounts of new geography encouraged subjective response, personal interpretations of the landscape. The category "Mountains," in fact, instructed: "Obtain bearings, by compass, of the limits of the range, and of all remarkable points, masses, gaps, etc.," a reminder that interestingly subsumes empirical observation in the rather subjective judgment of what precisely the term *remarkable* might actually mean. People, even explorers, after all, remark on very different things.

By the time the seventh edition of *Hints* was published in 1893 under the editorship of Douglas Freshfield and W. J. L. Wharton, it had exploded to 497 pages. The then-new president of the society, Clements Markham, no great admirer of Freshfield's, commented that "the little book had become overloaded, and a receptacle for the hobbies of various people." Singling out two mountaineers for criticism, he added that "the ideas of Freshfield, Whymper, and Johnston [who was not a mountaineer] about outfit are not of use to a man when he has started" ("Royal Geographical Society," 168). But despite this criticism, *Hints* continued to be the standard explorer's textbook it had been for almost forty years throughout the dynamic Victorian period of geographical exploration. But of equal importance is how the 1893 edition suggests how the nature of exploration was changing. In their preface the editors, Freshfield and Wharton, mention the need to "meet the, in some ways, higher requirements of a new generation of young travellers, many of whom had received scientific instruction in the Society's office before leaving England" (xvi).[19] The nature of the information offered in the 1893 *Hints* was significantly more specific than it had been in the first edition thirty-nine years earlier. Instructions for recording the results of expeditions are no exception.

"Record your observations on the spot," admonished Freshfield and Wharton, "keeping for the purpose a note-book with numbered pages and a map (where the latter is procurable) always at hand in a buttoned pocket" (7). They also offered the following, a "few words as to the method and form to be adopted by the traveller in preparing the permanent record of his journey after its completion" (7). They wrote:

The traveller, immediately on his return, should write out from his notes a full diary. This done, let him lay it aside for a short time, and read afresh all he can find on his subject. He will then be ready to take up again his own manuscript, and, if he sees his way to make an interesting paper or volume, to come to the important decision whether he shall retain the narrative form, or arrange his material otherwise. Should he retain the narrative form — and it has many advantages — let him erase repetitions; enlarge on, or mass together, typical and instructive experience, insert, where most convenient, condensed summaries of the results of his observations on special subjects, showing how and where they modify, or enlarge, the conclusions of his predecessors. (7)

At the turn of the century *Hints to Travellers* was by far the most important published source of general information for explorers and would-be explorers alike. At the end of the nineteenth century the demand for the kind of information offered in *Hints* became so insistent that the society initiated annual lectures on how to become an explorer, presentations that Ian Cameron suggests "gave many famous explorers an introduction to their calling" (200). More than simply a guidebook, obviously, *Hints* also represented a clear look into the ideology of exploration that animated the most influential organization presiding over geographical exploration in Britain and the United States. Additionally, with its clear aim of inculcating methods of narrative writing, *Hints* also represented the most specific, detailed statement of the aesthetics of modern exploration literature that we have at our disposal. It may certainly be the case, as Christine Kelly, archivist at the Royal Geographical Society once told me, that the best way to learn about the style of geographical narratives is to simply "sit down and read the *GJ*." But this reading can be significantly enhanced by understanding how *Hints* suggested its own self-conscious normative description of the "RGS Style" that goes well beyond the colorful but finally rather vague descriptions that have influenced reader perceptions of exploration writing up to this point. As I will show in a moment, the writing advice that filled *Hints* also instructed would-be explorers on how to provide information broadly useful to the imperial endeavors that Robert Falcon Scott and other heroes of exploration had already come to symbolize.

Peter Brooks situates exploration narratives in the category of literature that he calls "male plots of ambition," noting that the reading process for these texts generates a situation in which the "ambitious hero . . . stands as a figure of the reader's efforts to construct meanings in ever-larger wholes, to totalize his experience" (39). I must elaborate on this last remark. The style at work in modern mountaineering narratives is far from merely an insular and self-contained aesthetic. Individual perceptions operate beyond the private subjectivity of individuals. The "lived," or personally experienced, geographies of the mountains described by climbers gain a larger meaning as readers notice how they express more inclusive, collective, and culturally determined ways of understanding geography and adventures in distant lands. The various conventions of the modern mountaineering narrative, in fact, can be read as expressing the ideology of European and U.S. expansionism in the modern period, a phenomenon often referred to as the new imperialism.

The potential ambiguity of the term *imperialism* requires some clarification. Even during the 1890s, although *imperialism* tended to be used in a more neutral, moral sense than it usually is today, its meanings varied widely, suggesting in some contexts everything positive and forward looking about, say, the British presence in Africa or the benefits of the proposed annexation of Canada by the United States, and on the other hand everything negative about excessive expenditures on arms and colonial governments.[20] Only in the wake of the Boer and Spanish-American Wars around the turn of the century, and theoretically fueled by the work of J. A. Hobson and V. I. Lenin, did the term begin to carry its contemporary weight of opprobrium. A more precise understanding of this powerfully loaded rubric than that which arises from the well-known images of European exploitation and conquest informally associated with it may be useful. George Nadel and Perry Curtis define *imperialism* as "the extension of sovereignty or control, whether direct or indirect, political or economic, by one government, nation or society over another together with the ideas justifying or opposing this process" (1).

As a historical term, *new imperialism* generally designates the status and function of imperialism after 1870 and sometimes before the post–World War II period of decolonization. Following the collapse of trade protectionism in the British Empire after 1850 and a dramatic increase in European political rivalry in the last third of the century, the era witnessed the most dramatic extension of formal political and informal economic empire since the age of discovery. The best-known theories of the day to account for this phenomenon appeared in two widely circulated and influential studies: J. A. Hobson's 1902 *Imperialism: A Study* and Lenin's 1916 *Imperialism: The Highest Stage of Capitalism*, arguing, on one hand from a liberal and on the other from a socialist premise, that economic and commercial motives underlay the modern European "scramble" for new territory and spheres of influence. This argument has since undergone extensive critique and revision. In his 1964 essay, "The New Imperialism: The Hobson–Lenin Thesis Revised," the economist D. K. Fieldhouse took the position that new imperialism is fundamentally political rather than economic. Fieldhouse wrote that "one essential truth" about imperialism in the twentieth century is "that it had become irrational" (96), meaning for him that it was motivated by symbolic political and nationalistic abstraction rather than the prospect of commercial gain. More likely still is the observation that new imperialism is best distinguished not by a single tactic — the economic *or* the political — but by its unresolved mingling of the economic and the political, a situation apparent in the combined rhetorics of jingoism and commerce represented later in this study in specific twentieth-century mountaineering narratives.

An 1898 photograph of New York City's Newspaper Row serves as a kind of icon of how geography at the turn of the twentieth century emerged from a complex political and economic context. Above the main entrances of the offices of Hearst's *New York Journal* and *New York Tribune* next door, wooden staging holds huge slate boards festooned with streamers and crossed Stars and Stripes. Scrambling copyists stand on planking and quickly write the latest headlines in foot-high letters. In the street below a sea of bowler-hatted men follows the chalk of the newswriters as the day's war news covers the boards. The *Journal*'s man has written, SAN JUAN HOISTED THE WHITE FLAG. Fifty feet away the *Tribune* writer has chalked up: THE TRANSPORT GUSSIE LANDED AN IMPORTANT EXPEDITION AT CABANAS CUBA YESTERDAY. And at the far end of the building he has already ended the news with TRIBUNE WAR ATLAS 25 CENTS A COPY. CUBA. WEST INDIES. PHILLIPPINES. MANY OTHER COUNTRIES. FLAGS OF ALL NATIONS FOR SALE IN TRIBUNE OFFICE.

This was the era in which the explorations of missionaries and military men, the travels of Nellie Bly, and a foreign war in an exotic setting sold newspapers. This advertisement, designed to speak to a complex association between war, faraway places, and geographical representation at work in the public imagination, succinctly represents how geopolitics framed exploration narratives during the modern period. In practice, geographical writing in the period tended to follow geopolitical conflict, and readers, especially of popular magazines and gazettes, often learned geography in response to crisis. In Britain geographical writing traced threats to the margins of the empire. The public learned South African geography in 1898, Tibetan geography in 1903. Americans "rediscovered" the far Pacific when Adm. George Dewey landed in Manila, the Somme when the newsreels played, very much like when they became far better acquainted with the geography of the Persian Gulf nine decades later.[21]

The case of *National Geographic Magazine* illustrates this point. Ishbel Ross described the magazine's presentation of geography as strictly apolitical, as that of a "faintly rosete world" devoid of controversy (25). But this observation requires important qualification. Although Ross suggested, for example, that "few hints of the blood and muck of the World War got into the pages of the *Geographic*" (25), in fact the magazine geared its editorial mix to wartime, concentrating on the geography of the war-torn regions of Europe. The strategy was a success; *Geographic* circulation rose sevenfold during the war, which suggests how the reading public accepted geography as a vital backdrop to modern events. Ishbel implicitly recognized this in noting that "international complications," when combined with flourishing exploration and scientific investigation, comprised a formula for publishing success.

Well behind the popular gazettes and yellow tabloids, or even the *National Geographic,* theoretical geography also recognized the necessary involvement of the new and expanding discipline with international events. The most influential currents of thought placed the economic lives of the European states, and indirectly the United States and Japan, close to the center of priority in inducing and determining territorial expansion or informal influence during the period. By the time that Joseph Alois Schumpeter wrote his widely read essay, "Zur Soziologie des Imperialismus," in 1919, the provisional success of the Bolshevik Revolution resoundingly underscored the virtual necessity for coming to terms with the idea that the operation of economic systems controlled imperial behaviors. Although Schumpeter argued that expansionism can best be explained as learned behavior, as a kind of mass psychology predisposed to aggressive action, the climate of debate, to say nothing of international statist politics, required that he direct his argument with reference to Marxist and other economic theories.

From the time of his 1902 *Imperialism: A Study,* John Atkinson Hobson argued for an economic theory that he labeled "underconsumption." According to Hobson, since at least the middle of the nineteenth century the British had been investing surplus capital abroad, where it earned a high rate of return and consequently preserved domestic interest rates but did little to raise the standard of living of workers or more equitably involve them in the rewards of industrial production. Foreign investment, then, represented a strategy of diversion by which value could be withheld from labor.

This Hobsonian model was, when first advanced, open to dispute on the ground of debatable historical evidence. It continues to be. D. K. Fieldhouse, for example, persuasively argues that British trade in the colonies was simply not all it was cracked up to be in Hobson's theory.[22] But regardless of the final validity of the theory of "underconsumption," Hobson made his argument, readers evaluated it, and the theory became part of a heated dialogue of international scope concerned with the nature and circumstances of finance capital abroad, the most immediate culmination of which was the publication of Lenin's *Imperialism, The Highest Stage of Capitalism* and, by extension, the 1917 Bolshevik Revolution in Russia.[23] Hobson's thesis was part of an issue controversial to a broad range of interests during the early years of the century, including academics like Hobson, certainly, but also workers, labor organizers, politicians, financiers, and revolutionaries.

Additionally, however, constraints that drifted rather far from the bottom line of profit and loss guided imperial behavior during the modern period. The period following German unification under Bismarck was one of increasing rivalry among the imperial European states. In part this was expressed in open hostility but more frequently in a shifting, overlapping grid of initiatives, treaties, and alliances. For Britain, already burdened with historical rivalries with Russia and France, Bismarck's goal of a continental league, which took partial shape in the Triple Alliance of

1882, began a process of increasing diplomatic isolation that culminated in the period immediately before and after the Boer War of 1898–1902.

Although much of this tension was diplomatic and economic in Europe itself, it played out more overtly beyond Europe in a growing competition for colonial possessions. Between 1880 and 1910, for example, the European powers divided almost all of Africa with a startling rapidity. The confrontation of Jean-Baptiste Marchand and Sir Hubert Kitchener on the Nile at Fashoda (now Kodok) in 1898 in a French–British dispute about control of the Nile and Egypt, the British war with the Boers, and later the two Moroccan crises (1905 and 1911) were just a few of the more dramatic events that punctuated a long series of disputes about boundaries and spheres of influence.

In the United States a comparable combination of factors influenced the nation's foreign involvement. As attractive as foreign countries were to U.S. businessmen for trade markets and even for sources of raw materials, they were even more attractive to financiers. As the increasingly organized use of technology transformed U.S. industry, its efficiency increasingly generated surplus capital for investment in foreign ventures, where the returns were normally higher than in the United States. Yet during the modern period the Hobsonian theoretical model was not yet fully tested as an index to describe the foreign affairs of the United States. The economists Joseph Freeman and Scott Nearing observed in 1925 that "United States business investments abroad represent so novel an experience that they have not as yet been made the object of such exhaustive studies as J. A. Hobson's *Imperialism*" (15).

Although economics clearly was an important component of the emergence of the United States as an international power during the first years of the twentieth century, issues pertaining to national identity also played a role. A spirit that tolerated and encouraged increasing bellicosity in U.S. foreign policy dominated the era. Since the easy success of the United States in its 1898–99 war with Spain, three successive Republican administrations had bolstered U.S. naval strength and shown an increasing willingness to use it to enforce U.S. interests abroad, both economic and political.

In 1908, even as Annie Smith Peck climbed Huascarán, the U.S. fleet toured the world, carrying an unmistakable message of martial zeal between the lines of a professed goodwill. Perceiving European powers, especially Germany, as a threat to U.S. influence in the Western Hemisphere, Theodore Roosevelt drafted what soon became known as the Roosevelt corollary to the Monroe Doctrine, a policy that claimed for the

United States the right not only to prevent European intervention in Latin America but also to intervene in the internal affairs of Latin American nations to guarantee that they met their international financial obligations. This "Big Stick" foreign policy presided over U.S. intervention in Panama in 1903, the Dominican Republic in 1905, and again in Cuba in 1906. Arguably, its most significant result came when the United States assumed control of the Panama Canal Zone in 1903, when the U.S. Navy encouraged and then assured the success of a local "revolution" against a Colombian government reluctant to lease land to the United States for a canal. A 1908 article in the *American Review of Reviews* declared that the result of this aggressive posture was that South Americans viewed the "Yanqui" as a "Spoilsman, who has no respect for the laws of the country and who will stop at nothing to gain his ends" ("Progress," 147). The free exercise of the prerogative of power in and of itself increasingly came to influence U.S. imperial behavior.

The notion of *imperialism* evolved from the midnineteenth century on and carried a variable ideological and rhetorical weight in Britain. Even up to the moment of reckoning forced on the empire by Lord Kitchener's concentration camps during the brutal later months of the Boer War, the term could still be used to invoke national prestige, power, and wealth as embodied in such Victorian icons as the Suez Canal and India. On the other hand, in the lexicon of both radicals and liberals it could suggest destructive, roughshod land grabbing and exploitation.

During the last twenty years of the nineteenth century, Americans imported this debate and infused it with their own arguments. In the United States *imperialism* was equally divided between conflicting claims for national identity and purpose, both of which were problematic. On the one hand, Americans enthusiastically recognized how expansionism had left its mark on U.S. history and, some argued, character. Seeing continued U.S. territorial expansion as following in the hallowed democratic tradition of Thomas Jefferson, James Monroe, Thomas Hart Benton, and William Henry Seward, advocates of further U.S. expansion in the last years of the nineteenth century argued that separating territorial movement from national identity was impossible, and, as Theodore Roosevelt persistently maintained, that "this expansion is not a matter of regret, but of pride" (*Works of Theodore Roosevelt,* 15:337).[24] Further, the influential "frontier hypothesis" of the Wisconsin historian Frederick Jackson Turner, following the general late Victorian fascination for themes of progress and evolution, stressed westward movement of settlement as the determining factor in U.S. cultural and political life.[25] The Oxford geographer

Halford Mackinder's strategic "geographical pivot" theory, as well as Alfred Thayer Mahan's writings on the importance of sea power, had particularly disturbing effects on many prominent Americans in positions to shape policy, particularly Roosevelt, Henry Cabot Lodge, John Hay, and Albert Beveridge. In the scheme of Mackinder's political geography the United States was at the very margin of the world's nexus of power and influence, close neither to what he called the "World Island"—that is to say, the great linked landmasses of Asia, Africa, and Europe—nor to the "heartland," eastern Europe and the western steppes of Asia. Continued isolation, if Mackinder's theories bore themselves out, would unquestionably abdicate international prestige and leadership, perhaps even survival, for the United States.[26]

The clergyman Josiah Strong, in his 1886 book, *Our Country,* subtitled *Its Possible Future and Its Present Crisis,* included in his reading of American tradition the sense of an errand-into-the-wilderness mission felt by New England Puritans, affirming that God is "preparing mankind to receive our impress" (Healy, 38). Because it represented the interests of so many Americans in so many different ways, what the New York newspaperman John O'Sullivan had called "manifest destiny" in 1845 had not even begun to wane at the end of the century. In elaborating O'Sullivan's popular notion, William Gilpin, the first governor of Colorado and one of the nineteenth century's greatest boosters of expansionism, wrote, "Let us tread fast and joyfully the open trail before us! Let every American heart open wide for patriotism to glow undimmed, and confide with religious faith in the sublime and prodigious destiny of his well-loved country" (130), and his words continued to resonate in the contemporary terms of U.S. foreign policy twenty or thirty years later.[27]

Recall that at the beginning of this historical period, which was characterized by a growing clamor for power, financial gain, and national prestige by European nations and the United States, mountains were regarded as the backwaters of the geographical world. The first edition of *Hints to Travellers* acknowledged the tendency of nineteenth-century geography to see mountains merely in terms of finding the way through them. It advised explorers investigating mountain ranges to "mark the chief mountain-passes, and note if they might be easily defended against an enemy" (27). The 1906 edition of *Hints to Travellers,* edited by E. A. Rieves, first made the involvement of exploration with the material goals of empire explicit in an extended way. The section entitled "Industry and Commerce" attempted to outline ways of answering these questions of "resources, wants, and accessibility" regarding territory undergoing exploration:

(1) What are the available resources of the country that may be turned to industrial or commercial account?
(2) What commercial products can find an available market in the country?
(3) What are the facilities for or hindrances to intercourse between the country and the rest of the world? (Rieves, 1906, 138)

This section became a standard feature in subsequent editions of *Hints* through the modern period. It is interesting to note that this is the edition that Annie Smith Peck, the subject of chapter 3, would have read before making her "commercial" promotions of South America. The tenth edition of *Hints,* again edited by E. A. Rieves and published in 1921, is the one that John Noel, the subject of chapter 4, read before going to Tibet. It mentions that "some useful training" about the industrial and commercial development of recently explored territory could be obtained at the London School of Economics, an institution at which Halford Mackinder, the subject of chapter 2, played an important founding role.

In his 1931 book, *Told at the Explorers Club,* Blossom defined modern exploration in terms of its publicity and specifically linked exploration and commercial exploitation as well as exploration and dispassionate science: "A renaissance of exploration is here, recalling the golden days of the sixteenth and seventeenth centuries in western Europe. Surplus energy and wealth are seeking out the far corners of the globe, either as pioneers of industrial development or in behalf of disinterested scientific research (v)." Even if Blossom was a bit late in his assertion that a renaissance of exploration had arrived in 1931, we must recognize that he was correct in locating exploration in a context in which motivations are profoundly mixed and conflicted, where the disinterested and the deeply interested meet in the same adventure. Indeed, political considerations increasingly influenced the modern period's perception of exploration in general and mountaineering in particular.

Also a bit behind the chronological curve, I believe, was James Ramsey Ullman, who in *High Conquest* (1941) dated modern climbing from the end of World War I, noting that "its most interesting and important feature ... has been the expansion of the climber's domain to include virtually every mountainous region of the world" (77). For Ullman the expanded geographical range that signaled the modernity of mountaineering also incorporated its growing political significance. Although Ullman allowed that "ugly and senseless rivalries" have existed as long as mountaineers have plied their craft, he noted that "nationalism" was increasingly a factor influencing mountaineering after the war (79).

With European imperialism increasingly mediated by the rise of fascism and reactions to its rise, the nationalization of mountaineering reached a clearly identifiable climax during the late 1930s. "The Alps," Ullman observed, "had once been looked upon as a playground; then as a laboratory. Now they had become a battlefield. Climbers looked upon themselves as soldiers" (80). As a 1935 *Alpine Journal* review of Fritz Bechtold's *Deutsche am Nanga Parbat* pointed out, climbing mountains was taking on a "national character," becoming a "great patriotic effort" (399). The remark, sharply pejorative in the context of the rise of German national socialism during the 1930s, suggests how mountain space entered into symbolic codes of national identity during the period, even as German, Italian, and Japanese imperial strategies sought to expand colonialism through an anticolonial rhetoric aimed at other imperial nations. Mountains became ambushed in German notions of "living space" and Italian calls for "neo–Roman Empire."

German climbers were very active in the Alps during the 1930s, finally scaling the north face of the Eiger in 1938 after several almost suicidal attempts; they also were active in the Himalayas and Andes. Ullman, in *The Age of Mountaineering* (1941), told the story of two 1938 ascents of Illimani above La Paz, Bolivia, the first made by German climbers, who planted a swastika flag on one of the mountain's summits, and the second made a few days later by a group of English climbers, who quickly tore it down (147). As the fascist era opened, the political rhetoric attached to mountaineering intensified as well. In his 1935 *The Romance of Mountaineering* R. L. G. Irving suggested that for many Italians during the 1930s mountaineering expressed "the early exuberances of a nation in whom a great leader has seen the primary need of a consciousness of its own possibilities" (213). As early as 1930 the Italian mountaineering journal *Rivista del Centro Alpinistico Italiano* exhorted its subscribers:

A climber has fallen. Let a hundred others arise for the morrow. Let other youths strew edelweiss and alpenrose upon the body of the fallen comrade; and lay it with trembling devotion face upturned under the soft turf. Then up, once more to the assault of the rocks and of the summit, to commemorate the fallen one in the highest and most difficult of victories!

The medal for valour in sport, the highest distinction accorded by the Duce to exceptional athletes who break world records or are victors in international contests, will be awarded to climbers who vanquish mountains by new ascents of the sixth standard.

All Italians ought to know how to live in mountainous country. All our wars will always take place in the mountains, and the cult of mountaineering passionately pursued, and spreading more and more among our young men, will contribute to the military preparedness of the young generation. (quoted in Irving, 72)[28]

An anonymous British reviewer, commenting on a trio of German books on mountain warfare in a 1938 issue of the *Alpine Journal,* distanced himself and his country from the connection between mountains and war: "British mountaineers may be inclined, not without reason, to look with some distrust on the many works on mountain warfare which have lately appeared on the continent. They are accustomed to regard the Alps as a playground, and the connection between mountaineer and soldier cannot be as natural to them as to those who in defending their mountains have defended their homeland also" (161). Despite this evocation of Leslie Stephen and a predominantly nineteenth-century conception of mountaineering in the name of disinterested sport, the British joined in conceiving of mountains as political space. Irving argued that the British, before other Western peoples, were prepared to conceive of mountaineering in terms of exploration and discovery — and therefore territorial appropriation. In 1935 Irving revealingly mixed climbing routes and trade routes, comparing the highest piton pounded into a rock slab to "Gibraltar and others which secure our trade routes" (*Romance,* 199). Commenting in the *Alpine Journal* on a 1937 attempt on Kamet by a "small officerless party of three junior NCOs and a private of the East Surrey Regiment," Edward L. Strutt wrote: "We can indeed rest assured of a bright outlook in military Himalayan mountaineering" (5). As early as the period immediately before World War I, as a matter of fact, many Britons had actually conceived of the Himalayas as the exclusive domain of what the secretary of the RGS in a 1924 letter called "British field enterprise" (Hinks to Bailey).

It is perhaps no real surprise that the determinations of expansion and empire surface in the rhetoric of mountaineering as fascism reshaped neo-imperialism during the 1930s. It unfortunately limits our perspective on mountaineering history, however, to consider this a relatively isolated phenomenon associated with fascism and responses to it. In fact, the nationalist mountaineering of the 1930s was only the culmination of an early trend. During his first ascent of the Matterhorn in 1865, the legendary British climber Edward Whymper asked his climbing partner to roll rocks down on a party of Italians to make them realize their defeat. During the modern period the ideological loading of mountaineering steadily increased, gaining momentum with the accretion of empire as it moved toward the fascist era.

The ideology and practice of modern imperialism remained incompletely understood. As a 1910 *Saturday Review* writer said about Britain, "We conquered half the world in a fit of absence of mind" ("Real British," 748). The involvement of mountaineering in these larger processes also represented a comparable lapse in the complete understanding of modern history. The conjunction of the two is the topic at hand. The cases of Halford Mackinder, Annie Smith Peck, and John Baptist Noel, described in the chapters that follow, are intended to suggest that mountaineers and imperialists, rather strange and unexpected hiking companions perhaps, at least both shared a desire to set their tents up in the same place.

2

Halford Mackinder's African Pivot

Baggage is life.
—Richard Burton

IN 1907 WINSTON CHURCHILL SET OUT FROM THE COAST AT
Mombasa in the British East Africa Protectorate on what he called in
My African Journey "one of the most romantic and most wonderful
railways in the world" (2). Sometimes hunting from a seat rigged on the
cowcatcher of the locomotive, other times prowling for rhinoceros beyond the tracks, the then recently appointed undersecretary for the colonies made his way across the East African highlands to Uganda on an
official tour through what Sir Frederick Lugard, speaking for many Britons of the day, called "our East African Empire" (quoted in Churchill,
149).[1] For Churchill the train journey was pure pleasure. British settlement and plantation farming in East Africa had been seriously under way
for five years. The Uganda Railway, Churchill wrote, "with its trolley,
luncheon, sodawater, ice, etc." (8), provided "a sure, swift road along
which the white man and all that he brings with him, for good or ill, may
penetrate into the heart of Africa as easily and safely as he may travel from
London to Vienna" (3). After a brief stay with the governor of Uganda,
whom Churchill frequently kept awake by dictating loudly during late-
night baths, he continued down the Nile to Egypt and home.

The journey was not so sure or swift eight years earlier when the
Oxford geographer Halford Mackinder traveled through East Africa on

the same tracks on his way to make what would turn out to be the first ascent of 17,040-foot Mount Kenya, the second-highest mountain in Africa. Mackinder's 1899 journey on the Uganda Railway, then only partially completed, was through a newly organized British East Africa Protectorate, then wracked with famine, smallpox, and violent upheaval, a region around which the European powers postured in the ongoing "scramble" for imperial territory that marked the last twenty years of the nineteenth century. When Mackinder and his somewhat shoestring expedition reached Nairobi, then just a dusty railroad camp, and began their cross-country trek to Mount Kenya, they left the world of what would become Churchill's cocktail trolley to enter a roughly mapped region only nominally under British political control and still rather uncontaminated by British social and political custom.

"Mackinder enjoyed a large number of successful careers," writes one of his recent biographers, Brian Blouet (*Sir Halford,* 43). Today Mackinder is best known for his career as a geopolitical theorist, author of the important 1904 "geographical pivot" theory, a paradigm of geographical and strategic thinking important well through the cold war period and still debated today. He is also frequently remembered for the vital role that he played in the founding of geography as an accepted academic discipline in Britain, serving as the first director of the Oxford School of Geography beginning in 1899. When I visited Oxford in 1989, I found that Mackinder still enjoys there something of the status of the canonized founder of the order. As I turned the stained pages of Mackinder's journal in the Reading Room at Rhodes House and read through the typescript of his then-unpublished narrative account of his trip to East Africa, "Mount Kenya: Being the Narrative of a Vacation Journey in Equatorial Africa," I began to gain an intriguing understanding of this interesting and important figure in the history of geography. His vocation as a mountaineer and explorer is the least acknowledged of his careers and certainly the most brief. As one might expect, however, Mackinder's adventure in mountain climbing was hardly an isolated event. Instead, it gains its largest meaning when placed alongside his other activities as educator, academic, and political geographical theorist.

In Africa, Mackinder filled about eighteen notebooks, and on the return voyage to England he began to arrange his notes for a narrative account of the expedition. In 1900 two article-length accounts of the Kenya climb appeared in the *Geographical Journal* and the *Alpine Journal,* and Mackinder seems to have had every intention of publishing a book-length version as well.[2] Mackinder's correspondence suggests that in 1900 he was at work on the book and that as late as 1904 it was still anticipated.[3] Although Mackinder apparently arranged publication with Heinemann of Oxford, which went so far as to announce the book, nothing ever came of it, for reasons that remain somewhat mysterious today.[4] Mackinder's narrative, edited by K. Michael Barbour, finally was published in 1991 under the title *The First Ascent of Mount Kenya*.

The book, probably designed to promote Mackinder's academic career (and, by extension, academic geography as a whole) at the crucial moment of the founding of the Oxford School of Geography in 1899, reads almost like a textbook example of the conventions of the Royal Geographical Society style and how they shaped the topic of exploration and discovery within a much broader framework of then-contemporary geopolitics. For Mackinder, Mount Kenya rose from an excitingly wild and turbulent blank space on the map of imperial penetration into Africa. The politics of conquest, the strangeness of cultural difference, and the romantic quest for the summit mingle oddly in Mackinder's account of his East African expedition. Mackinder's writing is conspicuously unresolved in its awareness of the effect of the British acquisition of East Africa on indigenous inhabitants, and although Mackinder tries to focus on the mountain itself as the central topic of his narrative, the story goes curiously off track. So suggestive is Mackinder's account of East Africa of the larger context of the conquest and consolidation of European empire in Africa and its human costs that it simply cannot be read without acknowledging this complex network of events occurring around the mountain. The story of Mackinder's stunning and surprising climb simply outgrows itself as a simple adventure story. Furthermore, Mackinder's story seems to tacitly illustrate and anticipate the theoretical principles that would soon take their best-known shape in his influential 1904 pivot theory, a reexamination of the relationship between sea and land power in European imperial relations, as well as his later work in political geography. In both ways the narrative seems to negotiate the unfamiliarity of an unexplored landscape by incorporating it as an extension of the metropolitan European homeland. White mountains make sense through Whitehall.

Despite the differences suggested between Mackinder's expedition through East Africa and Churchill's later "official progress" there, in a certain sense Mackinder's 1899 trip is more representative of exploration in the twentieth century than the nineteenth.[5] During the nineteenth century

Africa was a major focus of European public attention and interest in exploration. In Britain the "opening" of the continent by missionaries working to suppress the slave trade and the more purely exploratory exploits of Livingstone, Burton, Speke, and Stanley, among many others, filled the popular press and for many came to represent the evolution of an enlightened and still expanding British Empire. But by 1899 the nature of European exploration in Africa was changing. The sources of the Nile had been discovered twenty years earlier. The continent had been traversed, the Niger and Congo charted. The emphasis was shifting to commercial development, colonization, and, by extension, the suppression of native resistance. Scientific study and survey work, rather than exploration in the sense of pure discovery, was increasingly becoming the work of geography. In 1899 two of the principal remaining problems of geographical discovery on the continent were mountains, the Ruwenzori range (Ptolemy's Mountains of the Moon) and Mount Kenya. When Mackinder solved one of these, the ascent of a mountain peak that Europeans had seen for fifty years but had never managed to reach, in a sense he had a foot in each century. He was the newest of all kinds of explorers, the mountaineer, yet he was one who could still inspire the kind of enthusiasm that had filled Britons as they read about the adventures of Livingstone and Speke. "My Sibyl [who was fifteen] worships you shyly and distantly as a hero," the Reverend J. G. Bailey wrote to Mackinder in 1900. "When the long account of your work came out in the *Standard,* she insisted on reading it to her governess instead of lessons" (Bailey).

To some extent Mackinder was an unlikely object of hero worship. He made only one serious climb in his life. Unlike other mountaineers, Mackinder is barely known for his mountaineering at all. Born in 1861 at Gainsborough on the River Trent, Mackinder's early life in Lincolnshire serves as a charming background to the events of his later life and is well documented in Brian Blouet's 1987 biography, *Halford Mackinder.*[6] But let us move forward and construct a beginning for Mackinder's life in 1880, when he came up to Oxford as an undergraduate. Because his exploits as a mountaineer are so closely tied to his role as an academic and educator, Mackinder's arrival at Oxford makes a useful primary benchmark. As an undergraduate, Mackinder studied modern history and geology, focusing, however, on biology. He learned zoology under H. N. Moseley, the naturalist on the *Challenger* expedition (1872–76), the epic oceanographic survey that set the standard for modern scientific exploration. After graduation Mackinder continued at Oxford, reading law; he was studying for the bar when he accepted a position as lecturer for the

Oxford University Extension. Blouet writes: "At the earliest possible stage he was displaying a characteristic which was to mark his professional life: that of running several careers at once" (*Sir Halford*, 9). Mackinder's lectures on what was then the rather provocative topic of something he called "new geography" attracted the attention of a group of Royal Geographical Society members in London who were intent on promoting geographical education and on formalizing geography as an academic discipline.[7] On January 31, 1887, Mackinder delivered before the society the paper that would launch his career as Britain's first academic geographer and, indirectly, send him to climb Mount Kenya twelve years later.

In his address, "The Scope and Methods of Geography," Mackinder argued that the time had come for a new conception of geography to match the closing of the earth's frontiers to exploration.[8] He called for the establishment of geography as a unified discipline that "shall satisfy at once the practical requirements of the statesman and the merchant, the theoretical requirements of the historian and the scientist, and the intellectual requirements of the teacher" (*Democratic Ideals*, 239). He suggested that because geographical conditions mediate human cultural practices, the often discrete areas of physical and political geography are in fact "two stages of one investigation" (212). Mackinder defined geography, therefore, as "the science whose main function is to trace the interaction of man in society and so much of his environment as varies locally" (214); geography is a human — that is to say, historical, cultural, and political — extension of place, not simply a matter of cataloging geophysical features.[9]

These were landmark ideas. In them we see forming Mackinder's vision of how the outlines of land and sea shape empire. We see an academic pioneer describing geography in terms of both intrinsic intellectual and practical political value. For his 1887 audience the combination played well. The members of the society were aware that Germany, an imperial rival to Britain, had already established a dozen schools of geography, and they listened carefully as Mackinder emphasized how education played a vital role in a broader scheme of political and economic affairs. But in this address what he finally stressed was the unifying capacity of geography. "In the days of our fathers," he said, "the ancient classics were the common element in the culture of all men, a ground on which the specialists could meet" (239). Geography would be the new classics, he suggested, synthesizing the best from all areas of human understanding. Mackinder's argument was very close to a suggestion that geography provided an inherent paradigm for closing the already widening gap between science and the humanities. Anticipating in this way C. P. Snow's *The Two Cultures and the Scientific Revolution* by about seventy years, Mackinder addressed this modern schism even while it was opening. Geography during the twentieth century was in fact largely successful in encouraging and practicing this synthetic, or multidisciplinary, orientation announced at its historical genesis as an academic field.

It must have been a marvelously exciting moment in the life of the twenty-four-year-old geographer as he rose to address the Royal Geographical Society, a body of men that was not only the foremost arbiter of geographical knowledge in Britain but also the very embodiment of the full tradition and achievement of Victorian exploration. The import of the moment must have been rendered more poignant by the fact that Mackinder's thesis fell directly in the middle of a debate that would continue to churn the Royal Geographical Society for years. The issue was, as Mackinder put it in his paper, whether geography could be "rendered a discipline instead of a mere body of information" (*Democratic Ideals,* 211). How was the society to weigh the roles of the educator and scientist against those of the more traditional figures of nineteenth-century geography, the explorer and the mapmaker? Although these roles certainly overlapped in the persons of individual members, the society in 1887 was pulled in three different directions as it contemplated how to expend its often limited resources in the name of what it ambiguously, but proudly, called geography. First of all, as Mackinder spoke, the society was still largely influenced by a certain conservative element of its membership that persistently thought of geography as it had been regarded from the age of discovery well through the great explorations of the nineteenth century. Geography, simply put, was mostly a matter of going out and finding something, of getting there first, blazing the trail, making the map, and claiming the natives for the king. A second group of members, perhaps best represented by Clements Markham, shared this desire to support exploration but wanted an increased emphasis on scientific investigation to go along with the planting of the Union Jack. A third group, headed by the mountaineer Douglas Freshfield; Francis Galton, a scientist and explorer; and Walter Bates, the secretary of the society, wanted the organization to involve itself more in the promotion of geographical education.

Mackinder's address had the desired effect of promoting the argument of the education faction within the society. The result was that the society underwrote the establishment of teaching positions in geography at Oxford and Cambridge, and by June 1887 Mackinder had been appointed as the first reader of the tentative and new discipline at Oxford, with the society paying half of his £300 salary. Early in 1899 the society solidified its support of geographical education by arranging with Oxford to support the founding of a diploma-granting Oxford School of Geography. Mackinder was appointed its first director. During these early years of British geography, in addition to providing the germinal direction for what was in Britain a new field of formal study, Mackinder traveled to the United States and Europe to meet with other geographers, took on a position at the new extension College at Reading, and began work on his 1902 *Britain and the British Seas,* which was to launch a series of regional geography studies to be published by Heinemann of Oxford.

Then in 1899, shortly after he began as director of the Oxford School of Geography, came what was both the most anomalous and the most typical event in his life. The biographer Brian Blouet may understate the remarkable nature of Mackinder's East African undertaking when he writes: "Amidst the teaching, writing, and educational administration he planned an adventure; an expedition to East Africa to climb Mount Kenya and collect materials in the surrounding country" (*Halford Mackinder,* 74).

Mount Kenya, which stands above the wooded highlands of East Africa, is an extinct volcano, weathered down to three jagged summits of exposed igneous rock, all named by Mackinder. The highest, Batian, is only thirty-six feet higher than Nelion, separated from it by a narrow notch, which Mackinder dubbed the "Gate of the Mist." The third summit, Lenana, stands at some distance and is six hundred feet lower. Rather than a straightforward "walk-up" like its East African neighbor, Kilimanjaro, which is 2,500 feet taller, Mount Kenya is a serious alpine climb. The first European to see the mountain was the German missionary Ludwig Krapf in 1849. For many years after this first sighting the main currents of exploration by Europeans broke around the mountainous regions near the source of the Nile; in fact, early reports of snow-covered mountains nearly directly on the equator were widely dismissed. The mountain was first attempted in 1887, when the Hungarian count Samuel Teleki approached the mountain through its surrounding forest belt from the southwest and reached an elevation of almost fourteen thousand feet. In 1893 the geologist J. W. Gregory of the British Museum left an aborted hunting expedition at the coast and attempted the mountain by a similar route. Reaching the Kenyan glaciers at around sixteen thousand feet, he reportedly abandoned the climb when his porters refused to wear the shoes that would have been necessary to move across the snowfields above.

The mountain itself was not the only difficulty. During these early attempts an equally serious obstacle to climbing Mount Kenya was how to get there. Krapf and Gregory had had to travel over land more than three hundred miles before even reaching the lower slopes. In 1899, with the Uganda Railway reaching beyond Nairobi to the south of Mount Kenya, Mackinder recognized a fresh and transitory opportunity to make the first ascent. If he acted quickly, before anyone else saw the same opportunity, the newly laid rail line might allow him to make a success of the climb where others had failed.

When the expedition arrived in Zanzibar on June 28, 1899, it consisted of six men. Mackinder had appointed his in-law and friend, Campbell Hausburg, as photographer. Edward Saunders would serve as scientific collector and Claude Camburn as taxidermist, both suggested by the British Museum. Douglas Freshfield of the Alpine Club had arranged the services of two Italian climbing guides, Cesar Ollier and Joseph Brocherel, to assist the relatively inexperienced Mackinder high on the mountain.

Mackinder hoped to reach the mountain with relative ease, but such was not to be the case. When the expedition reached the coast of the British East African Protectorate at the ancient harbor of Mombasa, it almost immediately began to encounter trouble that Mackinder seems not to have anticipated. The entire region had been gripped by famine for almost three years, and smallpox was epidemic. The interior of the protectorate between Mombasa and Mount Kenya, only loosely under British control anyway, was the scene of turmoil and violence brought on by famine and disease.

After only barely convincing a local administrator that the expedition should be allowed to proceed during the famine, the expedition proceeded upcountry on the newly constructed Uganda Railway to Nairobi. With about 170 porters, guides, and guards, a unlikely mixed group of Swahili, Kikuyu, and Masai, Mackinder set out cross-country to the north on July 28. For two weeks the expedition traveled toward the mountain, through a remarkable range of geographically diverse terrain, first through the treeless Kapoti plains, then through the fertile agricultural Kikuyu territory, the rich country of the Meranga, and, finally, on August 13 into the country of the Kikuyu warlord Wangombe, as Mackinder described him, "a terror to the whole neighbourhood" ("Mount Kenya," 462). The expedition had already had its difficulties with the people it encountered along the way. In Kikuyu a protectorate official had recently been killed, and tensions were high. Mackinder's porters were kept from deserting only at gunpoint, and the caravan was on one occasion fired upon.[10] Declining what seemed to be an ominous invitation from Wangombe to camp next to his village, Mackinder continued through the forests of the Kikuyu to the Laikipia steppe at the base of Mount Kenya.

That was when the food began to run out. The party made a base camp on the Laikipia, and Mackinder wrote that "our first attention was to commissariat" ("Mount Kenya," 464). Indeed, the expedition suffered chronic supply problems for the next month and a half. Cajoling, threatening, and finally detaining Wangombe, Mackinder obtained food and the promise of more. While a group of Swahili returned to Wangombe's village for the promised provisions, Mackinder left Hausburg to await their return and led the rest of the party through the thick forest band that surrounded the alpine zone of the mountain. Whereas Gregory had taken three days to penetrate the forest, Mackinder's caravan went through in one.

After making his eighteenth camp of the expedition on August 18, Mackinder wrote: "We made a rapid march and came in with good spirits, for at last we were to make the attempt for which we had come so far" (350). As the object of the expedition and intended centerpiece of that expedition's narrative, the mountain is described in some of Mackinder's most exuberant prose. Mount Kenya, after all, appears as

towering pinnacles of black and ruddy rock, the couloirs and some of the faces white with snow, and with the great falls into the glaciers. In strange contrast are the two great corries to the right with the great ruddy rock walls of a desert aspect, as if it were a piece of Sinai, and the whole is framed in by yet a third contrasted element, the valley slopes set with the green heads of stunted tree groundsel and the silvery tufts of creeping groundsel. (445)

Mackinder's excitement with the climb is evident at times. As he recounts the bivouac on his first attempt on the summit on August 30, the narration grows animated, urgent. He describes the view from the Mummery tent in a sentence that single-handedly takes on the scope of distance and the intensity of the scene:

We watched the last glows of sunset over Sattima, fifty miles to the west, looked across the vast, white, cold cloud roof to the south, saw the fires glow on the Laikipian plain at the foot of the dark forest, saw our deserted tent down in the great, bare, curving Teleki Valley nearer at hand, felt the chill of the white slope, and looked up at the towering pinnacles which were our ambition until the black vault was filled with golden stars, for there was no shade of blue left in the sky and the stars burnt steadily without blinking. (456–57)

Although Mackinder saw Mount Kenya as a window of personal opportunity, the small part of East Africa available for the somewhat specific aspirations that animated his expedition, it was an imperfect window at best. Mackinder's description of the upper mountain was extensively, perhaps anxiously, rewritten and revised. He was torn between a sense of the human isolation of the mountain and a nagging reminder of his ongoing predicament involving restive and uncooperative natives and strained supply lines. On August 20 they found human footprints inside the forest belt — "man Friday was on everyone's lips," Mackinder wrote but crossed it out (365). Later, Mackinder reports that a party of Wanderobo approached some of the expedition's members, commenting and complaining about the number of guns the Europeans were firing on and around the mountain (429).

Mackinder describes how "one's spirits go up and down in this solitude," couching his personal agitation in a indefinite pronoun while hinting at "a great crisis in one's life" (476). Shortly he wrote more directly: "How I long for civilization at times, and yet at others, despite anxiety, exult in the great nature around" (479). Mackinder reports reading *The Old Curiosity Shop* as a temporary escape: "Thank God for Charles Dickens" (481).

Between August 22 and September 13 Mackinder and the two Italian guides, Ollier and Brocherel, made three separate attempts on the summit. Their efforts were interrupted twice by trouble below. In late August two of the expedition's Swahili were ambushed and killed in a pitched battle with Wangombe's followers. Although the party on the mountain subsisted on boxed food brought from England, the base camp did not have sufficient provisions. On August 22 Hausburg sent a party of men to try to obtain food at the government station at Lake Naivasha, which was not only across the border in the Uganda Protectorate but also separated from Mount Kenya by essentially unmapped, untracked mountains. Mackinder later dispatched a second relief party to Naivasha under the command of Saunders. On August 30 Mackinder and the guides reached an elevation of 16,800 feet but were forced to spend a cold night tied to rocks above the Lewis Glacier before being turned back by a cleft in the ridge below the Nelion summit. Ollier and Brocherel later scouted a new route to the summit via the Darwin Glacier but again turned back.

With the food supply critical Mackinder was on the verge of evacuating the expedition when a food caravan arrived from Naivasha. On September 11 Mackinder, Ollier, and Brocherel made what would have to be their final attempt on the summit. The weather was not altogether promising. Mackinder recorded the readings in his journal and observed that the mountain was rapidly clouding over, the temperature chilling. Yet in camp that night Mackinder wrote in his journal: "What a beautiful mountain Kenya is, very graceful, not stern, but, as it seems to me, with a cold feminine beauty."

In the morning the mountain would prove more stern. The party again crossed the Lewis Glacier and spent another night in a Mummery tent huddled together "like sardines . . . stiff and cold-footed" (472). On the thirteenth Mackinder and his companions crossed a rock band to the Darwin Glacier and spent three hours traversing the "steep and intensely hard" ice ("Mount Kenya," 473), laboriously cutting steps most of the way. At the top of the glacier Mackinder found a biscuit tin discarded by Ollier and Brocherel on their earlier reconnaissance, and he wrote in his journal: "We now followed the arete above the biscuit tin." Finding this narrow ridge too steep to continue, the three men descended to a hanging glacier that looked like it might lead to the summit. Mackinder remembered later that "the glacier was steep, so that our shoulders were close to it. Had we fallen, we should have gone over an ice cliff onto the Darwin Glacier several hundred feet below." But the party chose their footing carefully, and as Mackinder tells it:

At last we reached the stone again, and almost exactly at noon set foot on the summit, which is like a low tower rising out of a heap of ruin. . . . On the top were two or three little turrets close together, and on these we sat. A small platform, a few feet lower, adjoined the south-eastern corner of the crag, and from this I got the shots with my Kodak of the summit with Cesar and Joseph upon it. (475)

With the mountain climbed, all seemed anticlimax. Mackinder led the entire expedition on to Naivasha, where he rushed on ahead to reach London on October 30. Despite the eyebrows raised when the director of the brand new Oxford School of Geography arrived late to teach his own classes, the expedition was a success. Mackinder not only achieved the summit but he had surveyed 150 miles of new ground, mapped the upper reaches of the mountain, and brought back valuable meteorological information and a wealth of photographic material, as well as collections of plant and animal specimens, including, as a matter of fact, a new species of gladiolus, christened *procavia mackinderi*. Write his name next to Livingstone's.

All this sounds right and true, the stuff of wilderness travel, the psychology of high altitude and being far from home. This was, after all, supposed to be a mountain-climbing expedition. As Mackinder maintained, the goal of climbing the mountain took precedence over everything, even scientific investigation. The reader of "Mount Kenya," however, is left with the strange impression that the sections of the narrative that treat the three summit attempts are brief and even anticlimactic in comparison to the larger processes of the expedition, the movement through the political landscape of East Africa, the troubled scrounging for food, and the eventual return to British civilization. It is something of a convention in mountaineering literature that the mountain be represented as a place set apart, a refuge for Europeans from the cultural strangeness of the alien world surrounding it or even from the complexities of life at home, a place where, as the mountaineer Samuel Turner put it, "the climber seems as free as Nature itself" (247). This is certainly a pleasing illusion. The illusion of freedom, of being part and parcel with nature, in "Mount Kenya" is thoroughly lodged within the machinations of culture and politics, and the twenty-two days that the expedition spent on Mount Kenya seem remarkably overshadowed in an expedition that took more than four months to grind back and forth from London.

When Mackinder read a brief account of the expedition to a meeting of the Royal Geographical Society on January 22, 1900, the then vice president of the RGS, Sir Thomas Holdich, praised not only Mackinder's work as an explorer and as a mountaineer but also the job he did in recording and publicly presenting the results of the expedition. "Mr. Mackinder's story of difficulties met and overcome in his plucky ascent of Mount Kenya," Holdich said after the reading of the paper, "together with the delightful series of illustrations he has given us, may, I think, be considered a model of descriptive illustration" ("Mount Kenya," 476). Holdich's remark can be read as more than casual approbation. In a broad sense it reflects the Royal Geographical Society's long-term commitment to encouraging and disseminating the narrative record of exploration. More specifically, Holdich's claim that the expedition's report and photographs could stand as a "model of descriptive illustration" suggests how they conformed to the conventionalized RGS format for exploration narrative. Young Mackinder was already showing his mettle.

It was, after all, quite an accomplishment for a young professor, perhaps especially in light of Mackinder's severely limited résumé as a mountain climber. Although he traveled outside Britain almost every year during the 1890s, this Kenya expedition would clearly be no hop across the channel. Furthermore, whereas Mackinder's trips to North America and the Continent centered around scholarly, or academic, projects or contacts, his Kenya expedition would be for the purpose of direct scientific investigation, to say nothing of adventure and exploration.[11] Mackinder described himself as "a professional neither in surveying nor climbing" (Mackinder, MS C-100). His written work before 1900 focused on geographical education, not exploration, and his specific area of geographical expertise before the turn of the century was close to home — the British Isles. Indeed, his two initial published accounts of the Mount Kenya climb that appeared in 1900 (a reminiscence about the climb was published in 1930 on the occasion of the mountain's second ascent) stand out among his more than one hundred published articles and books dealing with geographical exploration. Apart from the Kenya expedition in 1899, Mackinder was simply not an explorer. Nor was he a mountaineer. Only after he decided that he would travel to East Africa did he begin to climb, practicing near Zermatt for several weeks with an Alpine guide during the summer of 1898. His interest in mountaineering clearly was based on the one-time goal of getting to the summit of Mount Kenya.[12] The climb almost seemed to have come out of nowhere.

Mackinder was most likely influenced in his decision to attempt Mount Kenya by his in-laws. Sidney Langford Hinde, one of Mackinder's brothers-in-law, had for several years pursued a career in African colonial affairs and in 1895 had received an administrator's appointment to the East African Protectorate. Hinde and his wife, Hilda, became experts on East African languages and cultures, collaborating in 1901 on the book *The Last of the Masai*. It was probably from the Hindes that Mackinder not only gained insight into the beauty and interest of Kenya but also came by the more specific piece of information that doubtlessly shaped the nature of his expedition — that the Uganda Railway, then under construction, would soon reach the new town of Nairobi and the mountains in the east-central part of the protectorate where Mount Kenya was located.

The advance of the railway dramatically changed the logistics of climbing Mount Kenya. The distance and difficulty of the terrain between the mountain and the coast had been a background factor in the failure of the Teleki and Gregory parties of a few years before. From Mackinder's point of view the railway put the mountain within striking distance, making its ascent a little more like an Alpine climbing problem and a little less like an extended wilderness trek. For a university teacher who had only the summer months free from the classroom, this was a must. Additionally, Mackinder must have realized that he was not the only one who would recognize the transport potential of the Uganda Railway. His journals from the trip, in fact, contain a number of worried references to rumors that other expeditions were approaching Mount Kenya. In 1945 Mackinder remembered that while trying to promote the expedition among the *right* people at the RGS, he also tried to hush it up among others, for, as he put it, "I had no wish to find myself competitor in a race up a virgin peak" (quoted in "Annual General Meeting," 231–32).

Mackinder may have had purely personal reasons for wanting to climb Mount Kenya. Blouet suggests as much:

> Mackinder was, in a phrase of today, an over-achiever. Many of the people he knew were soldiers or explorers who had demonstrated skill and courage in difficult circumstances. To have worked with Lord Wantage, V.C., the soldier; Markham, the explorer; Henry Bates, the naturalist of Amazonia; Douglas Freshfield, the alpinist; and Mosely, the scientist on *Challenger,* made it difficult for Mackinder not to show that he was capable of similar feats. (*Sir Halford,* 77)

In this sense Mackinder's expedition to Mount Kenya, although his only foray into exploration and although he never did anything like it before or after, was typical of his life's work. Mackinder never did one thing for long. Like many another restless student, he moved through a series of disciplines, from biology to law to geography. He left an extension instructorship to found the Oxford School of Geography, only to drift away to help found Reading University and later the London School of Economics. By 1908 Mackinder had left academe altogether, for, as he described it later in life, "spheres of wider experience" ("Annual General Meeting," 232), entering politics and, later, private business. Mackinder had a pioneer's sense of initiative and perhaps impatience, a "love of beginnings," Blouet calls it (*Halford Mackinder,* 202). Achieving one goal, he was soon ready to pursue another. It is consistent with much else in Mackinder's life to consider the Kenya trip in this context. Also, as Mackinder contemplated his East African adventure, he was becoming increasingly estranged from his wife, Bonnie, who had returned to live with her family in 1897.[13] The increasing distance between husband and wife could very well have created a situation in which Mackinder felt that the time for another, very different sort of undertaking was ripe.

Furthermore, Mackinder was propelled to exploration more by concrete personal inducements than by a temperamental drive to achieve. As I have already suggested, the Royal Geographical Society was moving through a period of transition during the late 1890s.[14] For many of the more traditional, one might even say, Victorian, explorers within the organization, exploring the unknown was the condition of geographical credibility. The current president of the society, Clements Markham, was convinced that the business of the society was exploration and not education. In his handwritten book about his tenure as president of the society, Markham wrote that RGS monies were being "recklessly lavished on educational experiments from 1886–1893" (194). He elsewhere expressed his distrust of geographers who lacked direct experience in pushing back the earth's unexplored "blank spaces."

With the society's financial support of the fledgling geography programs at Oxford, Cambridge, and Manchester up for annual review, and with the powerful faction headed by Markham increasingly impatient with the whole notion of academic geography, Mackinder felt that not only his personal position but the unsteady status of British geography as a whole may have been at stake. As newly elected president of the Geographical Section of the British Association, he began to argue in 1895 for the establishment of a permanent school of geography at either London or Oxford. As part of the promotion of this scheme, Mackinder decided on a new tactic to win over Markham and the RGS exploration boosters. As the foremost geographical educator of the day, he decided, in short, to prove his worth "both 'in the field and in the study,' " as RGS president George Clerk put it ("Annual General Meeting," 230). Mackinder let it be known that he would explore and climb Mount Kenya and began making preparations for the expedition. When he was awarded the society's Patron's Medal in 1945, Mackinder plainly admitted that his motivation for going to East Africa was to establish credibility with the society. "I was given a leave of absence to visit East Africa," he recalled, "because at that time most people would have had no use for a geographer who was not an adventurer and explorer" ("Annual General Meeting," 231). The strategy was a success. During the summer of 1898, when Mackinder was practicing his mountaineering in Switzerland, Markham wrote to the vice chancellor of Oxford, proposing to split the difference financially in founding a school of geography there. Although Mackinder's arguments, as well as his explorations, played a part in persuading Markham in favor of the school, it is significant that the trip to Kenya and the beginnings of the school coincided almost exactly. In fact, Mackinder left the expedition still in Africa on September 30, hurrying back on the first steamer from Mombasa to begin his teaching well into the school's first term. When his report of the expedition came out the next year, no one was surprised to learn that Mackinder had named a "raised strip" in the Aberdare Mountains west of Mount Kenya the "Markham Downs" and alluded to the "presidential character" of the range ("Mount Kenya," 475).

In many ways the presence of Halford Mackinder on Mount Kenya perfectly embodies the spirit of "lateness" at play in the relationship between mountaineering and exploration during his day, an era when, as E. A. Rieves put it, "the days of the pioneer explorer of the old type are fast drawing to a close" (*Hints,* 1921, vii). If the earth was perceived as just about all discovered and explored, mountains came to represent remnants of unknown and untraveled terrain that still presented opportunities for would-be explorers, who often had been raised on the exploits of Cook, Franklin, and Livingstone. Africa, in particular, in the late nineteenth century was a rather crowded imperial venue. It was rarely conceived of as vacant, that is to say, empty of white men or "civilized" European-style governments and therefore inviting free-for-all conquest. Instead, it was an arena for "effective occupation" as the Berlin West Africa Conference defined it, an area where European governments competed with each other for first economic and then political control, a kind of Europe once removed. Even though its coastlines, river systems, and trade markets had been discovered, explored, and contested — in some cases for hundreds of years — its three principal mountainous areas, Kilimanjaro, Kenya, and the Ruwenzori range, had not even been seen by Europeans before 1848 and, when Mackinder set out in 1899, with the exception of Kilimanjaro, had still not been climbed.

This is especially interesting because in Africa the relationship between mountaineering and exploration had a literally ancient history. One of the great problems for Europeans exploring Africa, locating the source of the Nile, had for two thousand years been associated by rumor, legend, and classical writ with a mysterious and elusive range of mountains. Aeschylus referred to "Egypt nurtured by the snow"; Aristotle spoke of the source of the Nile as being "a silver mountain"; and Herodotus wrote that the river came from between "sharp-pointed peaks" far to the south. During the second century the Roman geographer Ptolemy (Claudius Ptolemaeus) described the source of the Blue Nile as a lake to the east and named the source of the western White Nile as a pair of lakes fed by the melting snow of the "Mountains of the Moon." Only in the midnineteenth century were Europeans in a position to put these assertions to the test.

Ptolemy's geography proved remarkably correct. While working at their mission in Mombasa, two German missionaries, Ludwig Krapf and Johann Rebmann, heard stories from Arab traders about mountains deep in the interior covered with a white substance — perhaps salt, they were told. In 1848 Rebmann saw one of these mountains, Kilimanjaro, from a distance, and the next year Krapf saw Mount Kenya, capped with a substance he more accurately identified as snow. Despite the traditional association of the Nile source with mountains, the reports of Krapf and Rebmann of snow-covered mountains within only a few degrees of the equator were widely dismissed. But in 1855, when Rebmann reported native stories of a huge central African lake, a "Sea of Ujiji" perhaps as large as the Caspian, the possibility of corroborating Ptolemy's description of a lake source for the Nile met with a more sympathetic response.

This rumor, and the map that Rebmann and a colleague, Jacob Erhardt, produced showing this massive body of water, set loose the most energetic and best-known period in European African exploration since Mungo Park's death on the Niger River in the west in 1806.[15] Within a year Burton and Speke had set out on a remarkable journey that would lead them in February 1858 to Lake Tanganyika and would lead Speke in August to Lake Victoria Nyanza, which Speke believed, at the time largely on faith alone, to be the source of the White Nile. In 1863 Samuel and Florence Baker traced the river to Lake Albert Nyanza, to the west of Lake Victoria. After pioneering routes across the continent by way of the Zambezi River system to the south during the 1850s, David Livingstone traveled farther into central Africa in 1866, searching for the source of the Nile in the area of Lake Nyasa and Lake Tanganyika, and as far as the Lualaba River far to the north. As it turned out, Speke and the Bakers were on the right track. In 1863 Speke located the Victoria Nile, which empties from Lake Victoria, and the Bakers followed the western tributary of the river much farther than it had ever previously been. But as Samuel Baker stood at the shore of Lake Albert, he reported that "on the west, at fifty or sixty miles distance, blue mountains rose from the bosom of the lake" (quoted in Newby, 207). Twenty-two years later Henry Morton Stanley would prove that these mountains far to the south of Lake Albert were the other source of the Nile, Ptolemy's "Mountains of the Moon," known locally as the Ruwenzori.[16] In 1906 a party led by the duca d'Abruzzi climbed the highest peaks in the range and mapped much of the region around them.

For the better part of twenty years during the middle of the century, the vast region of mountains, plains, and desert east of Lake Victoria remained an obvious omission from European exploration of the continent. Compared with other areas on the continent, the Niger, Congo, and Zambezi basins, Ethiopia, the Sudan, and the Great Lakes, East Africa was something of an exploratory backwater. But despite a comparatively slow start, the pace of exploration in the region east of the lakes picked up dramatically in the 1880s. From the early years of the decade, when German trading concerns actively began to develop their commercial interests south along the coast from Zanzibar, German explorers began to make discoveries across the vast distances of the East African interior. The early reports of Krapf and Rebmann about unlikely equatorial mountains were confirmed by Karl Klaus von der Decken during 1861–62 as he explored the region immediately around Mount Kilimanjaro. Gustav Adolf Fischer also operated in the area during 1882 and during 1885–86 farther south of Masai country to the southern shores of Lake Victoria. Scientific exploration of Tanganyika began in 1880 as three German explorers worked their way from Zanzibar to the western fringe of the Congo basin. In 1885 Teleki discovered Lakes Rudolf and Stefanie to the north of Lake Victoria.

The British, for their part, were just as active. In 1883 the Royal Geographical Society sent Joseph Thomson to find a route from Mombasa to Uganda, past Mount Kilimanjaro, Lake Naivasha, and Mount Kenya. The route presented a variety of topographical difficulties, but the most significant obstacle was the intimidating presence of a number of indigenous peoples who showed a marked hostility to European invasion. Although other groups, most notably the Nandi and Bunyoro, actually resisted the British takeover of East Africa more strenuously than did the Masai, Thomson's trouble with the Masai established their reputation as the most dangerous "hostiles" on the East African plains. Only by joining a large trading caravan for protection after a number of close calls with war parties did Thomson succeed in crossing the Masai country to Lake Victoria.

By making this three-thousand-mile round trip, Thomson in effect became the trailblazer for British colonial activity between Uganda and the coast. In 1891 Capt. J. R. L. MacDonald began to survey the route pioneered by Thomson for a projected 657-mile railway between Mombasa and Lake Victoria, and construction of the line began in 1895 under the direction of a young English engineer, George Whitehouse.[17]

In the midst of a region that in 1899 had been explored only recently, Mount Kenya was a particularly obscure point on a still rather sketchy map. After Krapf's 1849 glimpse of Mount Kenya the mountain was largely ignored for thirty-eight years. Although the experienced Africa explorer F. G. Dundas had disappeared in the forest belt south of the mountain some years before, it was not until 1887, as British and German commercial activity in East Africa brought more attention to the region, that Teleki, and shortly afterward Gregory, made the first serious attempts on the mountain. Mount Kenya had, after all, only inadvertently been discovered by Europeans while they were searching for something else. Krapf in his 1860 *Travels, Researches, and Missionary Labors . . . in East Africa* described Mount Kenya (which he originally named Mount Albert) parenthetically in his discussion of rivers that might be parts of the Nile system.[18] It was a marginal place in a marginal landscape.

In essays published both before and after his Kenya expedition, Mackinder acknowledged, and perhaps suggested that he shared, the conception of an earth whose geographical mysteries were shrinking. In his important and career-founding 1887 address to the Royal Geographical Society, "The Scope and Methods of Geography," Mackinder used the extent and success of exploration as an occasion to redefine geography not so much as the practice of exploration as a matter of education. He wrote:

> For half a century several societies, and most of all our own, have been active in promoting the exploration of the world. The natural result is that we are now near the end of the roll of great discoveries. The Polar regions are the only large blanks remaining on our maps. A Stanley can never again reveal a Congo to the delighted world. For a time good work will be done in New Guinea, in Africa, in Central Asia, and along the boundaries of the frozen regions. For a time a Greeley will now and again receive the old ringing welcome, and will prove that it is not heroes that are wanting. But as tales of adventure grow fewer and fewer, as their place is more and more taken by the details of Ordnance Surveys, even Fellows of the Geographical Societies will despondently ask, "What is geography?" (*Democratic Ideals*, 212–13)

In his 1904 "The Geographical Pivot of History," Mackinder not only updated this conception of exploration as being in its latter days but suggested its intimate involvement with political, strategic acquisition:

> Of late it has been a common-place to speak of geographical exploration as nearly over, and it is recognized that geography must be diverted to the purpose of intensive survey and philosophic synthesis. In 400 years the outline of the map of the world has been completed with approximate accuracy, and even in the polar regions the voyages of Nansen and Scott have very narrowly reduced the last possibility of dramatic discoveries. But the opening of the twentieth century is appropriate as the end of a great historic epoch, not merely on account of this achievement, great though it may be. The missionary, the conqueror, the farmer, the miner, and,

of late, the engineer, have followed so closely in the traveller's footsteps that the world, in its remoter borders, has hardly been revealed before we must chronicle its virtually complete political appropriation. (*Democratic Ideals*, 241)

Mackinder connected the end of the age of European exploration with the beginnings of the world as a "closed political system" of "world-wide scope" (*Democratic Ideals,* 242); exploration determines, in Mackinder's thinking, modern political actuality. In a rapidly closing Africa, Mount Kenya was in 1899 at least one of the white spaces on Europeans maps, a minor open question in an increasingly closed system. It was situated in a region of Africa that had not received the early and intense exploration that other areas had, and that in fact held huge tracts of unmapped terrain, and the mountain itself was an island of obscurity even in a relatively poorly known surrounding landscape. Mount Kenya represented a small piece of geography where real discovery and achievement could occur. For Mackinder this represented a unique opportunity. By 1898 he was making plans to seize it.

Mackinder's "Mount Kenya" tells the story of movement from the familiar, comprehensible, controllable environment of London to one of difficulty, conflict, danger, and often cultural incoherence. Although "Mount Kenya" was ostensibly about a mountain climb, only a small share of the problems that the expedition encountered have much directly to do with the rock and ice of the mountain. A full half of Mackinder's narrative, for example, goes by before the expedition even arrives at the mountain. "Mount Kenya," in fact, implicitly embodies the argument that mountain climbing has significance in the larger context of a full range of European activities at the boundaries of empire and their effect on native populations.

Inside the back cover of the original typescript of "Mount Kenya," Mackinder prominently included Benjamin Kidd's *The Control of the Tropics* on a list of "authorities on East Africa." Kidd's 1898 book was a recent addition to imperialist literature on Africa. Kidd maintained that in the 1890s European colonial rivalry no longer concerned itself with places suitable for European habitation. The tropics, in Kidd's view, had only limited value for the kind of permanent relocation that had been important in the colonial development of, say, North America. A European in the tropics, according to Kidd, tended to degenerate physically and "sink slowly to the level of the races amongst whom he had made his unnatural home" (50–51).

Mackinder's narrative, perhaps inadvertently, displays East Africa as just such an "unnatural home" for Europeans, a place where the landscape is characterized by a very superficial, even tenuous, veneer of European influence and control. Mackinder's account of his journey from London to Zanzibar to Kenya establishes a geopolitical context in which German colonialism, British naval might, racial difference, and the imminent South African conflict operate to reveal a geography at the very political and cultural limits of the British Empire. In Mackinder's East Africa nothing is settled. Mackinder's emphasis on the prominence of the military and the proselytizing church in East Africa suggests this. Mackinder reports that other passengers, while sailing down the coast of East Africa, were mostly military men and missionaries headed for various posts in Africa. Twelve days out of London the British imperium begins to assert itself in the narrative as Mackinder reports a British warship at anchorage at Jibuti (Djibouti) in Ethiopia "dressed with flags, in honour of the queen's accession" (6). Similarly, when Mackinder sails into port at Zanzibar on June 28, "the Queen's Coronation Day," he mentions the predominance of the Royal Navy, which had three appropriately decorated men-of-war in the harbor, compared to a lone German warship. Mackinder regards the masts of the sunken "Sultan's ship" protruding from the water in the harbor as a "valuable reminder to the Arabs" (13), a "reminder of England's power" (20). With perhaps inadvertent symbolism Mackinder writes that with British officials in Zanzibar, he "talked of the bombardment, which is the equivalent of 'the year of the earthquake' here, and we ate corned hump of beef."[19] He observes: "HMS *Thrush* left today for Delagoa Bay in connection with the Boer difficulty. The Germans have three men-of-war on this coast" (26). In a rough sketch of the skyline of Zanzibar, which Mackinder included in "Mount Kenya," the images of consulate flags and European churches predominate (20). In the captain's stateroom aboard the British warship *Philomel* at Zanzibar, Mackinder writes, "I noticed that Bearcroft's books included Hall's *International Law* and realized why a navigating officer is needed. The captain of a man-of-war fights his ship, maintains discipline, acts as a travelling diplomat and magistrate, and only supervises navigation" (38). One might wonder at this point in the story when the mountain climbing will ever begin.

In particular, the colonial rivalry that by 1899 had been playing itself out in East Africa between Britain and Germany for almost twenty years figures prominently in Mackinder's representation of the margins of the empire. In Zanzibar Mackinder learns that the boundary between British and German territory is in local dispute again, around Kilimanjaro as well as at the coast (31). Adopting the mistrust that increasingly characterized the British perception of German foreign policy during the era, Mackinder writes cryptically in his notebook: "The German man-of-war always has steam up" and jots in the margin "why?" (*Journals*, 1:32). This political orientation merges with personal interest in "Mount Kenya." The German explorer Hans Meyer, who had made the first ascent of Kilimanjaro in 1889, is Mackinder's implicit rival in East Africa. Mackinder mentions that while he was in Zanzibar a German exploring party under Lionel Decle arrived by mail boat (29) and that a German hunter told him that Meyer meant to climb Mount Kenya the next year. In his notebook Mackinder mentions that Meyer had just climbed Mawenzi and writes with unusual feeling: "that Meyer estimates Mount Kenya to be 500 feet higher than Kilimanjaro!!!???" (1:41).

Just as European interest in central Africa focused on the search for the sources of the Nile and marginalized the interior of East Africa, so did European political aims center around the same geographical nexus, an area where British, French, German, Italian, and Belgian exploration had created a zone of conflicting claims and interests. East Africa was an imperial backwater for Britain long before it was the mountaineering backwater so attractive to Mackinder in the late 1890s.[20]

"Modern European imperialism," D. K. Fieldhouse writes, "produced few more extraordinary episodes than the rapid occupation by Britain, Germany and Italy of the vast regions of East Africa" (*Economics*, 362). And rapid it was. Before 1884 none of the European powers held actual possessions or administered colonies in the region. The Italians and Belgians had no contact at all with East Africa south of Ethiopia before 1880. The Germans and French, in many cases overshadowed by Americans, maintained trading interests along the coast, especially at Zanzibar, the island commercial hub of the region. The British, also operating only minor trading concerns at Zanzibar and focusing most of their political and exploratory attention farther to the west and north on Egypt, the Sudan, and the sources of the Nile, did not manifest much of an interest in East Africa, although they considered it an informal area of influence. In short, in 1880 Europe seemed to have only the sketchiest reasons for imperial expansion in the region. Yet within a span of six years that is exactly what occurred. In 1886 the Anglo-German Agreement drew a political line from the coast south of Mombasa to the eastern shore of Lake Victoria, excluding the claims of other European nations, demarking British and German spheres of commercial interest, and dividing East Africa into a British protectorate to the north of the line and a German protectorate to the south.

British interest in East Africa reflected a combination of perceived humanitarian and strategic motives. Since the 1820s the African slave trade had been a public issue and affront in Britain, and its suppression had sent waves of European missionaries into the continent. Yet the perception was widespread that in East Africa, Britain did not need to rule in order to discourage the slave trade; from 1822 on, the British could act through the sultans of Zanzibar. In West Africa, Britain had acquired Sierra Leone as a naval base for the suppression of the slave trade, but in East Africa the Foreign Office was satisfied that Zanzibar already afforded the same opportunity but without the expense of formal colonial acquisition. A more complex issue arose with respect to the geographical position of East Africa. As I have already suggested, much of Britain's interest in Africa during the mid- to late nineteenth century centered on the Nile and its sources, simultaneously a strategic concern, romantic mystery, and national symbol. But with no land route open from the east coast to the lake region of the interior before the 1880s, East Africa was perceived as barely tangential to the Nile. A more immediately pressing issue with respect to East Africa was that announced later by Mackinder, its relationship to the British route to India. Long occupied with securing and maintaining lines of sea and land transport to its Indian possessions, the British Foreign Office saw East Africa as a link in the tenuous communications, trade, and military chain that connected London with the subcontinent. As long as no other European governments showed signs of extending commercial influence or political control over East Africa, particularly its ports, no problem existed. Certainly, in the view of most Britons direct political administration and colonization did not seem at the time to be called for. As late as 1884 the government turned down a proposal by Harry Johnston to turn a tract of land that he owned near Mount Kilimanjaro into a chartered British colony. Before 1886 Britain apparently had no intention of imposing formal colonial rule there.

Yet the economic underpinnings of empire were already developing in the 1870s. In 1876 the shipping magnate William Mackinnon and anti-slavery leader T. F. Buxton had begun construction of a road from Dar-es-Salaam to Lake Nyasa, with the dual purpose of developing commerce and suppressing slavery in East Africa. In 1877 Mackinnon had come close to negotiating the concession of large tracts of land from the sultan Barghash for the British India Steam Navigation Company, then operating a steamship service between Aden, Zanzibar, and Natal.[21] In 1884 when the German imperial entrepreneur Carl Peters obtained similar concessions while representing the Gesellschaft für Deutsche Kolonisation (soon to be transferred to the Deutsche-Ostafrikanische Gesellschaft), Mackinnon was finally able to act on his plans, forming the Imperial British East Africa Company. Both commercial organizations, German and British, soon came under the direct control of their respective governments as formal protectorates were established in the area.[22]

So what explains the rapid evolution of territorial empire in East Africa? Bismarck's 1884 decision to impose German protection on East Africa speaks to an intermingling of economic and political motives too complicated to present here. Although German traders had established operations in the region, and in fact European trade and shipping were generally expanding before 1880, Fieldhouse suggests that German bankers and financiers did not back political annexation there.[23] While German businessmen sought support from their government in keeping East Africa open to trade, they did not pressure Bismarck for colonization.

It is inviting to read British political expansion in East Africa as essentially reactionary. Although schemes by British financiers to develop the already established but marginal trade situation in the region began to take shape in the 1870s, demand for British intervention on economic grounds alone was not sufficient to prompt the government to extend imperial protection. Many investors in East African trade and proponents of political takeover probably acted as much from a patriotic desire to limit German expansion in the area as they did the desire for financial profit.[24] In addition, the loose trade and consular influence that Britain had enjoyed in East Africa for years was regarded as worth preserving not only for the purpose of suppressing slavery but also for the practical purpose of watching over the sea lanes to India. Granting a trade concession to the Imperial British East Africa Company was seen as an inexpensive way of achieving this without government involvement.

However, another important consideration was affecting British policy in East Africa. By 1890, when Britain and Germany signed a firm agreement dividing their protectorates, the Foreign Office had made important strategic reassessments about Africa. Egypt, occupied by the British since 1882, had long been the hub of Royal Navy operations in the Mediterranean. With the French, Belgians, and Italians increasingly showing signs of extending their control closer to the Nile, British strategists viewed the upper reaches of the river with growing concern. By 1890 official policy was to exclude other powers from the Upper Nile. In 1894 British and French desires to consolidate their holds over their African possessions collided at the Nile. Word reached London that France was planning to use political unrest in Egypt as a fresh occasion to challenge British control of the Nile and therefore Egypt. At the time the only British presence on the Upper Nile in Uganda was the loosely organized trading operation of the Imperial British East Africa Company, clearly not much of a redoubt against a feared French military incursion from West Africa. The government decision to take over Uganda from the company in 1894 was seen as the only practical means of stemming French designs on the region. In 1898, when a French military expedition under Jean-Baptiste Marchand marched to the Nile at Fashoda in the Sudan, the security of Egypt again became an issue played out far upriver. The extension of political control over Uganda served to forestall the immediate possibility of a similar confrontation.[25] In the final analysis, the geographical position of East Africa in relation to larger British strategic concerns transcending the region itself raised the value of maintaining sufficient control of East Africa to overcome what had been a long-held reluctance to extend political responsibility there.

As Mackinder's emphasis on East Africa as a European naval outpost may suggest, the European presence in East Africa is to a large degree marked in "Mount Kenya" by its preoccupation with the technological means of achieving and maintaining that presence. The involvement of transportation and communication at the fringes of the empire is a persistent theme in exploration literature of the period. With Mackinder railroads are the particular focus. The pattern of reference to military vessels, so distinct in Mackinder's discussion of Zanzibar, carries over to his absorption in the topic of ground transportation as he narrates his progress after landing in the East Africa Protectorate at Mombasa, where he begins the transport of his expedition inland on the Uganda Railway.

"Mount Kenya," after all, begins in a train station. The narrative's first line, announces: "We left Charing Cross by the evening mail on the 8th. of June 1899" (1), and establishes the primary relationship between modern transportation and mountaineering that not only provides the expedition with its occasion and means but also suggests one of its principal themes. Mackinder continues his emphasis on railroads in the entry for June 20 when he notes the large number of Italian workers on hand at Jibuti in Ethiopia. "Surely a very southern spot for white navvies [*sic*] to do the work of railway construction," he comments (6). In Zanzibar on June 30 Mackinder learns that from the Uganda Railway the Somali Tippu Tib "had seen Kenya from a distance" (35). Of the few remarks Mackinder makes concerning his brief stop in the German protectorate port of Tanga on July 3, he does mention that it is the terminus of a German railroad and notes rumors of the unusually large number of German troops in the capital of Dar-es-Salaam (53). In Mombasa "the air is never free from the panting of a locomotive or two" (93).

East Africa in "Mount Kenya" is in part, then, a technologically determined geography, in which the machines that move the explorer and the empire to and past its bounds measure his perceptions of distance and shape. Like the warships at Zanzibar, the Uganda Railway is a part of a transportation network linking London with its possessions and interests abroad. Mackinder traces, for example, how the coal used to power the railroad comes by sea, from Cardiff through the Suez Canal (78). While narrating the rail journey inland from Mombasa, Mackinder has the predictable movement of the train to structure the narrative. Each entry is fixed according to its progress.

But this predictable yardstick of the railroad is lost to Mackinder when the expedition takes to foot. The narrative divides rather sharply at the point that the expedition leaves the Uganda Railway. "At last we were away," Mackinder writes for July 28 (170). The extent of hand corrections to the typescript increases markedly on page 170 of the manuscript, just at the point that the expedition leaves on foot from Nairobi. Spatial orientation had been clear, essentially linear, while on the train, marked off in the narrative by reference to mileage on the railroad. Anxiety comes to infect the perception of the landscape while on foot in strange country; the mode of fixing location becomes more complex, relative, no longer the two-dimensional plot between Mombasa and Nairobi. Mackinder notes that the elevation of the country increases "imperceptibly" as he advances (200); the barometer reveals the change in elevation even if it is not apparent to the senses. With the "vast, gently curved slopes of Kenya" (200) visible in the far distance, and the "gate of Meranga" rising in the middle distance, Mackinder increasingly begins to fix location on a vertical, as well as a horizontal, axis.

As Mackinder recounts the expedition's trek toward the mountain, his use of comparative language in "Mount Kenya" further reflects his perception that this new landscape harbors mixed and conflicting elements. As "the country grew" (200) in elevation while the expedition climbs from the unfamiliar dryness of the East African plains to the mountain highlands, Mackinder increasingly stresses what reminds him of home. Increasingly, the forests and agricultural areas of Kikuyu and Meranga prompt Mackinder to comment on the "English appearance of the scene" (313). For August 12 Mackinder writes that in Meranga, fields "had all the appearance of an English ploughed field" and that the paths "were like English by-ways" (293).[26] On one hand, while the Kenyan highlands are botanically and climatically more similar to England than either the tropical coast or the dry interior of East Africa, what is remarkable about this pattern of comparison is that references to similarity actually increase as the landscape becomes less culturally familiar.

For July 24 Mackinder writes that around Nairobi "the Masai sacred trees are conspicuous landmarks" (163). Whereas railroad mile markers and protectorate outposts provided convenient gauges to space along the Uganda Railway, cultural difference orients space away from the railroad. While traveling on the railroad, Mackinder and his party had carried Europe with them into the wilderness in a very conspicuous, powerful, and effective manner. They had "ridden" on Europe, extended technologically into the interior of Africa. The relative ease and habituation afforded by the railroad postpones the recounting of difficulty and danger that soon dominates the narrative. Yet by his August 15 entry, Mackinder must finally admit that his comparisons to England have failed to render East Africa coherent and that he "longed for the eyes of the natives, and for the knowledge of the naturalist to recognize all that could be seen and heard" (321).

Since the midnineteenth century railroads had both symbolized the industrial revolution sweeping Europe and carried it in real, practical terms. Railroads were also coming to be seen in terms of their military and strategic significance. In 1873 the effective military use of rail transport had been a decisive factor in the victory of a newly united Germany over France. For many in Britain the construction of the Trans-Siberian Railroad during the years 1891–1903 represented Russian expansionism in Asia and thus its potential threat to British India, dangerously bolstered by technology. Not until the Japanese defeated the perilously overextended Russian forces in the Far East in 1905 would this fear be somewhat allayed. Even then, as a traditional sea power, Britain was the odd man out in the strategic application of rail transportation in Asia.

It was not the case in Africa. British imperial aims quickly became involved with rail transport. From the 1880s on, the romantic notion of a vast British empire embracing much of the continent had grown up with the quest for the source of the Nile, the territorial ambitions of Cecil Rhodes in South Africa, and the desire to retake the Sudan after the death of Charles George Gordon at Khartoum. For Mackinder, in terms of his 1919 version of the pivot theory, British imperial expansion in Africa represented cashing in on the potential for Africa to act as a southern "heartland," with presumably some capacity to offset the northern, Asian heartland, which obviously was in the hands of Russia and perhaps Germany.

To a significant degree these ambitions were involved with actual and fanciful rail construction projects. In the 1880s Rhodes had offered to build at his own expense a railway north from the Cape Colony to Zambesia as a means of solidifying British influence in the area against the conflicting claims of the Portuguese. Ultimately, Rhodes's designs extended much farther. He hoped that Britain would forge a dominion from South Africa all the way to Egypt, a vision that he expressed in his advocacy of a Cape-to-Cairo railway, an idea originally suggested by Gordon while serving in Egypt. Although this southern version of the German "Berlin-to-Baghdad" line never materialized, what Rhodes thought of as one of its spur lines, the Uganda Railway, in fact did.

Called a "gigantic folly" by many both in and out of Parliament, the railroad was first of all a feat of engineering and human endurance. Under George Whitehouse's energetic direction construction took six years. The 581-mile line (about eighty miles shorter than originally projected) crossed terrain that resembled, as Eric Newby suggests, "the temperature chart of a patient who is suffering from an undulant fever which grows steadily worse" (214). The thousands of Indians working on the railroad were ravaged in turn by malaria, dysentery, and the tsetse fly as construction moved from the coast into the Taru Desert. At Tsavo lions ate twenty-eight men. By 1900 the tracks had crossed the Great Rift Valley and by 1901 the ten-thousand-foot Mau Escarpment, only to encounter disease and menacing native predation on the western downhill leg of the route to Kisumu on Lake Victoria.[27]

The construction of the Uganda Railway was in many ways both the result and the instrument of a complex and evolving political drama being played out in East Africa from the 1880s on. Although a succession of

British governments had been reluctant to take political control of East Africa, between 1893 and 1895 the so-called liberal imperialists under Prime Minister Lord Rosebury extended official British protection over a half-million square miles of the region.[28] When Lord Salisbury's Unionist government inherited this vast territory, incorporated into the Uganda and East African Protectorates, it almost immediately began to promote the construction of a railroad linking the interior lake region to the coast. Salisbury argued that such a rail line would encourage commerce and settlement in the new British territory while working against the slave trade by bringing British authority and the reach of missionaries closer to its roots. Furthermore, the Salisbury government pointed out, the railroad would consolidate British control of the Upper Nile and ultimately of Egypt and the Suez. The argument was not universally convincing, however, and from the beginning the Uganda Railway stirred controversy. A widely read poem published in London in 1895 summed up the views of many prominent opponents of the railroad when it declared: "It clearly is naught but a lunatic line" (quoted in Marsh, 141).

When Mackinder traveled to Mount Kenya, the British public widely regarded Africa as an imperial arena in which the issue was the role of railroads in European expansion and control. For the British the construction of a Cape-to-Cairo railroad carried all the imperial, nationalistic import that the Berlin-to-Baghdad railroad did in Germany. As late as 1907 the plan was still under discussion. When Winston Churchill argues in *My African Journey* for a "Victoria and Albert Railway" as an extension of the Uganda Railway from Lake Victoria through Uganda, he fixes the scheme in a much larger context of imperial construction and control. Extending the Uganda Railway would become more profitable by opening up trade with Uganda and would also allow for a rail hookup with the water and rail systems of the Upper Nile and Egypt.[29] Finally, Churchill speculates: "Perhaps by the time that the junction between the Uganda and Soudan [*sic*] rail and water systems have been effected, The Rhodes Cape to Cairo railway will have reached the southern end of Lake Tanganyika" (150). The dream of a transcontinental line still lived.

Although all the talk at the time was about opening the interior to trade, about plantations at Nairobi whose freight fees would pay for the Uganda railroad, strategic military motives underwrote its construction. Lord Salisbury admitted this after the fact in 1900 when he explained to the House of Commons that the French challenge to British control of Egypt and the Nile had prompted the construction of the Uganda railroad to provide rapid transport of British troops from the Indian Ocean to the

Upper Nile. After all, the Uganda Railway was built by the government, not private investors; the gauge of its track matched that of the Egyptian railways. It might have opened Kenya and Uganda to commerce, but that was merely a dividend to the interests of the British military in securing a line of supply to Egypt and the Nile. Winston Churchill unequivocally pointed out in 1908 that the Uganda railroad had been "projected solely as a political railway to reach Uganda, and to secure British predominance upon the Upper Nile" (*My African Journey*, 4).

Although the territorial claims of the French, Belgians, and Italians also put stress on Britain's African empire, at the turn of the century Germany was most often perceived as the greatest threat to British imperial interests in East Africa. After his return from his second transcontinental journey in 1889, Henry Morton Stanley had been attempting to "prod the British lion" (quoted in Hollingsworth, 41) to counter what he perceived as German imperialism in Africa.

Rail transport was a significant part of this rivalry. In 1908 Winston Churchill wrote of the Uganda Railway, in obvious reference to the massive increase in German naval construction initiated by Adm. Alfred von Tirpitz in 1898: "Other nations project Central African railways as lightly and as easily as they lay down naval programmes; but here is a railway, like the British Fleet, 'in being' — not a paper plan" (3).

"In Africa, as elsewhere," James Ramsey Ullman writes in one of his histories of modern mountaineering, "human history is made in the lowlands" (*Age of Mountaineering*, 155). Clearly, Mackinder's "Mount Kenya" supports Ullman's observation by suggesting how mountaineering experiences, and the narratives they prompt, grow out of a rich and complex web of historical events.

Easily one of the most provocative and controversial geopolitical theories of the twentieth century, Mackinder's pivot theory first appeared in a 1904 paper, "The Geographical Pivot of History," presented at the Royal Geographical Society on January 25, 1904. It was later more fully developed in light of World War I in the 1919 *Democratic Ideals and History* and brought up to date to explain the events of World War II in the 1943 essay, "The Round World and the Winning of the Peace."

Mackinder's stated purpose in the 1904 pivot paper is to suggest "a correlation between the larger geographical and the larger historical generalizations," a correlation that he quickly defines in terms of "geographical causation" (*Democratic Ideals,* 242). In short, Mackinder argues that European history has largely been shaped by a series of invasions from the steppes of Asia, a region he therefore identifies as the geographical pivot of history. For Mackinder this heartland (*Democratic Ideals,* 255) would increasingly represent the key to military power in the twentieth century, and the nation that controlled it held the potential for world empire. In advancing this proposition, Mackinder was implicitly refuting not only the conventional wisdom of the day but also the then well-known argument made by Alfred Thayer Mahan for the strategic preeminence of naval power. Mackinder suggests that the "Columbian epoch" (*Democratic Ideals,* 241) during which sea power reigned supreme was rapidly drawing to a close. "Trans-continental railways," he writes, "are now transmuting the conditions of land-power" (*Democratic Ideals,* 259), providing continental land-oriented nations with the capacity for commercial and military transport and integration previously enjoyed only by maritime nations. Although the capacity of these nations to exercise naval power along the "inner, or marginal crescent" (an area roughly consisting of Europe, India, and the Far East) surrounding the pivot region continued to hold Asian land power in check, the balance of power was shifting away from maritime nations. For Britain, which had historically founded its influence and empire on its navy, and which was already engaged in a loud popular debate about national decay prompted by the Boer War, the message was an ominous one.[30]

The pivot essay very much reflects British concerns at the turn of the century regarding the expansion of the Russian Empire in Asia as well as the unification and growth of German power and influence. Mackinder portrays an alliance between these two rivals to British power as the most disturbing threat to the delicate balance that British sea strength still maintained with the potential for Asian land strength. If such an alliance came about, he writes, "the empire of the world would then be in sight" (262). Like many Britons coming of age in the late nineteenth century, Mackinder had a sense of international relations that had been deeply influenced by the Crimean War with Russia and, in the case of Mackinder, even more by the Prussian defeat of Napoleon III in 1870, an event that Mackinder refers to in "The Round World" as "my earliest memory of public affairs" (596). Russian advances across Asia, solidified by the recently constructed six-thousand-mile Trans-Siberian Railway and the Germans' much-discussed Berlin-to-Baghdad railway scheme only made the possibility of land-based mobility, and thus armed conquest, more immediate. If Germany and Russia allied, Mackinder writes in the pivot paper, the only means of forestalling ultimate conquest would be for the maritime powers to establish "bridge heads where the outside navies would support armies to compel the pivot allies to deploy land forces and prevent them from concentrating their whole strength on fleets" (262–63).

In *Democratic Ideals and Democracy* Mackinder expands the pivot theory to book length, developing a more specialized vocabulary to describe the geographical paradigm of history and contemporary international politics. In the wake of German designs he has expanded the crucial pivot region, now labeled the "heartland," to include eastern Europe. The focus of continental landmass has also expanded. Mackinder links Europe and Asia with Africa as what he now calls the "World-Island." Yet the formula for geographical causation remains essentially unchanged and is encapsulated in Mackinder's axiom:

Who rules East Europe commands the Heartland:
Who rules the Heartland commands the World-Island:
Who rules the World-Island commands the World. (150)

Twenty years after Mackinder's one excursion there, he had put Africa prominently at theoretical center stage.

In *Democratic Ideals* Mackinder defines the "World-Island" as "the joint continent of Europe, Asia, and Africa" (62). Furthermore, he goes on in this book to describe the interior of sub-Saharan Africa as "a second Heartland" or "Southern Heartland" (80) in which, as with the original "Northern Heartland," mobility is the key to political expansion and strategic success.

More specifically, then, East Africa, in the terms of the pivot theory, is part of what Mackinder calls in *Democratic Ideals* the "World-Promontory" (53), the vast Atlantic and Indian Ocean coastlines of Africa and Asia that led the sea powers of Europe to the Far East. "From the point of view of the traffic to the Indies," Mackinder writes, "the world was a vast cape, standing out southward from between Britain and Japan" (52). Mackinder observes that the "seamen" had historically established a series of "local bases" along this route, and he cites as examples Mombasa on the East Africa coast, as well as the Cape of Good Hope and Aden. Mackinder is more specific in describing the British stake in this notion of promontory. During the two decades leading up to World War I, Mackinder suggests, Britain had in effect sought to preserve the Indian Ocean as its own "closed sea" (57) as a means of protecting its routes to India. It is clear that at least in 1919 Mackinder saw, in part with the hindsight provided by the war, that Bismarck's prewar beachhead in Tanganyika posed a potentially dangerous disruption to this attenuated line of communication, trade, and reinforcement and therefore to the British defense against Eurasian conquest. Thinking of Germany as a land-oriented "pivot power," Mackinder argues in *Democratic Ideals* that it would be dangerous to allow any part of East Africa or Asia to be returned to the control of Germany, "the Power which took them with a keen strategical eye to the day when armies marching overland should find in each of them a citadel already prepared; which took them moreover, with the clear intention that the Chinese and the Negroes should be utilized as subsidiary man-power to help in the conquest of the World-Island" (174–75).

There is, of course, little evidence to support Mackinder's claim that Tanganyika in the 1880s was part of a clearly thought-out German plan for worldwide military ascendancy. But Mackinder clearly regarded East Africa as a region where the concerns of exploration and international politics mingled. And in point of fact, this way of understanding the geopolitical significance of East Africa corresponds closely to the kind of strategic thinking at the British Foreign Office beginning in the late 1880s that led to direct British political involvement in the region. Interestingly, when the British gained exclusive control of the Upper Nile in an agreement of 1890, they did so in part by granting to Germany the island of Heligoland as a North Sea naval base. Translated into the terms of Mackinder's pivot theory, this action amounted to Britain's bargaining sea access for the extension of land power, an attempt to reverse its traditional geopolitical position, not in Eurasia but in the relatively new imperial arena of Africa.

It is a truism, of the very kind that most aggravates theorists, that theories often omit people. In the case of Mackinder's pivot theory and the schemes and strategies of empire at work in East Africa, those most noticeably brushed to the side were the Africans themselves. While a temporarily bewildered Mackinder may have once announced his wish to see East Africa through the "eyes of the natives," it is precisely this point of view that is necessarily missing from his perspective, as it is from those of most Western explorers. As Mackinder moves deeper into East Africa, his direct contact with the region's native residents increasingly comes to shape and mediate his experience. Beginning largely as a set of cultural stereotypes, as expectations and rumors, East Africans in "Mount Kenya" finally become actual in Mackinder's personal contact with them, especially as he moves beyond the rather flimsy pale of British dominion in the East Africa Protectorate. From early in the narrative he presents Africans as objects of, or otherwise in association with, trouble and conflict. At Zanzibar Mackinder reports hearing vague rumors of an impending conflict between different groups of Masai, the "English" and "German" Masai (38–39), and the dispatch of German troops. Mackinder also notes the reports that he hears about the mutiny of the British East Africa Company's Sudanese troops in Uganda, still in progress to the west in 1897 (78).[31]

When he writes of his arrival in the East Africa Protectorate, Mackinder reveals these vague harbingers of trouble made concrete. The protectorate itself, an entity that sounds solid and stable enough before Mackinder actually lands there, seems on actual inspection to be only barely operational at all. "Mount Kenya" presents it throughout as mostly a thin and tenuous overlay of European authority over what remains an essentially unconquered land. The bureaucracy is only the sham of control. In Mombasa the expedition becomes immediately mired in red tape. Mackinder writes that when he presented letters of permission and recommendation for the expedition from the Foreign Office and the Royal Geographical Society, the acting commissioner of the East Africa Protectorate in Mombasa "expressed his wonder that the Foreign Office had allowed us to come out" (59).

Most important, however, is how "Mount Kenya" records East Africa's devastation by natural and human disaster in 1899. "Fever is a word unpleasantly frequent in conversation here," Mackinder comments upon his arrival in Mombasa. There he learns the full extent of the famine. Six thousand Waganda and Wasoga had been fed by the British at the railhead, he hears, mostly on bad water and uncooked rice, and "thousands of them died of enteric fever and dysentery on the way home" (79). He hears talk at the British Club in Mombasa that the Wanyika and Wakamba are mutinous (60). C. H. Craufurd, the agricultural commissioner and consul general in Mombasa, urges Mackinder to take an escort, perhaps even a political officer. The expedition is frustratingly held up in Mombasa; Mackinder writes on July 11, "I have now nothing to do but to wait" (92).

"Mount Kenya" measures the extent of the East African famine in two very different and finally conflicting ways, as a source of human suffering and horror for native Africans and as an inconvenience and impediment to the expedition. In both cases it is how indigenous Africans respond to the famine that provides the narrative with its way to understand the human geography of an East Africa devastated by starvation, disease, and the resultant violence. The former way of seeing the famine predominates as the expedition stays in British settlements and on the Uganda Railway and the latter after the expedition moves from Nairobi toward Mount Kenya on foot.

In conversation at Teita along the railway route, the railroad engineer Whitehouse tells Mackinder: "All the nigger wants . . . is food, drink, his wife, and liberty to raid by way of sport. We have spoilt his amusement, and he regards us as a nuisance" (109). Actually, the narrative suggests not only that the problem was far more serious than this racist, chauvinistic, trivializing characterization would suggest but that the involvement of the British in it was far more integral than simply being a nuisance. Mackinder observes that the Masai were angry that the government protected Kikuyu farmers' grazing land. He mentions that Lenana, a Masai chief, had moved his people away from the railroad for the express purpose of avoiding the spread of smallpox. Along the railroad corridor shunned by the Masai, Mackinder describes a bleak human landscape: "There were famine-stricken beggars at every station" (111); "we cross and re-cross the deserted caravan road, but the only natives are the beggars at the stations" (112). He sees a man "doubtless dying of famine" who was unable to continue after following a donkey caravan and picking up undigested grains of corn (119). He writes that "Hausburg shot a vulture which was feeding on a human corpse" (138). Gradually, Mackinder begins to draw conclusions. "Half way between Tsavo and Kibwezi," reads the entry for July 13, "was horrid evidence of the famine among the Wakamba": "Four skeleton women, with a child of perhaps six years, were begging, their skins all shriveled. Around, in contrast, were the Indian railway people, lackadaisical and hand in hand, and Swahilis, burly and laughing, buying food of the Indian traders. No wonder the Wakamba curse the white man and his railway" (113). Later, he notices "some well nourished and clothed Wakamba women" who could therefore only be "wives of railway men" (116). He observes that the famine had actually been made worse — the railroad and relief expeditions sent to Uganda to quell the mutiny had paid inflated prices for food that would otherwise have remained in the native economy (139, 148).

But from the midst of this lowland horror Mackinder looks to the horizon, where he sees "a bank of cloud, resting perhaps on Kenya Mountain"

(133), and on July 21 he writes simply: "We now saw the twin peaks of Kenya for the first time" (155). It is a predictive moment in the narrative. As the expedition moves away from the railroad toward the mountain, Mackinder marginalizes the famine's effects on the region's inhabitants and becomes preoccupied with his own problems — primarily obtaining food and defending the expedition from the mostly perceived, sometimes actual, threat of violent attack.

By the July 30 entry "Mount Kenya" begins to record Mackinder's sense of the expedition's vulnerability to Africans. Mackinder reports the first discipline problems of the expedition — its Wakikuyu porters refuse to march any farther that day. Mackinder concludes his day's entry by noting that he picked a campsite "safe from ambush" (184). After "long negotiations for food" in the village of Muluka, Mackinder's porters attempt, as he puts it, to "bolt" "en masse" (210), and the Europeans begin to hold them as virtual prisoners for several days. On the night of August 3 the sense of danger is acute. Mackinder has built a "strong boma" around the camp (222). While visiting a village, Mackinder describes what he considers the threatening behavior of the inhabitants, mentioning revealingly that "I took my Mauser from my boy" (227). On August 4 Hausburg and Camburn, the taxidermist, accidentally fire on a local man because they think he is a deserter from the expedition. On August 5 Mackinder mentions ominously that he is troubled by the number of natives around the expedition (237), natives showing what is to Mackinder the confusing attitude of "mingled fear and hostility" (230). He writes that he is "determined that an effort must be made to establish some sort of relations and to relieve the dangerous tension" (225).

Although the narrative openly and repeatedly acknowledges the problem of food, it only ambiguously suggests the origin of the problem. On August 15 Mackinder describes the situation this way: "Evidently there were some complicated political problems as between the Wameranga, Mgombe [Wangombe], the Masai, and the Wa-Tumu Tumu, and we had come in as a fifth factor" (325). The nature of this fifth factor remains unstated. The effect of this omission is the insertion of a kind of dramatic irony into the text. Although Mackinder lays all the groundwork for the obvious conclusion that the expedition's food and safety problems stem from the famine raging across the region, he does not openly announce that conclusion.

The Kenyan highland region where the expedition spent most of its time while in East Africa was plainly well-off in comparison to the drier, more marginally productive country around it. While Mackinder recognizes this, he does not go on to acknowledge how the famine might indirectly be placing the highland region under considerable pressure and constraint. Predatory incursions by the groups of hungry, dispossessed farmers roaming the East African countryside in 1899 represented a very real danger to the highland region, as did raids by profiteering traders and the threat of spreading contagion. Mackinder's own expedition, of course, with its habit of arbitrarily requisitioning food from local farmers, was itself a disturbing imposition on an already-stressed economy. "Mount Kenya" implicitly attributes the failure of Africans to meet the food requirements of the expedition sometimes to quaint, unaccountable, and superstitious xenophobia or sometimes to sheer native guile. The narrative hints at, but finally simply blocks out, other, more complete, explanations.

This peculiar silence in Mackinder's account is a symptom of its tendency to understand only the economic activity that is clearly recognizable in European terms and that is, in fact, participating in the project of European colonial economic expansion. The relationship that the narrative proposes between British commercial activity in East Africa and the indigenous economies of the region is perhaps best illustrated when Mackinder describes a marketplace in Meranga. Although the ground is literally covered with maize husks, to the extent that the expedition has trouble finding bare ground on which to camp, Mackinder does not stress the apparent existence of an indigenous native economy but rather what could be done to transform it into a European-style cash economy: "These markets constitute a chance for the trader, especially for the Indian trader. Once the rupee penetrates this far there should be a sale of goods to the Wameranga, and a purchase of produce wholesale for the export to other parts of British East Africa" (286).

This of course is in part railroad talk, the rhetoric that helped speed the budget of the Uganda Railway through Parliament and Cecil Rhodes's Cape-to-Cairo railroad scheme into the popular imagination of the day. More specifically, it reflects all that Mackinder had recently been told about the possibilities for making the Uganda Railway a commercial success. But in "Mount Kenya" it serves as the theoretical foundation for the narrative's ultimate dismissal of native East African concerns.

Mackinder presents the failure of Africans to fully and peacefully cooperate in supplying the needs of the expedition as an inconvenient and

dangerous anomaly, essentially beyond rational explanation and attribu-
table only to intractable native backwardness. The underlying causes are
more complex. As suggested earlier, Central Africa initially eclipsed East
Africa as the focus of European exploration. It also was the principal
object of Arab trade and commerce. By the 1880s the increasingly heavy
long-distance caravan traffic that was passing through East Africa as it
moved farther inland began to play an important role in the regional
economy. East Africa was increasingly distinguished by a network of trade
routes and caravan supply stations. Even before the Foreign Office extended political control over the region, British trade and patronage began
to follow the same lines. As the number of caravans moving through East
Africa to Uganda increased dramatically in the 1890s, the demand for
food and labor also rose sharply, causing East African farmers to increase
production markedly, often substituting maize for traditional crops like
sorghum and millet and diverting food from domestic consumption to
commercial export.[32] Whereas previously only surplus food was available for sale to Arab and European caravans, by the late 1890s cash
cropping was clearly replacing subsistence farming in East Africa. The
results ranged between local food shortages and the dangerous environ-
mental and social consequences of agricultural overproduction, problems
exacerbated by rapidly increasing population density in many areas.

Furthermore, the economic instability initiated by European activity
in Africa often translated into local political change as well. As this supply
network evolved, the provisions as well as porter and artisan services
available to trade caravans increasingly came under the brokerage and
control of local strongmen, a situation that tended to undermine the traditional political autonomy of East African communities. Wangombe,
for example, a local leader whom Mackinder reports as being the great
nemesis of the expedition, occupied a strategic location on the northeastern edge of the Gikuyu highlands through which most caravan traffic
passed on the route to what is now northern Kenya. Although Mackinder
does not acknowledge it, and most likely was not aware of it, Wangombe
was far more than simply an uncooperative local despot. He was actually
an important figure in East African economic affairs. Already a powerful
broker of food and other commodities, Wangombe used the scarcity imposed by the famine to consolidate and expand the range and depth of his
power. Wangombe's reluctance and perhaps hostility to the Mackinder
expedition must be regarded as nothing less than a calculated political and
commercial strategy, not the brute churlishness that Mackinder makes it
out to be. The effect was that East Africa was primed for catastrophe. In

his study of the effects of European occupation on traditional East African communities, Charles Ambler writes that "during a decade marked by drought and cattle disease, the development of commercial agriculture clearly left the region as a whole more vulnerable to natural disaster" (115).

The scarcity of food experienced by Mackinder was far more than simply a personal inconvenience. As Mackinder was beginning to plan his expedition to Mount Kenya, he could not have been aware of the extent to which conditions there were turning horribly wrong. In 1897 drought, famine, and epidemic smallpox began to spread across much of the region through which Mackinder would eventually travel. By 1899, when Mackinder actually reached East Africa, uncounted thousands had died from the combined effects of hunger, disease, and desperate social turmoil. In fact, the worst year, without a doubt, was 1899. A number of European travelers and officials in the region have left horrifying reports of the famine.[33] The devastation was so extensive and long lasting that Charles Ambler reports that many survivors he interviewed seventy years later refused to talk about the years that they simply recalled as the Yua ya Ngomanisye, "the famine that went everywhere" (123, 144–45).

As the famine spread, the countryside became a frightening scene of chaotic and random violence. Throughout the protectorate traditional social fabrics broke down altogether as desperate and starving people began to prey on anyone they thought was better off than they were. With the land traveled by refugees who might be carrying smallpox, and marauding bandits ready to kill to eat, suspicion reigned; strangers and outsiders were immediately considered threatening. Understandably, many starving people blamed the growing European presence for the catastrophe. Called "the great serpent" by many of the people whose land it traversed, the Uganda Railway was in fact a particular focus of resentment and dread and was frequently blamed as a source of the destruction spreading along its path.

When a series of lion attacks stopped the construction of the railway at Tsavo in 1898, many railroad workers claimed that the lions were the spirits of two dead chiefs angry about the trespass of the railroad through their domains (Patterson, 20–21). By the end of 1898 protectorate authorities had begun to distribute rations of rice to the starving, and the Uganda Railway was the primary means of bringing food to the interior.

By the time Mackinder left Africa, more than five thousand people were living on rice distributed by the government and missionaries, and the relief effort became such a distinguishing element of experience that in Ulu, southeast of Nairobi, traditional accounts of the years 1897–99 sometimes refer to Yua ya Magunia, "the gunnysack famine." The rice rations saved many lives but probably also contributed to the breakdown of traditional economies and the entrenching of British political power in the protectorate.

Mackinder's subordination of the effect of the Kenyan famine on Africans to his own relatively minor and transitory difficulties betokens the broad tendency of European imperialist thinking to overwrite indigenous cultures, to see human and physical geography at the margins of the European world through the subjective filter of European perception. This essentially abstractive gesture amounts to little more than a reduction of place and peoples to concept and theory. The famine and political unrest in Africa are still with us today — Ethiopia, Sudan, Somalia, Rwanda — and high-priced tours operate in Mount Kenya National Park, advertised around the world.

Mountaineers will not be surprised that Mackinder describes the retreat from Mount Kenya as an anticlimax. The luminous images of the mountain and the historic moment of mountaineering achievement are behind him. Mackinder writes that after the ascent, evenings "were spent monosyllabically, warming our hands and feet at the fire, amid the mysterious shadows of the tree groundsels" (539). He explains: "Our thoughts and rare words were divided between our conquest and the red cinders which spoke of home, until presently the scene around would break silently into our dreams compelling our worship" (540). Yet Mackinder retains sufficient language on September 19 to describe the expedition as a kind of inventory:

This day our journey culminated. My survey of the peak and its immediate neighborhood was complete and the circuit had closed on the plane table with only a very small error. We had been to the summit of the mountain. We had discovered new valleys and glaciers at the northern foot. We had looked down onto all the outer slopes except the northern in rear of the Terreri Crags. The structure of the mountain was clear. . . . We had observed its meteorology for a month. . . . We had also collected specimens of many of the characteristic animals and plants, a few of which at least we felt sure would prove to be of new species. Finally Hausburg had

taken a series of large-plate photographs which I was certain would develop successfully if he were able to get them safely home. Some things which we had
intended had failed or been omitted, but on the whole, we had snatched victory
from what was likely at one time to be a bad defeat. And now we were sated and
impatient to be home. (577)

For Mackinder, leaving the mountain becomes a process of reentry
into the European presence in East Africa and ultimately the metropolitan
motives and concerns that it embodies. As the expedition approaches
Naivasha, the mountain recedes daily. But while the expedition has been
gone, the Uganda Railway had progressed. The tracks are now only
twenty-five miles from Naivasha. At Naivasha Mackinder again becomes
entangled in colonial red tape after he receives an official letter from the
government of the East Africa Protectorate that was somewhat belatedly
recalling the expedition, a message that Mackinder describes as "rather
comic" (643). One day out of Naivasha, Mackinder sees "the first evidence of the railway" (645), and by the time he reaches a railroad camp,
he had, as he puts it, "passed out of Africa into Asia, out of this bwana
country into this sahib country" (646), a remark that reactivates the racial
and cultural hierarchy that he had used earlier to describe the geography
of the rail route.

Mackinder is quickly propelled back into the world of European affairs. While he is returning to Nairobi by train, Mackinder is entertained
in the new saloon car by Mr. and Mrs. Whitehouse. Of Nairobi, Mackinder writes, "There I found everything changed, a galvanized iron town
was rising; the hill was already crowned with bungalows; a club had been
organized" (647). While there Mackinder met Sir Harry Johnston, on his
way to take up a post as high commissioner of Uganda. At one point
during a dinner party thrown by Johnston, someone randomly picked out
a record for the gramophone, and to everyone's surprise it "ground out
Gladstone's last speech in the House of Commons! Johnston, I believe, is a
liberal! A hyaena in the outer darkness punctuated the resounding periods
in condemnation of the House of Lords" (654). In Mombasa, Mackinder
meets former pupils from Oxford, observes a French warship in the harbor, and sees a British troopship headed for South Africa in the wake of
the "Boer ultimatum" against reinforcing the British garrison in South
Africa (662). On his return voyage to France Mackinder learns of impending hostilities between Russia and Japan. He listens with interest to con-
versations about China, where, he is told, Britain's European rivals are at
work. "We are very strong in the Yangtse" (664), he learns, but "not a mile
of railway has in those regions been begun" (665).

More than most narratives of mountain exploration, "Mount Kenya" is explicit in emphasizing the culture shock that mountaineers experience in returning from the wilderness. As a component of the narrative, in fact, mountain climbing is clearly bracketed within the larger context of colonial expansion established at both the beginning and end of the text. The mountain is the site of personal ambition and achievement that the narrative seeks to keep separate from the large, difficult political world below. As Mackinder comments, "You cannot reverse the rule by coming down" (477).

We have no evidence that Mackinder's 1904 pivot theory developed in response to his 1899 journey to East Africa. The most that can be suggested is that the argument of the theory and the final meaning of his "Mount Kenya" narrative overlap and modify each other. Consider this remark: "One of the results of the rapid multiplication of lines of ocean steamers and of railways in distant seas and far-off countries has been to make it easy for men of comparatively brief leisure to undertake a share in exploration in the course of a vacation tour" (1). This comment sounds like a summary of Mackinder's East African expedition, his explanation for choosing Mount Kenya for his brief dabble in exploration, a Baedeker view of the pivot theory. In point of fact, the remark actually appears in the 1893 edition of *Hints to Travellers,* the one that Mackinder used while planning his trip. The guidebook clearly left a few things out. They always do. As Mackinder's "vacation tour" so conspicuously implies, East Africa in 1899 was a patchwork of international political and economic interest, an unstable, volatile, political geography where shifting or vaguely defined European boundaries were laid over an indigenous political landscape occupied by a native population often justifiably hostile to European occupation, to say nothing of a dangerous and difficult climate and terrain.

When Mackinder left London's Charing Cross Station on June 8, 1899, only three months had passed since the British and French had come to a tentative agreement settling the incident at Fashoda. The Uganda mutiny was still not completely settled.[34] During Mackinder's visit the British military actively pursued pacification of the native population of the interior of the East Africa Protectorate. British clashes with Nandi and Bunyoro tribesmen were ongoing, and war had broken out in Buganda. In 1899 Francis Hall led repeated punitive military expeditions against the Kikuyu and Muraka in the region between Nairobi and Mount Kenya.[35] Farther afield, three days before Mackinder left London negotiations broke down between the British and the Boers at the Bloemfontein Conference, moving events toward the exchange of ultimatums and the beginning of fighting in South Africa in October. Africa was no place for the disinterested explorer, if such a one existed then or now. It was instead a crucible of political conflict against which exploration was understood at the time.

For readers of "Mount Kenya" today it is difficult, and ultimately limiting, to segregate Mackinder's "Mount Kenya" from this disputed setting. At its opening and close the narrative pointedly hints about geopolitical affairs in and around East Africa. As the narrative progresses, it makes a conspicuously strenuous attempt to ignore the larger facts of the East African famine then in progress, as well as the context of European imperial friction enveloping all activity in the region. Instead, it attempts to focus on its account of pure and apolitical science, exploration, and mountaineering. The attempt fails. The inherent subjectivity of the Royal Geographical Society's style functions in Mackinder's narrative to refigure private geographical perspectives in the far-reaching milieu of public events.

In "Mount Kenya" Mackinder reports that when he arrived at Naivasha after his ascent of Mount Kenya, the first telegram he sent was to Sir John Keltie of the Royal Geographical Society, who was then attending the International Geographical Congress in Berlin, to inform him of the success of the expedition (642). Mackinder's telegraphed message, which was announced at the Congress, clearly spoke to the assemblage in multiple languages of personal achievement, geographical advancement, and international geopolitical ascendancy.

3

Annie Smith Peck and
the Economic Apex

A vast cone, with its apex pointing away from us, seemed to be
suddenly cut out from the world beneath; night was within its
border and the twilight still all round.
— Leslie Stephen

SEDATE TEACHER OF THE DEAD LANGUAGES IN THE PUR-
due University," an *Outing* writer called Annie Smith Peck in
1903, on the eve of her first trip to South America ("Men and
Women," 623).[1] But as the profiler was fully aware, this intentionally
ironic characterization conspicuously misses the mark in capturing the
true character of a woman whose exploits and interests extended far beyond the college classroom and were certainly far from sedate. Like Dorothy Pilley and her English professor husband, I. A. Richards, in the next
generation, Peck found glaciers and alpine tundra an attractive counter-
balance to the college quadrangle. But unlike Pilley and Richards, Peck
did not content herself with the already covered ground of previously
established routes in the Alps, the Lake District, or Wales.[2] Instead, Peck
established altitude records and made well-publicized first ascents. She
figured prominently in the popular press of her day, famous certainly as a
mountaineer but, what was more significant and important, as a female
mountaineer, still a rather rare species during the early twentieth century.
As the roles of women in and beyond the home were hotly debated in
every American venue from the pulpit to the press to the streets, Peck
repeatedly drew attention to the ways in which climbing mountains could
be interpreted as a political act within the context of the suffrage move-

ment. She and Fanny Bullock Workman, sometimes rivals, were recognized in the first two decades of the twentieth century as the two most famous female climbers in the world. Today Peck still sometimes surfaces as a heroine of the women's movement. Several Internet sites feature portraits of a rugged-looking Peck, and the *Discovery Channel Online* calls her the first woman audacious enough to climb the Matterhorn in knickerbockers instead of a skirt. Like perhaps the majority of women mountaineers during the nineteenth century, Annie Smith Peck undoubtedly began as what Janet Robertson in *The Magnificent Mountain Women* calls a "recreationist" (xii), but Peck quickly leavened with her interest in climbing as sport an intense personal ambition and a clear political motivation.

Although Peck wrote fairly extensively of her travels and explorations, during her lifetime her most widely known work was her 1911 *A Search for the Apex of America,* a three-hundred-page narrative of her four trips to South America between the 1903 and 1908 and the eight major climbs that she undertook during that period. The book focuses on her attempted ascent of Illampu in Bolivia and first ascent of Huascarán in Peru. In this book Peck fashioned a distant mountain landscape inextricably and provocatively involved with issues of gender, economics, and national identity, in which the "incompleteness" of the explored map has direct social and political implications. Peck placed her witty and engaging narrative voice at the center of an exploration narrative that is also an economic survey of South America, interwoven with an unresolved attitude about interventionist politics in the "dollar diplomacy" era of the Taft administration.

Annie Peck was born in 1850 in Providence, Rhode Island, to an "old" and traditional New England Baptist family. Her father was a lawyer and businessman, and her mother traced her roots all the way back to Roger Williams. Perhaps the intense competitiveness that Peck felt for her three older brothers was an early sign that she would not content herself with the conventional domestic role that her family envisioned for her.[3] In any case, this seemed to be suggested in 1874 when, against her parents' wishes, she took the train west to enroll at the University of Michigan as it first opened its doors to women. After graduation in 1878 Peck became the first female student at the American School of Classical Studies in Athens. She became a high school teacher in Providence and went on, as the

Outing editor described, to teach Latin at Purdue University and Smith College. She was an outspoken advocate of women's suffrage and control over property, and most of her adult life represented a persuasive illustration of female independence and initiative.

As shocking as her political persuasions and decision to have a career might have been to her family, that was only the beginning. While in her midthirties Peck developed a keen interest in travel. After her return from Greece she gave parlor lectures on archaeology and antiquities, often illustrated with her own stereopticon slides. She seems to have relished what she calls in *Search* the "unconventional situations" (40) that a "lady traveler" of her era might have found in the world's exotic and far-flung places. If travel represented for Peck a kind of liberation from the social constraints of traditional female roles, she was most drawn by the peculiar freedom of alpine landscape. On her way to her studies in Athens in 1885 she passed through the Bavarian and Swiss Alps by train. The experience would change her life forever. She wrote in *Search*, "On my first visit to Switzerland, my allegiance, previously given to the sea, was transferred for all time to the mountains" (ix). Peck immediately dedicated herself to becoming a mountaineer. In 1888 she made her first important ascent, of Mount Shasta, a graceful 14,162-foot volcano at the southern end of the Cascade range in northern California.[4] Peck achieved world fame when she climbed the Matterhorn in 1895 when she was forty-five. Two years later she trudged to the top of Mexico's Orizaba and at 18,696 feet established an altitude record for women in the Americas. Like Workman, Peck sometimes planted a banner or unfolded a flyer proclaiming VOTES FOR WOMEN on the summits of the mountains that she climbed. But it remained for Peck to extend her fascination with mountains further, beyond mountains already climbed by male climbers, to genuine exploration. She turned farther south, to the Andes, which in the early years of the century were a largely open theater for climbing achievement. After attempting an ascent of Mount Illampu in Bolivia, in 1908 Peck focused her attention to the north, to Mount Huascarán, the highest peak in Peru. Although the imposing twin summits of Huascarán had not yet been triangulated, they were rumored to tower to twenty-five thousand feet amid the Cordillera Blanca range two hundred miles north of Lima. If that contemporary estimate were correct, or even close to correct, it made Huascarán the tallest mountain in the Americas, about two thousand feet higher than Aconcagua, fifteen hundred miles farther south, which was then thought to be 22,800 feet (in fact, Huascarán is 22,205 feet and Aconcagua is

22,834 feet). If Peck could reach the summit of Huascarán, she would achieve a new record for high elevation in the Western Hemisphere for both male and female climbers, and she would surpass the world record for women climbers. Refusing to recognize the limitation of what was considered to be her respectable age of fifty-eight, Peck was convinced she could do it.

As it turned out, she was more or less correct in her confidence. When she returned successfully from Huascarán in 1908, Peck was widely recognized for her achievement. The Lima Geographical Society officially renamed the north peak of Huascarán Cumbre Ana Peck in her honor and at a gala banquet presented her with what she called a "pleasing souvenir." Peck described this memento as a "solid silver stirrup in the form of a slipper, a relic of colonial days, when it was doubtless used by some maid or matron of high degree in her horseback rides" (*Search*, 369). Although she conspicuously holds the slipper in her hand in the frontispiece photograph of *Search*, it was characteristic of the irrepressible Peck that she concluded the book by provocatively musing that by a "curious incident" she had happened to receive the gift while wearing *only one shoe*, having stepped on a nail the day before the banquet. I like to imagine Peck at the banquet, receiving her award with a combination of self-confidence and acceptably ladylike propriety, all the while limping on a bandaged foot. As this anecdote may suggest, and as a closer look at her experiences and writing will illustrate, Peck was a person willing to wear that ironically delicate and ornate silver slipper of exploratory success only on her own specific and idiosyncratic terms.

In addition to *Search*, Peck wrote many magazine articles, some climbing and travel narratives, and several of what we would now call "how-to" pieces related to travel. Additionally, she went on to write three other books. *The South American Tour* (1913) is essentially a guidebook providing practical information on such matters as fares, lodging, and food along a then–well-recognized tourist route through the continent. *Industrial and Commercial South America* (1922) is a handbook of political, economic, and historical statistics designed to assist U.S. businessmen working in South America. Finally, *Flying over South America* (1932) makes an appropriate postscript to Peck's literary career, narrating her "pioneering" tourist excursion around South America during the first year that commercial air travel became available on the continent. In 1911, when she was sixty-one, she made the first ascent of Peru's 21,079-foot Nevado Coropuna, and three years before her death in 1935 she made a final and more modest climb, New Hampshire's 5,367-foot Mount Madison. She was eighty-two when she reached that last summit.

The twin windswept summits of Huascarán rise ten thousand feet above the well-populated and densely farmed Callejon de Huaillas in the Cordillera Blanca of the Peruvian Andes. Although the east side of the mountain is protected by difficult and exposed rock, the west face is broken by a heavily crevassed glacier that drops down from the saddle between the two summits. After two reconnaissance expeditions to the mountain, in 1904 and 1905, and in the wake of a near miss on Illampu, Peck settled on the west face for what she hoped would be a final attempt on what she thought was the highest mountain in the Americas. Convinced that the native porters who accompanied her on her first trip to the mountain did not have high altitude experience nor inclination to make the summit, Peck hired two Swiss guides from Zermatt, Gabriel and Rudolf Taugwalder, who joined her in New York and traveled with her to Peru. Leaving on foot in early August from the town of Yungay in the Huaillas valley beneath the mountain, within a week Peck and the Taugwalders, supported by a team of porters, had established a camp at eleven thousand feet on the west face. From there Peck hoped to traverse to the glacier and follow it to the saddle between the two summits, where she would decide which summit might be more readily reached.

Their first obstacle was the wind, which scoured the exposed snowfield where they camped. Furthermore, the altitude had already begun to have its effect. Rudolf Taugwalder was suffering severely from what the local Indians called *soroche*, "mountain sickness," and was too unwell to continue. Leaving Rudolf in camp, Peck, the remaining brother, and two Indian porters traversed to the glacier. It was tough going. Deep, soft, late-season snow covered the crevasses, making progress slow, difficult, and perilous. The wind picked up again. Struggling to their waists in the light snow, they made their way between the two massive pillars of rock that marked where the glacier narrowed and steepened in a final slope to the saddle. The next morning the party began the last pitch toward the saddle, which turned out to be a 60-degree ramp of hard, brittle ice. Exposed on the high windswept ice field without crampons, Gabriel Taugwalder began the laborious task of cutting steps with the adze of his ice axe, and only on the third day did they reach the wide sloping saddle that extended for a half-mile between the peaks. From their camp in the saddle Peck evaluated the prospects of the two summits. Both were menacingly coated with glare ice for perhaps three thousand feet, but Peck thought she saw a route to the summit that would traverse the north peak.

In the morning the wind was steady and intensely cold, far colder than Peck had anticipated when she provisioned the expedition with clothing. She and Taugwalder left the Indians in camp at 6:30 A.M. Gabriel, roped to Peck below him, began cutting steps up the ice of the north peak. By two in the afternoon, with the summit still out of sight, the guide was too exhausted and sick from altitude to continue. Peck ordered a retreat, and the two felt their way down again to the saddle. Although Peck had hoped that Gabriel might improve enough to mount another attempt the next day, his condition only seemed to worsen, and two days later the party evacuated the mountain, following their trail back through the glacier and down into the Huaillas valley below.

When she returned to Yungay, Peck learned that she had been reported missing on the mountain and that news of her disappearance had already circulated widely. Like Mark Twain, Peck assured local officials that rumors of her death were greatly exaggerated. Moreover, she informed them, she was going back. After obtaining more food and whatever warm clothing she could purchase at the local mines, on August 28, after only ten days' rest, Peck led her guides once more up the valley to Huascarán. This time Peck insisted that they move more quickly and take a more direct route to the glacier, often doubling the pace of advance from the first attempt. On the second day they pitched their tent beneath the ice field that guarded the approach to the saddle and the next day negotiated a thin snow bridge to cross the giant bergschrund that had opened at the top of the glacier.

At the saddle the wind was worse than ever, dangerously cold, with the windchill, had there been such a term in 1908, well below zero. For their second summit attempt Peck and the guides put on every piece of clothing they had brought, layers of it. It was not enough. The steps they had cut up the steep ice slopes of the north peak on their previous attempt had long since disappeared, and the slow relentless process of step cutting took as long as ever, with the Taugwalders taking turns in the lead, Peck following. One misstep meant disaster. The gusting wind continually threatened to blow them off their precarious stances. When they paused to catch their breath, the cold blew through the layers of wool. At midafternoon, with the guides on the verge of total exhaustion, the angle of the ice above them suddenly seemed to drop off, and through the wind-driven snow Peck could see the summit, maybe only a hundred feet above them.

As they stumbled to the top of Huascarán, what might have been a moment of triumph seemed hollow, anticlimactic. Blowing snow obscured any view. Peck for the first time realized that she had no feeling in one of her hands. The prospect of descending the grim ice fields below began to seem appalling. Still, Peck's sense of purpose survived. Fumbling with awkward, freezing hands, Peck and the men tried to light a hypsometer stove to determine the elevation of the summit. As they crouched beneath a blanket to shelter the hypsometer from the wind, they were unable to light the stove. There was no more time. If they did not start down immediately, they would die. Without the altitude reading that she had longed for, Peck threw the useless instrument back into the rucksack. "There was no pleasure here," she later wrote (quoted in Styles, 64).

The descent to the saddle was as horrific as Peck had imagined. For hours, to keep control over their stiff and trembling bodies, the climbers fought to concentrate on every small movement in the technical descent. The wind drove through them. As darkness began to fall, every step downward became less sure, more a matter of frightening guesswork. Nearing the steepest pitch of the ice field, Rudolf lost both of his gloves and continued the slow, painstaking climb down with bare hands gripping the metal head of his ice axe. At 10:30 that night they finally fell exhausted into their tent as dim moonlight filtered through the churning snow. Almost too spent to move and unable to find fuel to melt snow or cook, Peck and the guides weathered two days in the worsening storm, eating snow and raw meals. Rudolf's hands blackened. When the storm began to lift, the party broke camp and within two days had trudged back into Yungay. The climb was over. Even before she left Peru, the draft of what would be *A Search for the Apex of America* was beginning to take shape in Peck's mind. She had much to say.

The bicycle was the sensation of the 1890s. During the decade as many as ten million Americans tried their luck on the seats of towering five-foot wheels or "ordinaries" and later on the more easily managed and lower-wheeled "safeties," which more closely resembled today's bikes. Bicycling clubs sprang up in every major American city, and crowds of twenty-five thousand watched championship races that sometimes outdrew attendance at major league baseball games. More than a mere sport, however, bicycling had its social dimensions as well. In 1892 Frances Willard, the founder of the Women's Christian Temperance Union who was then fifty-three, took up the wheel to promote the healthy outdoor sport as an alternative to the dissipated pleasures of the saloon. For women bicycling had particular significance. Throughout the decade bicycling became an increasingly acceptable recreation for middle- and upper-class U.S. women, traditionally barred by social conventions from strenuous activity. Skirt hems rose above the ankles to accommodate pedaling, and bicycling became one of relatively few public activities considered appropriate for the two sexes to pursue together, with men and women often riding on two-seat tricycles. Photographs from the era show that sometimes the women even got to steer.

Not surprisingly, Annie Smith Peck experimented with the trendy new fashion as it first gained popularity. But it was not to be her sport. In 1901 Peck playfully wrote: "It was my own opinion before beginning to ride a wheel that to bicycle was more dangerous than the Matterhorn, and when I broke my knee-pan while learning I felt quite sure of it" ("Practical," 695). The velodrome's loss was mountaineering's gain. But the highly visible experiment in shifting gender roles that played itself out in Gay Nineties bicycling was far from absent in what Peck wryly called the tamer sport of climbing mountains. Just as the bicycle became an occasion for controversial changes in women's activities and dress, the same hotly contested issues arose surrounding the appropriate behavior and clothing for women climbers. For Peck this became a great debate between the arrayed forces of propriety, patriarchy, utility, and self-determination for women. She vociferously and persistently entered the contest on the side of liberating women climbers from social constraint, including the impediment of the skirt.

The tweeds and knickers of gentlemen climbers have, of course, become symbolic of early mountaineering. Similarly, photographs showing lines of women climbers trudging up carved steps carrying long alpenstocks and wading through billowing wool skirts characterize the imagery of early mountaineering for women. During her lifetime Peck became famous for breaking the gendered dress code of high-altitude climbing. As early as 1838 the early Alpine climber Mlle. D'Angeville wrote that after her porters left, she customarily exchanged her "ordinary feminine garb" for "that of *la fiancée du Mont Blanc*" (Irving, *Mountain Way,* 159). Peck repeatedly chafed at the restrictions imposed by conventional female clothing, but, like D'Angeville, she at times presented herself as concerned with the intricacies of propriety. On her first approach to Illampu, she explained that, although she rode her horse astride and wore her knicker-bockers, she concealed all this with a long ulster, which, as she put it, "gave somewhat the appearance of a divided skirt and I trust prevented my shocking the sensibilities of anyone" (*Search*, 37). But embedded in the closely worded irony of this comment is Peck's very real affront to the sensibilities that required such elaborate precautions and, inside that, her awareness of the larger political and gender implications of the kind of costume trickery that was common practice among working and other-wise active women of her day.

Peck addressed female clothing most extensively in a short article that she wrote for *Outing* in 1901, called, significantly, "Practical Mountain Climbing." Here Peck argued that mountaineering is good for the physical health of women, and as far as assertions to the contrary went, she re-torted: "One lady whose physician told her she must never walk when she could ride, or stand when she could sit (he might as well have added, nor sit when she can lie down) nevertheless developed into a climber who could take longer walks than the average" (700). During an era when doctors confined women to bed for extended periods of "rest cure" for a variety of conditions, Peck added with what must have been remarkable understatement, "some physicians possess excessive caution" (700). For Peck, however, women's activities in the mountains raised in their own specific way the issue of the constraints placed upon women by their attire:

Women . . . will declare that a skirt is no hindrance to their locomotion. This is obviously absurd, and though a few ladies have climbed mountains like the Mat-terhorn in extremely scant and abbreviated skirts, I dare assert that suitably made knickerbockers (not so scant as men's and yet not too full) are not only more comfortable but more becoming, whether to stout or slender figures . . . and for a woman to waste her strength and endanger her life with a skirt is foolish in the extreme. (698)

Peck's argument here rested on serviceability in clothing. The flowing skirt might be suitable garb for women sampling the pleasing and sublimely dis-tant vista of the Alps from the patio of a Lake Como hotel, but for the women who ventured into the mountains, they were impractical and ridic-ulous. She mentioned the aesthetics of design only rhetorically. She con-cluded her case by reflecting, "It may not be necessary to add that no one should climb mountains or even hills in corsets" (699). For Peck the moun-tains suggest realistic limitations to gendered conventions, a kind of geo-graphical borderland where the argument of practicality challenged the nineteenth-century "cult" of True Womanhood and all its trappings. In effect, because as a climber she associated mountains with a vigorous physical activity, mountains both provided the occasion to free women from the burden of their traditional clothing and in a larger sense erased all limitations on women's freedom, opportunity, and capacity for achievement.

Anticipating a deference she would later sometimes show in *Search* for the low scandal threshold of the day (a deference that most likely was just as much a practical strategy for achieving the summit goal of the expedition as it was courteous regard for local sensibilities), Peck in the *Outing* article provided some advice: "For high climbing many ladies wear a skirt of moderate length until out of sight of the hotel or beyond the path of ordinary tourists, then they leave the skirt under a rock or in the mountain hut until they return. If the descent is by another route, the guide without a murmur adds it to his well-filled ruck sack" (698). For anyone who has examined the many photographs of Peck published in *Search* or in the periodicals of the era showing her posed resolutely in knickers with her ice axe in hand (including the often printed and staged studio "summit" photograph of her Huascarán ascent), the image of her skirt stuffed under a rock assumes almost iconic significance.

The issues, of course, went far beyond the symbolism of fashion. As Peck's account of her expeditions to South America makes plain, mountains were hardly places of safety and refuge beyond the vagaries of modern life that perhaps were symbolized by the bicycle. The customary mode of late nineteenth-century mountaineering was guided climbing from comfortable Alpine hotels. Professional guides did much of the work for their clients and took the lion's share of the risk. Although Peck climbed with guides and cut her mountaineering teeth on established and often straightforward "walk-up" routes, she pursued her passion for climbing into the wilderness. In tackling an untried route at extreme altitude on a remote and glaciated peak like Huascarán, Peck willingly abandoned, in the name of pioneering exploration, the margin of security and comfort that traditionally padded the climbing experience for many of her predecessors.

Furthermore, for Peck, as for Mackinder a decade earlier, just getting to the mountain at all was, in its own way, a hazardous and circuitous project. After a long but relatively uneventful journey by steamer through Suez and then by rail to the interior of British East Africa, Halford Mackinder experienced elaborate and frustrating logistical problems in moving his expedition across country from the railhead at Nairobi. Peck, on the other hand, found her way to Peru in relative luxury and comfort as a "lady traveler." She also accomplished her trek overland into the mountains in a reasonably straightforward manner. The distance and difficulty of the immediate approach simply did not compare to that which Mackinder had encountered a few years before in East Africa. Peck's problems were of a different order. She mentions in passing that during her 1903 trip she had been "involved . . . in the tribulations and uncertainties of bubonica, quarantines, etc." and that in 1904 she hoped "all this would be over and the country again in its normal condition, if any other condition *is* normal" (*Search,* 129). Throughout *Search* Peck's frequent mentions of how her route to and from the mountains took her through and around regions in Central and South America beset by contagious epidemic disease emerge as a minor theme. Conditioned to regard the northern latitudes as more healthy, European and North American travelers at the turn of the twentieth century associated the tropics with disease and contagion. Peck is no exception. When she learns, for example, that a young engineer is planning to build a spa in the Canal Zone, she remarks, "I had never thought of Panama as a health resort" (127). Peck does her best to downplay the dangers, her sense of "tribulations" more a matter of inconvenience than biblical scourge. She leads readers to believe that her most pressing worry is that the sulfur fumigation of her baggage will damage her photographic equipment. She writes at times with nearly classic RGS-style stoicism of her willingness to confront the dangers. "Travel at this time was unusually light on account of the paralyzing effect of the bubonica," she notes (160); clearly, plague was something that discouraged other, less stalwart travelers.

But the intrepid traveler does not take chances with exposure to disease. She repeatedly alters her plans in the interest of safety. The persistence of epidemics as a topic in *Search* suggests that disease is one kind of information that Peck uses to understand the geography through which she passes. Unlike Mackinder, who seems unwilling to acknowledge that his supply problems stemmed from widespread regional famine, Peck is much more inclined to place her situation in the context of prevailing local health conditions. She presents her readers what we might call verbal "disease maps" of South and Central America, which prescribe against areas of infection and limit her range. In 1903 a yellow fever epidemic prevents her from visiting the port city of Guayaquil in Ecuador. After her successful ascent of Huascarán in 1909, an outbreak of malaria prevents her visit to the agricultural Yungas Valley in Peru. The geographer Yi-Fu Tuan writes in *Landscapes of Fear*: "Sickness forcefully directs a people's attention to the world's hostility" (87). As a social phenomenon, widespread disease orders spatial information, divides places that are safe from those that are not. For Peck the *cordons sanitaire* of Latin American contagion are invisible boundaries that are even more transitory than national borders or the frontiers of terra incognita; they shift unseen across the landscape, varying from year to year and according to the resolution of the traveler. The uncertainty of infection creates conceptual wilderness, even in the midst of human inhabitation — in fact, because of it. The only reliable and secure quarantine line in Peck's mind seems to be that drawn around the mountains she climbs. I imagine too that her conceptual lines are topographical contour lines implying elevation. In *Search* the specific kind of danger represented by widespread epidemics is to a significant degree a function of low elevation.[5] She associates plague exclusively with the coast, port cities, and valleys. She clarifies this perception best in her description of the area around La Oroya in Peru, in which she clearly depicts a vertical gradient of disease: "In the fertile valleys . . . are a number of pleasant towns, with an agreeable climate where tuberculosis may speedily be cured. Farther down it is warmer and in places malarial. . . . Certain regions still lower are afflicted with beriberi and other dreadful diseases" (106). Clearly, the margin is with elevation gain. Once she passes through areas such as these to the alpine zone and begins her treacherous climb, she is safe, at least from infection, and epidemic disease gives way before the more immediately pressing concerns of the mountain.

These concerns were complex enough. Although Peck may leave behind the hazards of infectious disease in climbing a mountain, she faces not only the objective dangers of a serious ascent but she imports to the mountain the full problematics of her situation as an early twentieth-century woman and spatializes the gender conflict inherent to it. From the beginning of her narrative she defines mountains as the particular arena in which her self-identity would be defined and as an arena where that identity would necessarily have to emerge from an established context of male activity, behavior, and language. On the first page of *Search* Peck describes what she had thought in 1898 might be the first setback to her plans to climb Illampu:

A few months later my heart sank within me, as I read in a Boston paper that Sir Martin Conway had left England to do some climbing in South America, for I felt quite sure that he was going to try *my* mountain. "Now," said a friend, rather inelegantly, who shared the knowledge of my purpose, "your cake is dough! Of course Conway will climb it, and if he doesn't, you can't." (1)

Conway did in fact attempt Illampu but was twice forced to retreat. He did, however, acquire a kind of literary ownership of the mountain when his subsequent book, *The Bolivian Andes,* established his credentials as an explorer of Illampu, albeit an unfortunate one. For Peck, who announced that Illampu was *hers,* this represents a serious threat. Peck accepts Conway's experience on the mountain as a provisional claim by virtue of the privilege of prior visitation so honored by twentieth-century explorers. She anticipates the difficulty of the climb as measured by Conway's failure (*Search,* 19). She takes his advice to approach the mountain from the south (132). She considers his suggestion that the Indians living at the base of the mountain may be dangerous and responds to his speculation that the Indians may be superstitious about ascending Illampu (137) by constructing crosses for them to plant at the point of their highest progress, to sanctify what otherwise might be considered an intrusion on the sacred mountain. Peck so repeatedly makes reference to what Conway-said-about-this or what Conway-did-here that the Illampu sections of *Search* sometimes almost seem to take the Bolivian Andes as their ultimate topic, presenting a geographical schematic of a literary text rather than the other way around. In any case, the figure of Conway *haunts* Peck's narrative under the legend "Conway had proceeded" (148). Peck's male rival functions in *Search* as an absent figure of authority and object of anxiety who can be displaced only by a successful ascent.

In 1899 Halford Mackinder gendered Mount Kenya in its "cold feminine beauty." One can only speculate on the psychological state and personal experiences that underwrote such a comparison, such a pointedly specific — perhaps from a male standpoint, daunting, intimidating, and threatening — construction of female identity. More broadly, of course, Mackinder's metaphor can be placed in relation to the long Western tradition of representing the natural world as feminine, a tradition thoroughly described by Annette Kolodny in her 1975 *The Lay of the Land.* As Kolodny and more recent scholars have elaborated, the pastoral imagery of a nurturing maternal garden underlies much of our deeply embedded thinking and archetypal structures pertaining to the natural world. The imagery that emerges in the literature of discovery, exploration, and conquest is often infiltrated with the symbolism of psychosexual mastery of a new land, as Kolodny puts it, "possessing the charms inherent in the virgin continent" (5)—a virgin that is vulnerable, available, and—as Kolodny quotes Thomas Morton, an early colonist of Massachusetts who ridiculed the strictures of Puritanism, as suggesting— "longing to be sped" (quoted in Kolodny, 12).

Being successfully and conventionally male at the turn of the twentieth century, of course, was just as much a matter of correctly reading the gender codes of the time and performing accordingly as being female was for women. We can have little doubt that complex homosocial gender dynamics conjoined the interests of imperial and institutional politics with those of mountaineering, all of which then participated in defining the overlapping contexts of the public "sphere" of male identity and activity. The conquest of traditionally female-gendered mountains and other geographical features and regions represented a conveniently effective way for men to solidify masculinity within the conventions of the times. Although written in a moment of doubt and anxiety about the success of his expedition, Mackinder's characterization of Mount Kenya as coldly feminine is in line with the tradition of representing "virgin" geography as easily had, even willing. In a sense, the imagery is not radically far from Coleridge's notion of a "kingly Spirit" and "Great Hierarch." The suspicion lurks that for an Englishman like Mackinder, who was living during the closing days of the long reign of Queen Victoria, the image of a coldly feminine hierarch might not have been altogether inconsistent with a certain construction of female gender. Peck, on the other hand, although she does not gender Illampu itself, still labels it with possession and contests its possession by another, Martin Conway. In this regard the deep archetype remains largely intact, the lack of gender-specific imagery for the mountain displaced in Peck's struggle to deny its control by a rival who represents the traditionally male fraternity of climbers. Illampu, therefore, becomes in Peck's thinking not so much a female place but a place for the assertion of a new and expanding definition of what constitutes the female.

The sense of rivalry and of belatedness that defines Peck's relationship to Conway, the successful and well-known male mountaineer, carries an almost prognostic significance that is vital to the main current of her narrative. The book is, after all, a victory celebration, and its early sections, those relating the accomplishments of Conway, although they follow a chronological sequence, are finally just preface to Peck's eventual first ascent. When she moves beyond Illampu, Peck's narrative extends to Huascarán, where the shadow of Conway does not follow. When Peck achieves the north summit, she can describe her feat as "the conquest of a mountain at least 1,500 feet higher than Mt. McKinley, and 2,500 feet higher than any man residing in the United States had climbed" (*Search*, 358). But long before she reaches that essentially comparative or relative goal, Peck's mountains are places that she identifies in terms of male/female confrontation. The more abstract rivalry Peck feels with Conway acts as a cross-reference to her more mundane or direct conflicts with her male climbing companions.[6]

Like virtually all climbers, male or female, during her time Peck inherited the tradition and practice of climbing with professional guides, who were, as might be expected, exclusively male. The departure from guided climbing, as noted in chapter 1, must be considered one of the benchmarks in the transition of mountaineering from sport to exploration. For women climbers the transition was even more gradual. In fact, women did not begin until the late 1970s to challenge the most difficult rock-climbing routes without male climbing partners (Robertson, xii). But for Peck the reliance on professional male guides proves repeatedly problematic and, in its own right, challenging. In the first place, by venturing alone into the wilderness with only a team of Indian porters in many cases, and with the Taugwalder brothers in 1908, Peck flew in the face of all convention and decorum. In particular, it was unheard of to actually sleep in the same tent with male companions, as Peck did. Moreover, she quickly learned that the audaciousness of her behavior did not automatically translate to credibility and authority with her climbing partners. In his sketch of Peck in *Outing*, the writer noted that she had failed to reach the twelve-thousand-foot summit of Grossglockner because "the guide, like the proverbial angel, feared to rush in" ("Men and Women," 623).[7] This reference to a timid guide most likely drew upon an interview with Peck and reflected a theme that she frequently describes in her mountaineering. The figure of the reluctant male guide is almost conventional in Peck, and the theme of male faintheartedness permeates *Search* from first page to last.

Peck first describes this difficulty when she recounts her first expedition to Illampu in 1903. When her Indian porters refuse to continue farther up the mountain, her Swiss guides and the unnamed American "professor" accompanying them suddenly seem strangely aloof and cannot be persuaded to admonish the Indians to proceed, in part because they too want to turn back. The effect of the professor's inaction is to encourage the mutiny. Peck explains: "Doubtless the Indians supposed him to be the leader of the expedition and believed that he had already abandoned it"

(51). Her irony is clear when later she snaps, "To manage three men seemed beyond my power. Perhaps some of my more experienced married sisters would have done better" (51).

This scene sets a pattern carried on throughout the book. "Oh how I longed for a man with the pluck and determination to stand by me to the finish!" (152), she writes when the males along on her 1904 expedition to the same mountain show a similar lack of resolve, complaining that "the men showed far greater alacrity in coming down" (152). At a number of points in the narrative she makes a sharp comparison between *her* desire to climb up and what she perceives as a general male affinity for going downhill. When she descended from her third unsuccessful attempt on Huascarán, Peck had in fact been forced to turn back by the unwillingness of her male companions to continue after a minor fall. She reports learning that one of the men had been saying that actually it was "the Senorita" who had "sat down and wept and declared that they could go no farther" (243).

Although she employed Gabriel and Rudolf Taugwalder in 1908 and led the expedition, she found her decisions constantly questioned and undermined by Rudolf, who was unable to accept the open leadership of a woman. Dealing with Rudolf, as Showell Styles so aptly puts it in his account of Peck's climb in *On Top of the World,* required "tactful handling" on Peck's part (58). Peck reports that on her third attempt on Huascarán, the Taugwalder brothers "were rather impatient of what they considered unnecessary advice or suggestions from a woman, even an employer" (*Search,* 341–42) and were consistently demanding about food, drink, and other creature comforts, seemingly, in fact, incapable of providing for themselves. Peck mentions that, more often than not, she is forced to "look after the men" (318), even to the point of having to cook for her guides. Distanced by thousands of miles and in a situation far different from the kind of for-hire Alpine climbing that they were accustomed to leading—a milieu that was based upon and rigidly enforced the station and class differences from their usual male clients—the men seem to have found that deeply ingrained gender roles sometimes overwhelmed their sense of class subordination. For Peck the final insult comes on the last slope of Huascarán. As Peck works with her instruments, one of her guides slips away and steps to the summit first. "I *was* enraged," she writes. "I had told them, long before, that, as it was my expedition, I should like, as is customary, to be the first one to place my foot at the top" (344). Although she later downplays the incident, at the time her disappointment is intense. "I had been robbed," she reports (344).

As a counterpoint to this tendency on the part of Peck's male companions to shuttle her into a more traditionally subordinate female role, as Peck tells it the males themselves at times take on behavioral and personality characteristics stereotypically associated with women. They nag and whimper. They profess helplessness to get their way. Their "continual chatter" (166) forces Peck to travel out of earshot and, compared to Peck's own quickly efficient preparations, they practice what she calls "an elaborate toilet" (303). With these references the men become vehicles for a critique of patriarchal clichés concerning women, as well as perhaps a coordinated and self-conscious commentary on what she considers conventional, as well as politically uninformed, in female behavior.

In short, Peck's presentation entails an uncomfortable quandary. Although she presents her male mountaineering companions as having proved almost uniformly annoying, burdensome, and onerous, she sees her reluctant reliance upon them as necessary. Initially in *Search,* her perception of the *utility* of male companions divides along well-defined racial and class lines, a version of the familiar elitist "chaps" and "lads" hierarchy that pervaded expeditionary climbing in its early years and even survives today in the client–native porter relationship. She requires Indian porters simply for transporting the expedition's equipment up the mountain; she requires non-Indian males to assist in the actual summit bid. When in her account of the first attempt on Illampu she is told that no local "European" men are available to accompany her, she dramatizes the moment for emphasis: " 'Alone!' I cried in amazement and some horror, 'you don't mean that I should go all alone with an arriero ninety miles to the *finca* (where there was no really civilized person) and go up the mountain with Indians and cholos only?' 'Yes,' he replied, 'I do' " (58). Although she shortly confides ambiguously that "this idea almost took my breath away" (58), Peck's question here most likely serves as a last ditch attempt to persuade a local landowner that he should accompany her and as a result may lean a bit toward the intentionally hyperbolic, designed perhaps to prey with appropriate melodrama on white male anxiety about the safety of white women among Indians, an anxiety that the landowner may have shared. Although she continues to express certain reservations, later, on her second attempt of Huascarán, Peck does in fact climb only in the company of Indian porters and concludes: "I have no doubt but that I was much safer than I have been at times in our great cities" (195), making in her own way the conventionally unfavorable comparison between civilization and mountain that so frequently appears in modern mountaineering narratives.

A generation later Miriam Underhill, in *Give Me the Hills,* sounded more confident about climbing without the support of men. "I saw no reason," she writes, "why women, *ipso facto,* should be incapable of leading a good climb" (149), and she described how during 1929 she "decided to try some climbs not only guideless, but manless" (150), including her ascent, with Alice Damesme, of the Matterhorn.[8] Note, however, that Underhill referred to climbing relatively short and well-established Alpine routes and that she had the benefit of twenty years' improvement in climbing equipment and technique. Peck, in fact, in a 1901 article allowed that "many ladies . . . climb high mountains with their husbands, and many who have none, without" ("Practical," 700). But a mountain of the scope of Illampu was at the time another matter. Peck, attempting an unclimbed multiday route with complex approach and logistical problems, was quite simply attempting a much larger project than those undertaken by Underhill's or Peck's own climbing ladies.[9]

Professing herself from the beginning of *Search* to be a "firm believer in the equality of the sexes" (xi), Peck seems both to be seeking out unclimbed mountains as places still free of male conquest and to be seeking participation in kind in that conquest. Although she achieves the latter, her success with the former is far from clear-cut. Her perception of topography tends to import gender conflict to what theoretically might be the "neutral" ground of the mountain. The conflict followed Peck home. The severe frostbite that resulted when Rudolf Taugwalder dropped his gloves on the descent from the north summit of Huascarán required the amputation of his left hand, as well as parts of his fingers on the right hand and a portion of a foot. When Peck publicly accused Taugwalder of carelessness after the climb and held him responsible for his own misfortune, she was accused of callousness, and many stalwart male members of the American Alpine Club felt vindicated in proclaiming this further evidence of the inherent inability of women to lead serious mountaineering expeditions. Again, in the reaction of the male climbing community the overlapping categories of gender and class find interesting expression. While the tradition of guided Alpine climbing was comfortable with the "alienated labor" and sometimes even death of paid working-class guides, in the case of Peck, the protective, even paternalistic, advocacy of the "chaps" for the "lads" Rudolf and Gabriel Taugwalder provided an occasion to publicly reassert the mountains as a geography rightly within the male sphere. While Peck has survived as a pioneer figure in women's mountaineering, during the last years of her life her own sense of resolution and instinct for self-promotion, as well as the vehemence and sometimes stridency of her published remarks, left her reputation to a certain degree clouded in a society not prepared to hear the perspectives of strong, independent-minded women. She was a flashpoint for larger cultural debate about the roles of women in a society fighting what would prove to be a rearguard battle against full equality.

In the forward to *Search* Peck mentions that when she first planned a climbing expedition to Illampu in 1898, she had tried to finance it by soliciting the sponsorship of various manufacturers whose products she, as a successful, famous, and somewhat notorious woman mountain climber, would endorse in advertisements. She had no takers. "What a chance was lost for saying 'Soapine did it!' " she jokes (xi). Peck's promotional skills, however, do not go to waste. She announces that the goal of *Search* is "to aid in a small degree the cause of Peace by increasing our knowledge of countries with which we have too little acquaintance, a bond of sympathy and union taking the place of crass conceit and narrow prejudice" (xi). Soapine's loss is international harmony's gain, in Peck's telling of it.

For Peck the "bond of sympathy and union" is best forged through economic relations, and everything about *Search* shows that she designed the book to encourage such relations. That *Search* is a travel book and an exploration narrative we can have no doubt. That it has a clear subtext of feminist concerns we must be equally confident. But the peculiarly heterogeneous character of *Search* is finally what is most remarkable — how it combines these already mentioned concerns with pointed promotion of U.S. foreign investment.[10] Plainly, Peck is covering a lot of bases.

Possessed of a "zeal for improvement and growth" (360), South America, as Peck presents it, is a cornucopia of raw materials awaiting development and export by foreign capital. As Peck relates her travels to and from her climbs, she enumerates the opportunities available for investors from the United States. Concentrated in two sections of *Search* (after her first unsuccessful attempt on Illampu and after her ascent of Huascarán) but present throughout, Peck's preoccupation with the resource base of South America surfaces as one of the book's dominant topics. Peck surveys timberlands, sugarcane fields, and coffee plantations. She hints that the cocoa industry in Peru is "not yet largely developed" and "offers a great opportunity to investors" (107). She applauds the work of the capitalist Henry Meiggs in constructing railroads (222) and lists where American-style hotels could be operated at a profit. And why does she tell her readers all this in a book about mountaineering? Mountain climbing, after all, as she explains it,

for itself alone, to many, nay, to nearly all of our people, might not seem worth while; worse, it might appear folly: but as a means of drawing attention to a section of country that should be world famed for the splendour of its great mountains, no less for the mineral riches along their slopes, it seemed that my efforts might appeal in a practical way to practical men. (217)

Accordingly, Peck praises the quality of Peruvian oil and coal and describes sulfur, silver, and copper mines. Mountain climbing and resource inventory are as equally interwoven in her narrative as she announces them to be in her thinking. We get a clear glimpse of this as she describes her plans to travel in the mountainous region near Tinayhuarco, Peru. She observes: "The object of my visit was two-fold: first to see the celebrated copper property upon which more than twenty millions have been spent by American capitalists, a property containing what has been called the richest copper deposit in the world, and second, to make an ascent of some great mountain" (269). According to Peck, the only injury she receives in her travels through South America comes not from a fall down a crevasse but from a fall from a mule after she visits the Cerro de Pasco copper smelter (270). When all is said and done in *Search,* Peck closes not by emphasizing her mountaineering but by justifying it in terms of the book's advice to investors: "If they [her expeditions] shall have served in some degree to foster the awakening interest, to disseminate a little information in regard to a portion of what is fitly called the Land of To-morrow and the Continent of Opportunity, they will not have been made in vain" (370).

At least two of Peck's other works offer themselves as interesting cross-references to the economic arguments explicit in *Search.* A short article called "The South American Tour: Why, When, and Where to Go, What to See, and How Much It Will Cost" appeared in the June 5, 1913, issue of the *Independent.* This travel piece, adapted from her 1913 book of the same title, discusses leisure travel to South America in the context of international investment and trade. A trip south, Peck advises, will "cause some of the businessmen to open their eyes" (1292) and "investigate hitherto neglected opportunities before it shall be too late" (1285). Peck's 1922 *Industrial and Commercial South America* dispenses with the elements of exploration and tourism altogether and does nothing but boost foreign investment. The book is an economic and political geography of South America, a statistical inventory of resources and commercial activity designed to assist businessmen from the United States with such practical information as "the opportunity for investments of various kinds and political conditions affecting these; the instruments of exchange, banking and trade regulations; the means of communication and transport by land and water" (*Industrial*, xviii).[11]

Following Peck's writing from the turn of the century through the 1920s, the shift from the topic of travel and exploration to the topic of U.S. economic expansion is noticeable. *Search,* which falls chronologically at the midway point, represents the most provocative hybrid of the two genres. When Peck narrates her climbs on Illampu and Huascarán, she does not concern herself with commodities and investments but rather with the rigors and frustrations of the ascents. When she details her way to and from the mountains, her preoccupation with economics and investment plays itself out in her writing. Her exploratory narratives are in fact embedded within the larger matrix of a book that can best be identified as promotional literature. Not wholly unlike the intent of the compendiums of Richard Hakluyt and Samuel Purchas, that sought to sell Europeans on the potential of the North American colonies during the age of discovery, Peck's writing undertakes to convince Americans in a more contemporary "new world" of Latin American commerce.

Consider in more detail the dynamics of Peck's narrative structure. In her extended portrait of Latin America, Peck seems to identify certain places as presenting difficulties too obvious or serious to be swept under the expansive rug of her favorable impressions. Epidemic disease is, of course, one of these. As one of the most widely recognized dangers inherent in the world's "backward" regions, particularly the tropics, communicable disease in the early twentieth century represented an impediment not only to casual travel but also to potential trade and investment opportunities. Just a year before the publication of Peck's *Search,* S. P. Verner had scrupulously emphasized in his "Effective Occupation of Undeveloped Lands" the necessity of avoiding what he called the "pestholes . . . at the mouths of every one of the African and South American rivers" (833) and the establishment of trading centers in inland "High Colonies," preferably above nine thousand feet.[12] When *Search* was published in 1911, educated readers may still have subscribed to disturbing confusions about how contagious disease could "poison" the air itself.[13]

Peck's observations about epidemics openly acknowledge the reality of the common association between disease and equatorial regions, even if they do not play to the almost primal fear of it, as an essay like Verner's does. They perhaps even reference a broader traditional association between epidemic disease and social or moral degeneration. But a paradox is built into Peck's candid admissions. She notes at one point, for example, in the most abstract terms how the plague raging down the coast of Peru in 1904 dramatically restricted trade, but in the same paragraph she goes on to describe the port city of Samanco with a level of detail and a lively flavor of "business as usual" that suggests nothing if not bustling commercial activity (*Search,* 160). Is the effect of this rhetoric to mitigate the impression of the epidemic's severity? If so, the "disease map" that Peck overlays on Latin America may not be the patchwork of hostile zones of infection and friendly zones of security that it seems on first reading to be. In Peck's telling of it, the mountains she climbs, dangerous as they may be in other respects, are refuges from the lowland peril of epidemic. They are also, in a sense, the promotional high points of her writing, the sites of dramatic adventure that carry the argument for American commercial development associated with them, just as sex and prosperity may be used to carry the argument to buy an Infinity in a television commercial. But if the lowlands are not all that dangerous after all, if the dynamics of the narrative speak *through* the mere formal announcement that, yes, there is disease in Latin America, then the distinction between mountain and lowland breaks down in terms of disease. More important, the rhetoric of gaudy high-altitude promotion tends to merge with the down-to-earth, utilitarian thesis of investment opportunity. Peck's embedded sections of mountaineering narrative become less distinctly ornaments on the plain surface of argument, and we are drawn more innocently into those sections, prepared to read adventure stories. When this effect occurs, the goals of promotional writing are certainly fulfilled.

Whatever ends Peck might have wished to pursue in her book, it is clear that she had a significant reading audience at her disposal. Her calmly unconventional behavior and groundbreaking and well-publicized climbs had made her a public figure of some note, part role model and part oddity. When she sought financial support for her South American expeditions, she advertised widely for subscriptions. Her articles appeared in a dozen American magazines from 1895 on, including *Harper's,* the *Independent,* and *Colliers,* and in 1905 she appeared in a photographic essay in *Everybody's Magazine* entitled "Intimate Portraits: Men and Women Who Are Doing Interesting Things," along with Georgianna Bishop, the recent winner of the Women's National Golf Championship; Eva Booth, a commander in the Salvation Army; and Mrs. Cornelius Vanderbilt, whose "charms," the article's author assured readers, will soon be responsible for her husband's appointment as first secretary of the U.S. Embassy in Berlin (213). Peck's book was well received and in the United States widely reviewed, including reviews in the *A.L.A. Booklist, Literary Digest, Nation,* and *New York Times*.[14] "Well worth reading," concluded a writer for the *American Review of Reviews* (638), in general speaking for the rest. Peck clearly enjoyed a kind of popularity that provided her with a platform for whatever positions the book cared to take.

Early reviews give a sense of the response to *Search*. The *Educational Review* called it "fascinating as a novel" (428). The *Literary Digest* identified it as a book of "South American exploration" (1123). *Catholic World* predicted that "the volume will surely tend to promote the kindly relations which the author wishes to see established between ourselves and the South American people" (398). And notice how a writer for *Book Review Digest* characterized the book in 1911: "In addition to the chief interest of the book which attaches itself to the perilous business of mountain climbing, the people in the valleys, their manner of living and their resources are observed in passing" (368). This is an acknowledgment that Peck's is an intentionally hybrid work. Its mountain adventure story mingles with its cultural portrait, and with the curiously imprecise word *resources* the reviewer hinted at an even wider scope to the book's concerns. It is unclear whether *resources* refers to the material basis of life in South America or to resources as commodities, those raw materials and investment situations available *in* South America *to* enterprising Yankees. These early responses imply that the book's first readers most likely glossed it as an acceptable miscellany of daring adventure, economic promotion, and political assumption. We can reconstruct the context of their reading to better understand why they might have done so.

First of all, Peck makes plain her own conception of U.S. relations to South America. "The Spanish War," she wrote in *Industrial and Commercial South America*, "first inspiring many with the idea that the United States had become a world power with interests beyond its boundaries, served to arouse in others a disposition to have a share in foreign trade" (xv). With this observation Peck summarized the U.S. transition to world power at the beginning of the twentieth century and in fact suggested the most appropriate backdrop to a reading of *Search*.

The "splendid little war," as Theodore Roosevelt called the 115-day war with Spain, serves as a fascinating point of disjunction separating the aloofness and isolationism of U.S. foreign policy in the nineteenth century from what would prove to be the imperial posture it maintained throughout the twentieth. On one hand, it represents a real and sudden watershed between very different international roles. The war plainly precipitated events. Between the time that Spain ceded the Philippines to the United States in 1898 and the time that the United States transformed Cuba by treaty into a virtual protectorate in 1903, the nation had clearly adopted an extroverted international personality. This new orientation was variously announced in the rhetoric of the three Republican administrations of William McKinley, Theodore Roosevelt, and William Howard Taft and extended in many of the actions, if not in the idealistic verbiage, of the Democratic administration of Woodrow Wilson. It expressed itself in the first of the so-called Open Door notes written by Secretary of State John Hay in 1899 admonishing the European nations that had set up spheres of interest in China to respect the trading privileges of other nations. It moved through its popular crescendo in the consummate and bellicose nationalism of Roosevelt as his administration engineered U.S. control of the canal route through the Panamanian isthmus in 1903 and when he proclaimed the Roosevelt corollary to the Monroe Doctrine in response to Europeans' loan default claims on the revenues of the Dominican Republic in 1904. And it continued from 1908 to 1912 in the dollar diplomacy of the Taft presidency, which encouraged U.S. banks to displace European creditors in Latin America.

Yet, on the other hand, it is almost equally true that in an important sense the Spanish-American War was also a gaudy and well-exploited exclamation mark in a complex of economic and political events that had been moving the United States toward world power since the Civil War. The sudden acquisition of overseas territories simply provided expansionists with a new, urgent, and apparently largely successful argument for the policies that they had been advocating for years. As I outlined in chapter 1, political theorists, economists, crass jingoists, missionaries, and social philosophers all contributed in their own ways to creating a climate of public discourse in which expansionism seemed both a viable option and a controversial issue. When an advertisement appeared in 1899 showing Admiral Dewey in his battleship stateroom washing his hands with Pears' Soap, it signaled significant public acceptance of the mandate of expansionism.[15] "The first step towards lightening THE WHITE MAN'S BURDEN is through teaching the virtues of cleanliness," the ad enjoined.[16] One can only wonder whether Peck, a would-be soap promoter herself, fancied her image in the place of Dewey's.

This situation had its greatest influence on relations between the United States and Latin America, where in addition to its political and strategic expression, U.S. expansionism had a distinctly economic character. At the outbreak of the war with Spain, U.S. foreign commerce had risen to $223 million, double what it had been in 1880 (Freeman and Nearing, 242). Leading Republicans and business leaders increasingly came to see expanding commercial involvement with Latin America as what the Republican leader James G. Blaine called it: "the especial province of this country" (quoted Freeman and Nearing, 242), just as the European powers had theirs in Asia and Africa.

Even more important than trade activity in this period was that increasingly significant amounts of U.S. capital became available for foreign investment. And whether it resulted from the financial "glut" described by Hobson or simply the diversion of capital from less lucrative domestic investments, after 1900 exported American capital tended to stay in the Western Hemisphere. By 1913 more than two-thirds of the $2.6 million that Americans invested overseas ended up in the hemisphere, and half went to Mexico, Central and South America, and the Caribbean basin (Dunn, 3). With only 4 percent of the total investment going to the new territories acquired as a result of the war with Spain, U.S. money lurched toward the "commercial colonies" of politically independent nations (Fieldhouse, *Economics,* 61) — in short into just the sort of investment opportunities that Peck describes in *Search.*[17]

By the time of the Taft administration, what once might have been regarded as essentially a business investment situation had been formalized as the government policy generally known, then and now, as "dollar diplomacy." Taft's State Department initially extended its diplomatic influence in China on behalf of an American banking syndicate led by J. P. Morgan and Company and quickly turned the same kind of attention to Latin America. Taft explained to Congress in 1912:

> It is obvious that the Monroe doctrine is more vital in the neighborhood of the Panama Canal and the zone of the Caribbean than anywhere else. . . . It is therefore essential that the countries within that sphere shall be removed from the jeopardy involved by heavy foreign debt and chaotic national finances and from the ever present danger of international complications due to disorder at home. Hence the United States has been glad to encourage and support American bankers who were willing to lend a helping hand to the financial rehabilitation of such countries. (quoted in Freeman and Nearing, 265)

During Taft's presidency dollar diplomacy, soon practiced farther south as well, led to direct military intervention in Cuba, Ecuador, and Nicaragua as the most drastic extensions of "encouragement and support" for U.S. financial interests.

D. K. Fieldhouse rightly calls colonial rule "a complex improvisation" (*Colonialism*, 42). This characterization holds all the more true for the particular combination of economic encroachment and nationalist zeal that controlled the noncolonial relationship of the United States and Latin America during the period represented by Peck's *Search*. In the case of the United States, the flag clearly followed the dollar in the penetration of the region. Peck's book undertakes to describe only the first stage of this two-part process. But it is this very complex foreign involvement that speaks most distinctly through Peck's work. In the most general terms *Search* clearly operates as a document both *of* and *about* U.S. economic expansion in Latin America. It hints at this status with specific references to such prominent figures in U.S. foreign policy events as Theodore Roosevelt, Secretary of State Elihu Root, and Meiggs and contextualizes economic events with frequent references to the most famous U.S. foreign adventure of the era, the construction of the Panama Canal.

In 1906 Peck wrote an article for *Harper's Monthly* describing her attempt that year on Huascarán. This abbreviated piece, much of which later finds its way into *Search*, focuses almost exclusively on mountaineering, with little exposition of the peripheral affairs of the expedition, such as preparations, travel to the mountain, the regions and peoples encountered along the way. More to the point, though, is that in this article Peck does not even mention South American culture nor, even more pertinently, economics. On the scale of shifting emphasis from climbing to promotion noted earlier as a characteristic of Peck's oeuvre, this piece clearly falls as an early work. Does a more narrow editorial focus on the heroic and even bizarre exploits of a mountain-climbing woman account for this? It may. Peck lived in part by her pen; a survey of her journalism suggests a willingness on her part to adapt her subject matter to the editorial requirements of a range of periodicals.[18] It could also be true, though, that something had changed between 1906 and 1911 that would alter the context of Peck's experiences and somehow invite the conjunction of politics, economics, and mountaineering that her book finally records.

Little in the history of exploration between 1906 and 1911 accounts for the difference in the two pieces. The first decade of the century did see an expansion of mountaineering on what James Ramsey Ullman calls in his *The Age of Mountaineering* "an enormous scale" (80), particularly in

Africa, central Asia, and near the poles. But in the context of U.S. politics, 1906 and 1911 differed in two important respects. The year 1906 was the midpoint of Theodore Roosevelt's successful second term in the White House, a moment when economic boom times seemed to pace both domestic reform and increasing international influence. By 1911, however, the political climate of the United States had altered substantially. Concerned about Japanese expansionism in the Pacific, the Roosevelt administration had mediated a resolution to the Russo-Japanese War of 1904–5 at the Portsmouth Peace Conference. But the role played by the United States in that war did not begin then. Between 1904 and 1907 investment bankers in the United States carried the majority of Japan's wartime debt, virtually allowing the war to occur. In 1925 Joseph Freeman and Scott Nearing looked back at the financial events of 1907 as marking an important increment in what would continue during the entire modern period to be an accelerating U.S. involvement in foreign investment. For Freeman and Nearing 1907 was "the first real adventure of the United States . . . into the fields of international financing" (11).

Unfortunately, any lasting beneficial results of this experiment were cut short by inauspicious events at home. Beginning in mid-March 1907, Americans experienced the first important American economic crisis of the twentieth century, a "panic" that, by a contemporary estimate by the *American Review of Reviews*, sidetracked 200,000 railroad cars and saw securities decline in value by $5 billion in nine months (Speare, 465). As bank upon bank followed the lead of the prominent Knickerbocker Trust Company of New York in closing its doors, the nation entered a period of economic downturn, the effects of which still lingered as Peck wrote *Search*.

Most contemporary analysts attributed the 1907 crisis in confidence to excessive investment speculation, undermined by scarcity of capital and tight interest rates. But part of the legacy of the 1907 panic was that for most of Taft's term in office, Republican Party conservatives continued to blame the economic downturn on Taft's political mentor, Theodore Roosevelt. In 1902 Roosevelt had revived the Sherman Anti-Trust Act as a means of bringing suit against the monopolistic practices of forty-four major corporations. In 1906 Roosevelt supported the Pure Food and Drug Act, and the Hepburn Act, which regulated interstate freight rates. The president's critics claimed that these policies created an antibusiness climate that brought on the panic. This split between Roosevelt and the more conservative elements within the party, as well as a personal animosity between Roosevelt and Taft, finally led Roosevelt to contest Taft's reelection bid in 1912. When Roosevelt failed to gain the Republican nomination, he formed the splinter Progressive Party. Using this vehicle, Roosevelt campaigned on a platform of government regulation of business and what he called "New Nationalism."

As it turns out, in her advocacy of closer commercial relations between the United States and Latin America, Peck speaks a vague mixture of progressive Republican foreign policy and personal endorsement of Roosevelt that echoes, however ambiguously, the events of national politics in 1911. *Search* presents a certain amount of evidence that Peck did actually maintain personal links with the best-known expansionists of the era. She recounts her preparations for her 1908 trip to South America:

> A visit to Washington, with a call on President Roosevelt, gained his favorable interest, as I felt sure it would; since he was an honourary member of our Alpine Club, and by temperament would be appreciative of a real athletic and sporting event. Moreover, if not quite committed to Woman Suffrage, he was not of the sort to decry woman's ability, or when it had been proved, to throw stumbling blocks in her way. And his friendly interest proved of real service. (307)

Peck never explains the precise nature of this "real service." She does not mention Roosevelt when she lists the financial contributors to her expeditions, so we can perhaps assume that Roosevelt did not play the instrumental role that he did in providing for Robert Peary's 1901 Arctic expedition. However, that Roosevelt's name comes up in connection with both Peck and Peary serves to further solidify the relationship between mountaineering and polar exploration that existed in the minds of many people during the period and to which Peck repeatedly alludes. In any case, even if Roosevelt's assistance to Peck were of a completely intangible sort — the good name and goodwill of a still-popular president — the event of their meeting establishes Peck's activity in a milieu of promotion and publicity in which the two categories of Republican expansion and exploration plainly have common ground.

More specifically, though, Peck's open advocacy of U.S. investment in Latin America would have supported the political and economic policies of Roosevelt's handpicked successor, William Howard Taft. If conservative economists were correct in blaming the panic on a scarcity of capital, the diversion of money into foreign investment could actually have contributed to the political black eye that Republicans nursed after the panic. But on the other hand, foreign investment in 1911 also was perceived as a way to accelerate recovery. As during the economic crisis of 1893, the panic of 1907 prompted many Americans to see foreign export markets and lucrative, high-yield foreign investment as a way out of economic stagnation, as a kind of extension of the economic component of the ideology of Manifest Destiny that had fueled U.S. prosperity in the nineteenth century. Beginning in 1909, Taft's version of progressive Republicanism meshed nicely with the range of theoretical solutions current during his term in office. Hobson, for example, argued that British overseas investment was one available solution to economic depression. The high interest rates traditionally associated with overseas investment upheld domestic interest rates and profit levels. In proposing and supporting the export of U.S. capital, Taft was in effect laying the groundwork for investors in the United States to achieve similarly high rates of return, a situation that in the terms of Hobsonian logic would lead directly to economic revitalization.

In addition to the overarching theoretical presence of Hobson behind this reasoning, many U.S. economic and political theorists, politicians, and military men of the era, including Alfred Thayer Mahan, Whitelaw Reid, James Harrison Wilson, and Albert J. Beveridge, had pointed to the economic importance of foreign investment and trade. But perhaps the most influential and completely thought-out theory was that articulated by Charles A. Conant. In many ways Conant's 1900 *The United States in the Orient* anticipated both Hobson and Lenin in its discussion of capital; it provided an obvious game plan for the dollar diplomacy carried on by Taft.[19] A born-again Republican, Conant trained himself as an expert in currency and banking and acted as a close adviser to the designers of U.S. foreign policy between 1903 and 1912. Conant explained that the "glut" of overproduction was a result of surplus capital or "oversavings." Rejecting Hobson's ideal solution — increasing the buying power of U.S. workers — Conant argued for "the equipment of new countries with the means of production and exchange" (quoted in Healy, 196) as a means of dispersing investment capital. Conant's writing is a revealing mix of economic theory and ideological corroboration — he placed the "Anglo-Saxon race" at the pinnacle of human evolutionary progress and gave credence to and fueled U.S. fears of growing Russian power and influence. He embodied the diverse spirit of twentieth-century imperialism in its full range of motivations. Although he initially saw China as the ideal theater for this economic expansion, as Taft did later, Conant's theory plainly describes the inherent investment possibilities of Latin America as well. In fact, Conant formulated currency reforms for Panama and Nicaragua and died in Havana in 1915 while doing so for Cuba.[20] Conant's work provides a precise theoretical model for both Taft's dollar diplomacy and Peck's investment promotion.

Peck does not confine her name dropping to Roosevelt. In *Search* Peck describes how on September 10, 1906, she stood on a balcony of the English Club in Callao, Peru, as the man-of-war USS *Charleston* steamed into port. Aboard the *Charleston* was Secretary of State Root. Root was touring South America, Peck insists, "conveying to the several Republics the assurance of the sincere and disinterested friendship of the United States Government" (263). Peck portrays Root exclusively as a statesman, a universalist, a quiet intellectual man of peace. She points out, in fact, that Root was celebrated by the Peruvian government, as she describes it, by honorary induction into the faculty of political and administrative sciences at the University of St. Mark in Lima (265).

It is significant that Peck represents in so highly favorable a light a man who clearly was one of the principal architects of U.S. expansionism during the Progressive Era. As secretary of war under McKinley, Root oversaw the transfer of U.S. authority to the territories acquired during the war with Spain. As secretary of state under Roosevelt (1905–9), Root engineered a series of delicate negotiations with South American nations, with England over fishing rights, and with Japan over emigration control. He worked to strengthen the world court provided for by the First Hague Conference in 1899 and helped establish the Central American Court of Justice. He was awarded the Nobel Peace Prize in 1912, as the English edition of Peck's *Search* appeared in London.

Yet Root's foreign service was also motivated in large part by his acceptance of the assumptions of U.S. hegemony and his desire to deal practically with the obligations and requirements that it imposed. He seems to have believed that increasing U.S. investment in Latin America made the political expansion of the United States there inevitable. In 1908 he predicted that Haiti and Nicaragua would likely follow Cuba in becoming U.S. protectorates. And in 1912, the year he received the Nobel Prize, he told the New York Chamber of Commerce that "it is a question of time until Mexico, Central America and the islands, which we do not possess in the Caribbean, shall come under our banner" (quoted in Freeman and Nearing, 262). In this light Peck's description of the arrival in Peru by warship of Root's diplomatic mission seems less innocent than it otherwise might, at least from the standpoint of Latin American sovereignty. Peck's account of Root's diplomatic mission implicitly associates territorial annexation with the more limited and benign version of U.S. relations with Latin America that she seems inclined to privilege, one that could consist of just friendly "travel, commerce, and trade" (*Search*, xi). Peck describes in some detail Root's visit to Lima, including a gala banquet given by Peruvian president José Pardo. Peck reports that in the company of the mayor of Lima, Root and his family paid a visit to the city's cathedral, "of which Pizarro himself laid the foundation stone, January 18, 1535," and which houses "a coffin in which the body of the Conqueror, Pizarro, is said to repose" (264). In the context of Root's own belief in the inevitability of U.S. political domination of the region, this state visit to the tomb of the conquistador seems almost sinister.

By 1922 Peck seems to have been willing to make a much harder distinction between "imperialism" and commerce than she did in *Search*. She writes in *Industrial and Commercial South America* that through trade "we would enjoy the fruits of the whole earth, not by imperialistic conquest, but through friendly acquaintance, the sharing of ideas, and the exchange of products" (xvii). This distinction, however, seems less stringent in *Search*. With the history of U.S. involvement in Latin America in the backs of our minds, Root at the tomb of Pizarro becomes the most striking tableau enacted in the book. Peck's model diplomat, his work aimed at the same purpose as Peck's own persistent blandishment of U.S. financiers, seems poised at the threshold of a new conquest. *Search* involves Root in its complex amalgam of adventure and propaganda, and her mention of Root invites readers to draw her mountaineering and Root's politics into a common arena of understanding.

Peck does not hesitate to elaborate the shape of that arena. One of the truly interesting features of Peck's *Search*, as I have already suggested, is that it goes into real detail in suggesting the actual *how* and *where* of economic opportunity in Latin America. Consider the cases of the two South American countries in which Peck climbed. The investment opportunity in Bolivia and Peru advertised in *Search* represented an industrial and commercial climate already well tested by U.S. investors.

Silver had dominated Bolivian mine production for three hundred years, but as the demand for tin rose in industrial nations during the 1890s and the international silver market softened, Bolivia's mining economy shifted away from dominance by silver producers. By 1900 tin accounted for more than 50 percent of the nation's exports. Whereas a small native Bolivian oligarchy had traditionally controlled silver mining, the more capital-intensive nature of the developing tin ventures invited foreign investment and influence. This economic expansion was further encouraged by the proceeds of a large sale of Bolivian territory to Brazil in 1903 and the payments that Bolivia began to receive after a 1904 treaty with Chile for the coastal territory that Bolivia lost in its unsuccessful alliance with Peru in the War of the Pacific (1879–84).[21] Reparation income and the growth of tin production financed extensive railroad construction through the 1910s.[22] Peck noted in *Industrial and Commercial South America* that in 1903 La Paz, the largest and most important commercial city in the country, did not yet have rail service (221), but that by the time that *Search* was published, a rail line from Chile had reached the city.

The War of the Pacific contributed to industrial capitalization in Peru as well, although in a rather different manner. Almost bankrupt after the war, Peru was forced to accept Chile's imposition of the so-called Peruvian Corporation, a consortium of foreign (mostly British) bondholders that administered the Peruvian war debt and took over direct management of large segments of Peruvian rail transport and mining. Although this was a severe blow to Peruvian national pride, comparable to that inflicted on Germany in the stripping of its industry by the Treaty of Versailles, the longer-term result of this foreign economic intervention was dramatic industrial and agricultural development fueled by European and U.S. investment.[23] In particular, investors from the United States gained significant interests in the copper industry, which Peck recognizes in *Search* as she describes her visit with Americans at the Cerro de Pasco smelter and provides a litany of copper production in dollars and pounds (271). Peck, in fact, clearly seems versed in the economic status of Peru in the early 1900s. In portraying it as a dynamic investment environment, she accurately represents the times, and her writing is salted with references to specific figures in Peruvian business affairs. She repeatedly mentions the Andean railroad construction carried out by Meiggs in the 1870s as an index to the continuing growth of transportation, particularly with reference to what seems to be her pet project in South American industrial growth, the construction of a Pan American railway.[24] Peruvian president Augusto Leguía, whom Peck declares in *Search* to be "a man of unusual ability and great strength of character" (368), was closely aligned with business interests and an energetic advocate of U.S. investment in Peru-

vian industry and sugar and cotton production. Peck visits twice with
Leguía as she travels in South America, once to be honored for her successful ascent of Huascarán.[25]

Not unrelated to this was the construction of the Panama Canal, which
occupies an interesting position in Peck's narrative. She seems to have
regarded U.S. control of the Panama Canal as a distant, but still very clear,
background to the mountaineering events that she describes. *Search* pointedly presents Peck's travels as almost coincidentally intermingled with
events on the isthmus. If urban Americans were tired of hearing about the
construction of the Panama Canal by 1912, they would have had trouble
avoiding the latest news. Events from the canal were an almost ever-
present accompaniment to the sense of progress and energy that pervaded
U.S. public life. That this extends to Peck's *Search* as well is an important
testimony to how firmly the book is situated in its time. On her first trip to
Bolivia, Peck visits Panama for the first time in November 1903. She
reports in *Search* her impressions of the Culebra Cut, a "busy hive of industry" (120), then perhaps the most massive engineering feat ever undertaken and by 1911 a topic of immense interest to U.S. readers. Peck also
explains that she happened to be present in Panama on November 3, when
U.S. military forces gained control of the Canal Zone from Colombia:

> I saw on shore a few soldiers, mere boys, from a Colombian gun boat in the
> harbour. Near this was a United States war-ship to prevent the Colombians from
> landing soldiers to preserve order in their own territory. Of persons on the Isth-
> mus, a few only were responsible for the sudden Revolution which was hatched up
> in New York, most of the people even in Colon and Panama not being in on the
> secret. After sailing I found that the officers of our ship, the *Yucatan,* were well
> posted on the matter, and was told that the revolutionists were waiting to proclaim
> a republic only until the departure of this and a French steamer. (120–21)

Peck's straightforward account almost reads like revisionist history. Yet
she seems simply to be telling it as she sees it, without apology. Later in
Search she even acknowledges in passing that the United States "stole"
Panama, remarking that the Colombians therefore felt "*they* had a right to
steal from them [the Americans]" (309). Because she repeatedly docks at
Panama en route to and from Peru and Bolivia during her numerous
expeditions, Peck observes the Canal Zone in transition. "Things were
moving rapidly," she reports of her visit in 1906, "but while a political
revolution may be accomplished in an hour, a city or a tropical wilderness
requires time for complete transformation" (216). Peck seems to have had
no qualms about direct military intervention in the name of progress. On

the whole, her repeated commentary on Panama cross-references her interest in U.S. economic expansion with its historical concomitant — military intrusion.

By 1890, well before Peck developed her skills as a slide lecturer on exotic, faraway, and lost cultures, "working girl" societies across the United States had begun conducting another kind of public presentation. The so-called practical talks held by these popular organizations increasingly stressed self-improvement, education, independence, and, perhaps most prominently, financial guidance.[26] With such titles as "Money — How to Get It and Keep It," these lectures addressed the growing desire among U.S. women for economic independence and self-determination.[27] The period of Peck's South American exploration comprised something of an interregnum in the long-fought movement for voting rights for women. After early successes in the 1890s the suffrage movement lost momentum after 1896. Only in 1910, when women in the State of Washington gained the franchise, did the movement reestablish its pace, following shortly with success in California in 1911 and the massive and inspirational march along New York City's Fifth Avenue in 1912 that signaled the growing impetus to pass the constitutional amendment of 1919. It is in the excitement of this regained momentum that the publication of Peck's *Search* in 1911 must also be placed. Peck's polite evocation of Theodore Roosevelt certainly responds to his guarded political support for women's issues. Although he had rejected in 1908 an appeal from Carrie Chapman Catt of the National American Woman Suffrage Association to recommend suffrage to Congress, in the heat of his 1912 campaign Roosevelt had hastily added suffrage as a plank in his Progressive Party platform. Although Roosevelt gained some support from the almost one million women then eligible to vote in some states, Eleanor Flexner in her *Century of Struggle* insists: "It is doubtful whether Roosevelt's advocacy of woman suffrage won him many votes" (262). What is certain is that informed readers by 1912 would have seen the feminist Peck's slim connection with Roosevelt in the light of his equally slim involvement with women's issues. And, more important, they would have been sure to see Peck herself as an exemplar of female independence and self-assertion.

Peck's book rather adamantly speaks to a preoccupation with gender difference within the province of exploration. We also have reason to believe that this fundamental issue extends into the narrative's broad concern with economic promotion. Peck's mountaineering was bold and even outlandish in its day. Her narrative clearly takes up the enthusiastic affirmation that Olive Schreiner, the South African novelist and feminist, made the same year — "We take all labor for our province!" (quoted in Cott, 41). Peck's narrative is feminist in the sense that it destabilizes gender roles and describes a conspicuous usurpation of the more traditional male activity of exploration. It claims for women the prerogative of challenge, improvement, and adventure. Annie Peck on a mountain summit with a VOTES FOR WOMEN banner in her hands had important emblematic significance that should not be discounted. But what is perhaps especially intriguing about Peck's narrative is how it conjoins two important issues of its time — women's rights and the growing economic influence of the United States in Latin America.

During the first decade of the twentieth century the women's movement channeled much of its energy into forging ties with organized labor. With the founding of the National Women's Trade Union in 1903, women's rights advocates increasingly focused on wage earning as a marker of female individuation. The woman wage earner became a model of independence in an era when a woman's right to her own property and wages was still a contested issue in some parts of the country. Consequently, as Flexner points out, to many women during the decade *equality* came to have an increasingly more concrete meaning: "Better pay for their labor, security from fire and machine hazards or the unwanted attentions of the foreman, and a chance to get home to their domestic tasks before complete exhaustion had overtaken them" (247). The widespread efforts of women to unionize during the period of Peck's exploration clearly reflected this.

Beyond her disgruntled complaints about fainthearted and egotistical male climbing guides, Peck makes her most fundamental feminist argument in economic terms.[28] On one hand, the book displays its author as a woman largely on her own financially, as a college professor, author, and public speaker. That she is able to undertake her audacious expeditions at all argues persuasively for a woman's economic life not only beyond the home but several thousand miles beyond it. On the other hand, Peck's status as a "worker" is modified somewhat by the financial support that she sometimes raised for her expeditions, and her education and world travel can be seen as denoting class privilege. Most problematic of all perhaps is that Peck seems to describe herself as identifying primarily with *capital*, rather than labor, with the big business that resisted the suffrage movement rather than with the working women who provided the movement with one of its most powerful symbols and who filled its ranks.

But everything we know about her political positions, as well as her personal style and temperament, argues clearly that Peck was no female remonstrant saying "no, thank you" to equal rights. Although the American Federation of Labor under Samuel Gompers publicly opposed colonial expansion, organized labor generally tended to support the imperialism of the McKinley years (Healy, 222). While Gompers and other labor leaders worried about the importation of cheap foreign labor, Conant argued, in fact, that economic expansion per se (rather than necessarily colonial expansion) benefited domestic workers. He drew upon the growing numbers of working-class investors to argue that even the wise and careful laborer could have a capitalist's stake in foreign investment, and he more broadly held up the advantage of general economic prosperity available through overseas investment to Americans of all classes. As women increasingly argued from the position of their economic independence and financial prerogatives, they also involved themselves in this theoretical debate. It is fair to suggest, I think, that the feminism of Peck's narrative invited many of its first readers to understand the text's promotion of investment in light of how that investment might affect women.

A 1920 *Rocky Mountain News* cartoon shows a woman burdened with a yoke and two pails standing in front of a ladder. Each rung is labeled in ascending order: SLAVERY, HOUSE DRUDGERY, SHOP WORK, then, a little higher, TEACHER, STENOGRAPHER, GOVERNESS. Higher still is BUSINESS AFFAIRS, and barely legible, close to where the ladder disappears into heaven, EXECUTIVE. That a cartoonist after the success of female suffrage and at the threshold of the exciting business boom of the Harding and Coolidge era would have seen opportunity for women in these terms is not surprising. But it could be that Peck's narrative of exploration covertly suggests female opportunity in the same terms, that is to say, by suggesting that women have a role to play in international finance. In an important sense, *Search* operates rhetorically by blurring the distinction between gender and financial issues, in the very act of blending mountaineering with capital investment. Finally, its most notable impression may be of the confusion or perhaps *equation* of the spheres of male and female. Mountaineering becomes economic expansionism in a broad thematic sense. And when we are caught up in the rhetoric of exploration. we march to the tune of Elihu Root, dollar diplomacy, *and* Schreiner's feminism all at once. We buy into advertisement's casual association of otherwise unrelated elements.

But we must not lose sight of the way that *Search* makes its definite gesture toward distinguishing spatial "zones." If we accept at face value Peck's differentiation between those spatial zones set aside for mountaineering and those open to economic opportunity, the text refuses to neatly cohere. One could even argue that, for women, Peck sees mountains as *open* while the lowlands are *set aside,* closed, already claimed for economic purposes that at least functionally are male. "Were I a young man with $1000 to start, I can conceive of no more favorable place to go and make my fortune," she advises (225). Then why does Peck, so interested in the exploitation of South America's every commercial niche, explicitly award business opportunity exclusively to men when she herself is a vigorous middle-aged woman with at times a good deal more than $1,000 to start?

The answer inevitably is a complex one. Perhaps *Search* responds to the demands of what was anticipated to be a substantially male audience. Perhaps it speaks to U.S. economic expansionism as an issue somehow compartmentalized from gender. Perhaps it even looks far beyond the surface of capital investment to how economic resurgence might "trickle down" to the increasingly female work force of 1911. The evidence for any of these hypotheses is merely circumstantial.

If this poses a problem, it is because with her "map" of gender space, which so sharply draws the line between female and male territories, Peck may be marking off a very specific kind of terra incognita. When she writes of investment opportunities in South America, Peck, unlike most exploration writers, makes a direct appeal to her readers for a specific kind of response. Because she expressly wishes that her narrative will prompt "travel, commerce, and trade" (xi), she calls upon readers to take up her promotional clarion with their own concrete action. She invites readers in, by asking them to finish with their commercial activity what she began with her promotion. Peck's gesture here is inclusive, an attempt to familiarize South America rather than keep it exotic in the interest of highlighting the achievement of the explorer.

When she discusses herself, however, as a mountaineer and as a woman, she distinguishes herself not only from readers who have not been to the summit of Huascarán but also from the less stalwart males who accompany her. She confesses her desire to "reach a higher point than any where man had previously stood" and compares this impulse to that of

"Peary's getting a degree nearer to the North Pole" (xi). Female identity is less clearly readable in the cartography of male economic activity in South America. This is a purely metaphorical way of saying that at least on the surface of *Search*, Peck never explicitly defines a place for women in the economic dynamics of international investment.

Based on what we know about Peck's politics, such a conventional gesture of omission would seem vastly out of character. As an individual, her background and training as an academic and her vocation as a writer may certainly have played a part in accounting for the advisory distance she kept from the workaday matters of actual exploitation of resources and trade opportunities. Although she may implicitly have limited women as a whole to the margin of the traditionally male sphere of industry, trade, and finance, casting herself in the role of visionary and publicist rather than investor or manager, perhaps Peck was looking beyond international investment altogether, embodying in *Search* an alternative model for U.S. public achievement. For the average reader the memory of the scandals that prompted Roosevelt's progressive reforms still remained, as did the lingering aftereffects of the economic crisis of 1907. The financier and the industrial magnate were certainly symbols of burgeoning U.S. confidence and unbounded opportunity, but their image in U.S. society inevitably remained ambiguous, qualified in relation to the experience of common people lower on the economic food chain. At the same time, cultural heroes like Peary, Dewey, and Roosevelt himself competed in the public mind with giants of industry as national symbols. The Arctic, Manila Bay, and San Juan Hill were the theaters where U.S. *character* was revealed in its most basic terms, as if stripped for a moment of the baggage of politics, class, and privilege in such a manner that all Americans could imagine a little of that national character in themselves or at least aspire to it. Peck sought to add distant Huascarán to the geography of symbolic U.S. places. While male U.S. heroes decorated the pages of New York's *Tribune* and *Journal*, the great women in public life at the time were often perceived as agitators, militants, malcontents. Working toward her own specific vision of what she calls early in *Search* the "advantage to my sex" (xi), Peck seeks to establish herself as a woman among the ranks of bold and adventurous U.S. cultural heroes, and she does so not only by climbing her mountain but by writing an account of it that fully reproduces the mixture of political, economic, and heroic significance and achievement that characterized the sphere of public U.S. greatness after the turn of the century. To address the full range of what Americans looked for in their heroes, Peck's mountain could not stand isolated but had to be situated within a complicated, male-dominated world of gender, politics, and business.

So, as the mantle of her new fame, Peck accepted the silver slipper that she held in her frontispiece photograph, presented by men who stood for all these. The silver slipper, an icon of traditional privileged and sheltered female roles, became by virtue of the circumstance of her receiving it a personal emblem of how, through unconventional behavior, early twentieth-century women could participate in the cultural symbolism of greatness. "It may therefore be regarded as certain," Peck remarked, "that Huascarán is above 23,000 feet, hence higher than Aconcagua. . . . I have the honor of breaking the world's record for men as well as women" (quoted in Styles, 66). The news of Peck's success on Huascarán was cabled worldwide, and journalists marveled at the accomplishment of the "schoolmarm" from Rhode Island.

It turned out to be a short-lived honor. As Annie Peck limped on her injured foot from that gala dinner in Lima celebrating her success, she could not have realized what lay in store. The American Alpine Club and the Appalachian Mountain Club raised money by subscriptions to support the injured guide Rudolf Taugwalder, and Peck's ill-considered, although perhaps accurate, remarks about his irresponsibility continued to come home to roost. The worst blow, however, came in 1909 from Peck's rival, Fanny Bullock Workman. Exploring the Punjab Himalaya with her husband in 1906, Workman had reached a verified altitude of 22,810 feet on the Nun Kun massif and in so doing had become the world's then–highest-climbing woman. Reading that Peck had been unable to take a hypsometer reading on the wind-scoured summit, Workman was immediately suspicious of Peck's estimate of the elevation of Huascarán and hired two French surveyors to triangulate the mountain. They placed the north peak at 21,812 feet and the south peak 230 feet higher than that. Peck's claims were widely discredited. Huascarán was not as high as Aconcagua after all, and Peck had failed to establish any new altitude records. Moreover, she had not even managed to reach the highest of Huascarán's two summits. Although Peck responded to Workman in a 1910 *Scientific American* essay, she succeeded in convincing few of her doubters. She went on to write and publish *A Search for the Apex of America* as well as three other books, but the sting of disappointment remained.

Despite the devastating disappointment and controversy that attended the aftermath of her climb of Huascarán, in the long run Peck succeeded in becoming the symbol of personal and female accomplishment that she had longed to be. Today the controversy has faded and Bullock's well-orchestrated one-upmanship with it. What remains is the life of an intensely ambitious and reform-minded woman of action. As a woman who pursued her climbing well into her life, Peck was a predecessor to California's Hulda Crooks, who became famous for climbing Mount Whitney twenty-three times, for the last time at the age of ninety-one. As a woman who brought her critique of conventional female roles into the mountains, Peck stands in a long line of pioneering female climbers that culminates today with India's Santosh Yadav, who has defied tradition to become the only woman to have climbed Mount Everest twice.

Although long out of print, Annie Peck's remains a fascinating and knotty book. *A Search for the Apex of America,* like Halford Mackinder's "Mount Kenya," records personal motivations in dialogue with larger culturally determined perceptions of mountains, perceptions that move rather surprisingly far from the traditions and clichés that have shaped our expectations of what climbing a mountain is all about. Peck's legacy serves as an important reminder of this rich and far-reaching complexity.

4

John Baptist Noel,
a Summit Photograph

DRISCOLL: Think he's crazy, Skipper?
ENGLEHORN: Just enthusiastic.
—Ruth Rose, screenplay for *King Kong*

THE "SUMMIT PHOTOGRAPH" HAS LONG BEEN AN OBLIGA-
tory ritual of successful mountaineers. Blurry shots of climbers,
holding flags of their nations and universities, embracing, grinning
through their exhaustion with open space and glacier landscapes merging
into the vague distance below—in the twentieth century, photographs
such as these became perhaps the most conspicuous mode of representing
the mountaineering experience to the world below the summits. They
offer themselves as a vivid cross-reference to the stories that climbers tell,
not as mere illustration but as a medium capable in itself of conveying a
sense of the profound strangeness and rich incompleteness that mountaineers have found in high-altitude landscapes.

Since the pioneering work of Vittorio Sella, the photographer who accompanied Luigi Amedeo, the duca d'Abruzzi, on so many of his exploratory mountain expeditions early in the century, photography has emerged
as the conventional way of marking personal and group achievement in
the mountains.[1] Describing his first ascent of Mount Logan in 1925, Allen
Carpe wrote of how he and his party had stood exhausted on the summit,
only barely able to appreciate their success. "Almost automatically we
went through the appointed routine," he said, "hand-clasps and congratu-
lations, a round of motion pictures, the empty gesture of a record of names

and date thrust into the snow" (82). As Carpe's remarks suggest, by the 1920s summit photography had become de rigeur, if not always authentic or enthusiastic. Annie Smith Peck tells us that on reaching the summit of Huascarán, her first words were "Get the camera" (345). Although she photographed her guides, she failed to hand them the camera; the "summit photo" of Peck that appears in *A Search for the Apex of America* is plainly a contrived studio version of the event. But even this artificially posed tableau expresses the sense of personal authority and accomplishment that we associate with narratives of mountaineering exploration.

While photography has come to be used in this iconic fashion, it also has been adopted as a tool of realist representation, as a means of empirically documenting exploration. This strategy is perhaps best illustrated when it backfires. Peck writes in *Search*, for example, that she is "desolate" at the thought that she might not be able to "verify my story with photographs" (322). Even more interesting is the case of Frederick Cook. When Cook returned from Alaska in 1906, claiming to have reached the summit of Mount McKinley, he brought back as proof a summit photo of his climbing partner Edward Barrill. Because of the surprising quickness of Cook's ascent, Herschel Parker and Belmore Browne, two of Cook's former climbing partners, already suspected a hoax and found the photograph particularly suspicious. In the background of Cook's shot Parker and Browne thought they saw a mountain that should have appeared completely different had Cook actually photographed it from the summit of Mount McKinley. The angle and scale were all wrong. By ascending this mountain, which they called Fake Peak, and reconstructing the composition of Cook's photograph, Parker and Browne cast serious doubt on whether Cook had actually climbed to the summit of McKinley, a controversy that would develop more fully when Cook arrived in Greenland in April 1909 claiming that he had reached the North Pole about four months ahead of Robert Peary.[2] Events such as these suggest how the practice of summit photography speaks to the fundamental tension between the empirical and the subjective that plays itself out so thoroughly in exploration writing.

With these introductory considerations in mind, consider a summit photograph of a slightly different order. It is shaded in sepia, iron blue, and pale yellow — the colors of hand-tinted photographs from the 1920s. In the foreground the mountaineer is sitting on a camera box in the snow.

Rock ridges and glaciers in the background give way to clouds and empty sky. Dominating the shot is a large motion picture camera mounted on a tripod, its telephoto lens supported by another tripod and being adjusted by a Sherpa assistant. The camera points upward. Dressed in sweater and heavy wool trousers, the mountaineer appears to have momentarily turned away from operating the camera to have his own picture taken. His face below his climbing goggles is sharply featured and unshaven. His narrow eyes and mouth seem playful, even amused. It is tempting to imagine that this could be the face that we would see on the artist in Vermeer's *Allegory of Fame,* if he would only turn toward us.

But in actuality this mountaineer is Capt. John Baptist Noel, the official photographer for the 1922 and 1924 British expeditions to Mount Everest, the first serious attempts to climb the mountain. These expeditions culminated in the dramatic, tragic, and even mysterious disappearance of George Leigh-Mallory and Andrew Irvine only several hundred feet below the summit, probably the most famous event in British mountaineering history and on par in its public impact with the disappearance of the Franklin expedition in the Northwest Passage in the 1840s and the death of Robert Falcon Scott in Antarctica in 1912. The remarkable discovery in May 1999 of Mallory's body on the steps of the Northeast Ridge by a research expedition led by Eric Simonson — and the wealth of evidence, clues, and speculation that it has initiated among climbers and historians alike — serve in part to return our attention the 1924 expedition and Noel's work as he documented it on film. Thus this particular mountain photograph, an image not of a climber standing on the summit but of Noel filming the summit of Mount Everest from the North Col in 1924, at twenty-three thousand feet on the mountain's Northeast Ridge, while Mallory and Irvine were still climbing high on the mountain.[3] It is a would-be summit photo once removed, a reflexive image of its own means of production, a photograph of a photographer photographing the summit, almost like a platonic projection of summit photography.

Although most noted as a motion picture maker and photographer, Noel recorded his impressions of the early Everest expeditions and their fatal conclusion not only on film but also in print in his 1927 *Through Tibet to Everest.* Concentrating on the 1922 and 1924 expeditions, of which he was a member, Noel's narrative places his own relationship to Mount Everest in a context that extends back in time to the mountain's identification by the British Trigonometrical Survey of India in the 1850s. On one level clearly a mountaineering narrative, *Through Tibet* is also a film production narrative, intertwining the efforts of the expedition to climb the mountain with Noel's own efforts to film it doing so. *Through Tibet* reveals the complexity of the act of filmmaking, showing the work of the film artist as it records the tension between European and Asian culture, empirical and subjective representation, and varying visions of the role of the mountaineering explorer. Noel's account, conjoining mountaineering exploration with commentary, in turn responds to British public awareness of the status of imperial British interests in the unstable political arena of central Asia during the early 1920s.

Today Noel's camera apparatus is set up in the collection of the Science Museum in South Kensington, London. A dull silver rectangular duralumin box, maybe eighteen inches long and a foot high and mounted on a wooden tripod, it of course appears primitive to museum visitors equipped with sleek black video cameras. But in 1924 the 35mm Newman camera was state-of-the-art outdoor photographic equipment. Turned by battery power, in addition to the more conventional hand crank, the Newman exposed four hundred feet of Panchromatic film from magazines. Attached to the front of the camera body was a twenty-inch Hobson telephoto lens and to the top a viewfinder tube, a six-power directional telescope that Noel used to locate his distant subject matter for the closer field of the telephoto lens.

It was hardly the first camera equipment to find its way to Mount Everest. Several significant precedents shaped Noel's work. Although no European had approached the mountain before 1913, interest in climbing Mount Everest grew steadily after the turn of the century. Before World War I, a number of influential mountaineers, including Douglas Freshfield, Tom Longstaff, and C. G. Rawling, had proposed an expedition to Everest. But with both Nepal and Tibet officially closed to Europeans in the wake of the 1903 British occupation of Lhasa, political as well as geographical difficulties inhibited the pursuit of such a plan.[4] Under the circumstances the developing craft of long-distance photography suggested itself as an appropriate substitute for actual travel to the mountain. During 1911 or 1912 Dr. Alexander Mitchell Kellas, the noted Himalayan explorer, produced the first photographic image of Everest. He hired, trained, and equipped a Nepalese to travel to Tibet's Arun Gorge and photograph the eastern approaches to the mountain and then return the film to him in Nepal.

When the first British expedition to Mount Everest, the so-called reconnaissance expedition, finally gained access to the mountain in 1921, Oliver Wheeler, a young photographer with the British Trigonometrical Survey of India, was chosen to accompany the expedition. Wheeler took with him what was then the new technique of photo surveying and attempted a systematic photography-based mapping of the area surrounding the mountain.[5] In many ways the scope and intent of Wheeler's work is comparable to that of William Henry Jackson, of the Hayden Survey in the United States, who was the first to photograph Pikes Peak and the Yellowstone country. While Kellas's photographs were aimed at the very specific goal of gaining the information necessary to climb Mount Everest, Wheeler's work was part of a broader scientific survey of the mountain that amassed a variety of geographical information, much of it not directly related to mountaineering. In addition, George Leigh-Mallory took a great many photographs below the North Col of the Northeast Ridge, but unfortunately almost all these were lost because he put the photographic plates in the camera backward.

But by the time that the Everest Committee of the Royal Geographical Society and the Alpine Club began preparations for a follow-up expedition in 1922, one that would make a serious effort to reach the summit, the committee had already begun to develop a somewhat more pragmatic conception of what mountain photography could be. With the costs of the expedition beginning to far outpace its resources, the Everest Committee increasingly came to regard photography as much as a product — a promotional tool and saleable product in its own right — as it was a scientific geographic record. In 1922 the committee decided to produce a commercial documentary film about the expedition. This proposal was not without opposition from the conservative elements within the two organizations. Arthur Robert Hinks, a banker who was named honorary treasurer of the Everest Committee in 1921, had a deep personal aversion to publicity in any form. When fund-raising for the 1921 reconnaissance expedition fell short of the £4,000 the committee thought the expedition would require, Hinks sought the contracts that were eventually made with newspapers and magazines as a way of making up the difference. The *Times of London* and the *Philadelphia Ledger* published reports telegraphed from the expedition, and the *Graphic* printed its photographs.

Hinks was plainly out of synch with the very public role that the three Everest expeditions of the 1920s would play. What distinguishes them from earlier mountaineering endeavors is the extent to which these expeditions embraced their place at the convergence of high public exposure, financial interest, and political symbolism. After all, the British climber Norman Collie had even jokingly suggested that the committee approach a soap manufacturer for financial backing on the condition that its climbers plant on the summit a flag carrying the Sunlight Soap logo — an imagined scene redolent of the same combination of commercial and national authority obvious in Pears' Soap's Admiral Dewey ad and even in Annie Peck's unsuccessful schemes to land soap endorsements. For Hinks the era of the mountaineering soap opera had not yet arrived.

Although Collie's proposal was tongue-in-cheek, probably largely intended to provoke Hinks, it proved to be predictive. Today, for example, exploration is often financed by advertising, and climbers agent their skills and exploits to corporate sponsors. The Everest expeditions provide a convenient benchmark for measuring the shift from the involvement of exploration in the quest for resources and markets, as in Annie Peck's *Search*, to being, in a sense, a resource itself—for pursuing both economic and political aims.

It is significant, then, that the committee appointed Jack Noel to the 1922 expedition and placed him in charge of still and cinematic photography.[6] Noel's peculiar flair for promotion had already made its mark on Himalayan mountaineering. Among mountaineers, Noel's name had been linked to Mount Everest for some time, perhaps more closely than any other. In 1913, with Tibet tightly closed to foreigners, he had left the Sikkimese town of Gangtok in disguise and crossed the little-used Choten Nyi-ma pass into the forbidden territory. He found himself off the edge of any accurate map in his possession, but he also found that he had journeyed to within forty miles of Mount Everest, probably the nearest approach that any European had then made. In 1919, as the end of World War I renewed British interest in Himalayan exploration, Noel presented a paper, "A Journey to Tashirak in Southern Tibet, and the Eastern Approaches to Mount Everest," before the Royal Geographical Society on March 10, 1919, that described his furtive reconnaissance. After Noel was done speaking, such notables as Percy Farrar, president of the Alpine Club, and Sir Francis Younghusband, soon-to-be-president of the Royal Geographical Society, rose in turn to support sponsoring a series of expeditions to Everest. When Younghusband, himself long involved both in military and exploratory activities in the Himalayas, did become RGS president, he formed the Mount Everest Committee to do just that. Thus Noel's paper prompted the first expeditions to Everest in 1921, 1922, and 1924.

Noel was himself a curious mix of impulses. He grew up climbing in Switzerland in that era when the Alps were still the patrician "playground of Europe" of the critic Leslie Stephen's conception. Noel had early on come under the spell of mountain photography. "I worshiped a man called Vittorio Sella," he remarked in a 1974 interview (Brownlow, 452). Although Noel had been educated as an artist in Florence, he followed his father into the British Army and remained there until he resigned his commission to join the 1922 expedition. His 1913 adventure in Tibet had earned him a reputation as somewhat eccentric, and his 1919 speech had made him virtually the author of current British interest in Mount Everest.[7] Gen. Charles Granville Bruce, leader of the 1922 expedition, was particularly fond of Noel for this, admiring his entrepreneurial instincts — his fellow Everest climber Noel Odell called Noel a showman — and Bruce often playfully referred to Noel, a Catholic, as "St. Noel of the Cameras" (quoted in Unsworth, 146, 74). When the Everest Committee decided to partly underwrite the expedition with the proceeds of a film about it, Noel's buoyant personality and track record earned him a place behind its official cameras. Noel recalled:

> The Royal Geographical Society was a very conservative body; they didn't want an ordinary professional person from a film company to make the pictures. Half of them didn't want any pictures at all. It was just a scientific climbing expedition. They didn't want any vulgarity in the newspapers. So they invited me. The idea was that the film, when it was eventually shown, would produce money for the expedition. (quoted in Brownlow, 454)

Setting up a darkroom at sixteen thousand feet above sea level on the Rongbuk Glacier, Noel pursued his work as what he called a "photographic historian" (*Through Tibet,* 208) to the 1922 expedition. Following the glacier, the expedition gained the Northeast Ridge. George Finch, an Australian who was an experienced Alpine climber, and Geoffrey Bruce, a young climber who was a cousin of the general's, reached an elevation higher than twenty-seven thousand feet. The deaths of seven Sherpa porters in an avalanche below the North Col, however, effectively ended any hope that the expedition would reach the summit before the monsoon season closed in. Noel for his part was both an outsider and an insider on the expedition. On one hand, he was almost constantly busy with his own work. Developing film in a tent heated by burning yak dung and transporting his camera equipment to the twenty-two-thousand-foot level on the mountain, Noel endeavored to fulfill his plan for making a "complete photographic record" (*Through Tibet,* 157) of the climb. But Noel was not merely an objective observer. When Finch and Bruce were overdue on the mountain, Noel burned his spare unexposed movie film to signal them. Ever visual in his perception, he observes "this made brilliant illumination" (*Through Tibet,* 190). In 1974 Noel told Kevin Brownlow that when the avalanche swept away the Sherpa porters, "I didn't bring a camera—I just went out and helped" (Brownlow, 458). The 4,945-foot film that emerged from the expedition, *Climbing Mount Everest,* was first shown in December 1922 and made, as Walt Unsworth puts it, a "rather modest success" (146); it ultimately was released by film distributors in Britain and on the Continent.[8]

For Noel *Climbing Mount Everest* showed that the mountain had an alter ego as a potential commercial property. When he was asked to serve again as official photographer for the 1924 expedition, Noel formed his own film production company to make the film, buying from the Everest Committee the rights to film the expedition. He had learned from his first effort. *Climbing Mount Everest* lacked human drama and relied too heavily on static landscape shots—it was, in short, too much heir to the earlier work of Kellas and Wheeler. Noel reported in a 1927 *Asia* article that when George Bernard Shaw saw the film, he commented: "The Everest expedition was a picnic in Connemara surprised by a snow-storm" ("Photographing," 368). Furthermore, Noel's film advisers even warned him that "without a love interest the picture will be a certain failure" ("Photographing," 367). From the very beginning Noel conceived of his new film undertaking in the language of the feature film; consequently, in Noel's mind commercial success hinged on mountaineering success. He wrote to General Bruce in 1923 (in a letter now in the Royal Geographical Society's Everest Archives):

> Travel films have in the ordinary way little scope except as lecture films and it is almost impossible to get them into the cinemas which is the chief source of revenue for films, but next year by taking an elaborate and carefully produced film with more capital available for production and exploitation than the Expedition would ordinarily care to spend I expect to be able to make a film that can compete in the cinematograph trade with the usual productions and so obtain a large enough scope to repay the cost of producing the film. Success will depend virtually on whether the mountain is conquered. I will accordingly take two separate films, one the story of the Expedition which will be shown to the public only in the event of the mountain being conquered and a second film dealing with the life of the people in Tibet, Sikkim and Bhutan.

The ever-resourceful Noel plotted alternatives, other ways of packaging Mount Everest as a film—maybe an adventure film, maybe a travelogue—depending on how things went on the mountain. The result, however, turned out to be something of a hybrid.

Carrying his motion picture equipment to twenty-three thousand feet, a promontory that he christened Eagle's Nest Point, Noel filmed what was truly the daring rescue of four Sherpas trapped on a narrow ledge beyond an ice couloir. The day before the disappearance of Mallory and Irvine, Noel filmed the pair climbing into obscuring mist at twenty-six thousand feet along the Northeast Ridge. As the two climbers prepared to make their fatal summit bid the next day, Noel received a note from Mallory, "perhaps the last note he ever wrote in his life" (*Through Tibet*, 213), advising the filmmaker where to look for him the next day — three miles away on the summit ridge.[9] Noel strained through his finder tube for hours but never saw them again.

This was clearly grist for any documentary filmmaker's sense of high drama. When Noel's second film, *The Epic of Everest,* was released in December 1924, its title suggested the shift from the earlier film. Whereas the first film had dwelled on the colorful approach march through Tibet, with the actual climb "anticlimactic," as Brownlow puts it (464), and had spent too much footage on the purely scenic quality of Mount Everest, the second film represented the mountain as the milieu of mystic heroism. Abandoning his announced either/or approach to the film, Noel attempted to graft travelogue onto adventure with large doses of local Tibetan color. His aptitude for promotion came into play as the film opened at the Scala Theater in London. As he left Tibet, he had persuaded seven Tibetan monks from the monastery at Gyantse to accompany him to England. The monks toured with the film, appearing on stage beforehand, dancing in traditional costume and playing cymbals and horns. The entire effect was suitably exotic and provocative, to say the least. The film received favorable reviews from *Kinematograph Weekly* and the *Bioscope,* although, as I will make plain later, it met a somewhat less than cordial reception in Asia.

I should note that Noel's name is associated most with his work as a photographer and filmmaker. After all, his literary output was not extensive. His *Through Tibet to Everest* was published in London in 1927, and during the 1920s he wrote only a handful of journal and magazine articles about his Himalayan experiences.[10] I would like to suggest, however, that we can grant his association with the visual arts a kind of priority as we go on to examine his written work. Although the written work of a number of figures in British mountaineering could illustrate the public *use* of climbing mountains, the writing of none does so as pointedly and provocatively as John Noel's. *Through Tibet to Everest,* which appeared about three years after even his second film had eased into oblivion in the collapse of the British film industry in 1924, becomes an intriguing post-script to his film work.[11]

The expeditions to Mount Everest that Noel describes differ from Annie Peck's several trips to South America in their scope but most notably in their level and kind of organization. Despite her announced efforts to promote north–south understanding, Peck still climbed as a private individual, for the most part financing her own expeditions and traveling with at most only a few porters or guides. The Everest expeditions, on the other hand, not only were much larger — with thirteen British members on the 1922 expedition, for example — as well as, to quote the expedition leader General Bruce, "sixty of what may be termed other ranks" (51) — but had a distinctly soldierly flavor about them. Many expedition members had been army officers, including both Noel and E. F. Norton, an experienced traveler in Asia who emerged as the expedition's leader after Bruce became ill. The Everest expeditions were in fact a departure from the more individualistic nature of early British climbing, even that of Halford Mackinder's expedition to Mount Kenya, in their corporate character and method of running the climb by committee.

Nonetheless, *Through Tibet* remains steadfastly an *individual* account of the mountaineering events. Readers share in Noel's role in his story to an extent unusual in exploration narratives. Noel places himself in an intriguing intermediary position between readers and events yet still suggests his authoritative knowledge of even those events in which he did not personally take part or witness. He functions as a kind of preliminary reader of the text of the climb, filtering and refining material for those of us who come later.

Noel's role as narrator is complicated, however, by his persistent tendency to move freely between the narration of events in which he is directly involved and events in which he is not. He makes, in fact, no absolute distinction between what he "sees" and what he has been told. This is the rhetorical means by which Noel's voice controls the narrative. Even his accounts of Kellas's Himalayan expeditions and the 1921 reconnaissance have the same level of intimacy and detail as his accounts of his own travels to Tibet, the 1913 disguised trespass and the 1922 and 1924 expeditions, generally without the bother of conventional methods of attribution associated with indirect reporting.

Narrating the rescue of the Sherpa porters trapped on the 1924 expedition, an event he witnesses from a distance of 1.25 miles, Noel describes three British climbers — Mallory, Norton, and Howard Somervell — working their way toward the marooned porters. "One must try to realize their state of mind," Noel writes (245) and goes on to describe it. Here Noel allows his own imaginative reconstruction of other men's minds to control his telling of events. Several paragraphs later he acknowledges: "I could not understand the actions, although I continued to photograph them. Later, when they all got safely back to us, Somervell narrated what had happened" (246). Much more typically, however, Noel presents climbing events about which he is *told* in the same terms as those in which he participates. One of the most vivid examples of this comes as Noel describes himself filming Norton and Somervell on the Northeast Ridge. Shooting from two miles away, Noel explains how he lost sight of the climbers at twenty-five thousand feet — yet he continues to describe their actions without accounting for the change in the nature of this information — from pictorial or experienced information to indirect *narrated* information. "After this I lost sight of Norton and Somervell," Noel writes. "Next day they climbed 1,500 feet and built their highest bivouac at 26,500" (253). Noel's version of events shifts abruptly here from his own actions and experiences to his own very *constructed* account of those of the two climbers. Although he cannot see Norton and Somervell, Noel reports: "Up and up, higher and yet higher to 28,000 feet they went. Then heart and lungs found their limits. Slower and slower they went — only step by step now." He even adds: "Norton's pulse, normally slow and regular, was beating rapidly and irregularly" (253). This remarkably detailed report intriguingly dislocates Noel's physical position on the mountain, and the effect is to posit his own narrating voice as oddly central to the actions of others and to give a primary authority to his own subjectivity.

As part of its subjective presentation, Noel's narrative recognizes geographical incompleteness as the pretext to exploration and its narration, and, like other exploration narratives, it verbalizes the "progressive" experience of exploration, the recession of boundaries of physical movement and perception. Noel's narrative begins by emphasizing a marked distinction between Mount Everest and the Tibetan plain from which it arises. Even the title of the narrative effectively describes this landscape of distinction. "For weeks, we had toiled through the desolation of mountain and plateau," Noel writes in *Through Tibet*. "At last we sighted our goal and gazed spell-bound at the sheer cliffs of rock draped with ice which seemed to form part of the very heavens above us" (136). In this remark his subjective reference to an encounter with place mingles freely with his more "objective" geophysical terminology. The mountain, the site of exploration, is radically set apart from the experientially defined region of toil and desolation. The Royal Geographical Society style lived on.

But *Through Tibet* does not end with this distinguishing scheme. It describes a rich coextensive cultural geography as well. A rather rare occurrence in modern mountaineering exploration literature is that by the end of the narrative Noel is describing Mount Everest, in the heady language of spiritual abstraction, as a realm of seekers and heroes. Mallory and Irvine undergo apotheosis; their deaths cease to be corporeal matters of exposure and oxygen debt and become instead issues of spiritual refinement. On the narrative's last pages Noel quotes Pope Pius XI: "The soul trains itself to conquer difficulties; and the spectacle of the vast horizon, which from the highest crest offers itself on all sides to the eyes, raises his spirit to the Divine Author and Sovereign of Nature" (278).[12] Noel's narrative plainly connects this near Miltonian image to Mallory and Irvine. Moreover, the process is ongoing. "There are other men," Noel writes, "who feel an urge to the high places, men whose spiritual natures are drawn to them, irresistibly, and who there gain the spiritual sustenance their souls crave" (277). In concluding his narrative, Noel draws upon some of the most deeply stratified ideological layers of Western thought. Christian mysticism, moving by way of the romantic association of mountains with the sublime and nineteenth-century notions of individualism, surfaces here as a way of solidifying Noel's conception of the mountain as the legitimate province of the European explorer-seeker, as a geography that is symbolically British — and rightfully so.

Through Tibet, after all, emphasizes that the only genuine or significant spirituality associated with the mountain derives uniquely from Western culture. Noel casually dismisses the complexity and integrity of hundreds of years of Tibetan Buddhism as he describes the Tibetan people as "sunk in the most fantastic superstition" (63). He expresses "disgust" at Tibetan religious ritual and persistently stresses the filth and squalor that he sees as dominating Tibetan life.[13] Noel does allow that "in some of the Tibetan monasteries it is possible to find really cultured and genuine religious devotees of great intellectual and spiritual attainments" (84), but the general thrust of his commentary on Tibet suggests that while this remark may speak in the *language* of a kind of cultural relativism, it actually imposes a Western standard of evaluation. The Tibetans living below Mount Everest appear quaint and primitive in *Through Tibet;* Noel may listen to a monk describe Tibetan mythology, but he regards it as a "solemn fantasy" (143).

The Everest expeditions of the early 1920s, after all, were the ones that brought the mind of Europe to the Himalayas, bringing home, among other things the traditional story of the yeti that became transformed into the popular image of the Abominable Snowman. The yeti became a displacement of the human and cultural strangeness of this particular fringe of the empire, reconfiguring it into the subanthropological. The consistently described "human like" snow ape became the carriage of an inability to deal with human cultural difference.

Through Tibet takes as part of its purpose to elaborate what Noel calls the "contrast between ourselves and the strange people we found living there" (147), yet Noel tends to reveal a self-satisfied, even paternalistic, attitude toward cultural difference. The distinction between mountain and plateau is a distinction between hygiene and filth, between "the spirit of modern man," who climbs to altitude, and the "immaterial obstacle of superstition" (147) that presides on the ground below.

Twice in *Through Tibet* Noel indulges in the war-exploration metaphor so conventional in exploration literature, perhaps best exemplified, as noted in chapter 1, by Shackleton's World War I–era *South.* The more interesting of Noel's tropes falls in his account of the 1924 expedition as he describes his feelings about his storm-forced retreat from the mountain. He writes: "In a struggle between man and mountain, such as this — as in any other battle . . . the moral effect of turning away from the enemy, after having once challenged and opened the fight, is fatal" (228).

As Noel suggests here, the conception of mountaineering "war" presented in *Through Tibet* is not so much a conflict as it is a *commitment,* locking into a clinch with the threatening mountain. Consequently, the narrative expresses a mixed conception of mountain geography. As an index of this perception, consider Noel's references to the breathable air on the mountain, that consistently important topic in mountaineering narratives. Noel is most concerned with the ill effects of "mental confusion" (168) caused by the thin atmosphere on Everest. To be high on the mountain, he says, is to be "suffocated as if by some subtle, invisible, odourless poison gas" (168), a disturbing, claustrophobic comparison, to be sure. At its worst this exhaustion and "mental coma" fill Noel with "horror" at the thought of even trying to use his camera (186).

Noel further elaborates this conception of Everest's thin air when he relates how at first the expedition's Sherpa porters had laughed at the British for carrying bottled oxygen to the mountain. " 'The air in our country, sir, is quite good' " Noel reports them as objecting. But later, at higher elevation: "When they tasted it they realized how wonderful it was and how it stilled the heaving of the heart. Then often they would come to us and say: 'Sir, I — little sick to-day — please, sir — I want a little "English air" ' " (163). This charmingly patronizing little story is a commonplace in accounts of the Everest expeditions, appearing in the narratives of a number of members. Aside from its obvious cultural chauvinism, it also serves to further instill a sense of the foreignness of thin Himalayan air, both biologically and politically.

But the "English air" anecdote has a double valency. In his account of the 1922 expedition Noel refers ominously to Everest as "The Dead World" rising above the "region of life" below. This remark seems to contrast with the sense of refuge from tribal hostility that Halford Mackinder felt on Mount Kenya or that Annie Smith Peck felt from contagious disease on the flanks of the Andes. But although the mountain is "the kingdom of King Cold," Noel continues, "to the real mountaineer — that is, to a lover of mountains — mountains are always living and friendly things" (165). A climber should feel "at home and happy" (166) while on a mountain, he maintains. The frequently repeated anecdote about the comically dependent and backward Sherpa request for "English air" represents, as much as anything else, the mechanics of this familiarization. That the British have the capability of bringing their own air to the task of the mountain demonstrates in a very real sense how technology allows explorers to experience new places on terms that inherently are based on preconceived or familiar terms. The bottled oxygen in its small way tames the strangeness, hostility, and "deadness" of Everest, an attempted subjugation that the phrase "English air" concisely records. The intimacy of closure that is the war with Everest really amounts to altering the perceptional status of the mountain, bringing it "down" into an ideologically *European* world.

Noel makes this point of view even more explicitly in a 1926 article in *Asia*, "High on Everest." In this piece describing the 1924 expedition, Noel anticipates his readers' view of a mountain like Everest as a wildly forbidding and hostile world. Not only does he tell a cut-down version of the English air anecdote but he goes on to argue that, again, a "real mountaineer" can be at home on Everest by using the analogy of the Arctic, which, Noel writes, "people always used to consider . . . a dead world too" (1081). Noel puts an interesting wrinkle to the conventional comparison of mountain and polar exploration by evoking in this argument one of the most unusual texts generated by the European encounter with the Arctic, Vilhjamur Stefansson's 1921 *The Friendly Arctic*. Stefansson, the commander of the 1913–18 Canadian Arctic Expedition, lived for extended periods with the region's Eskimo inhabitants and came to see that adopting their traditional material economy and even, to some extent, worldview is the only way for non-Eskimos to successfully explore the Arctic. As its title suggests, *The Friendly Arctic* asserts that surviving in the Arctic is simply a matter of knowing how, not, as most of his readers might imagine, a matter of the objective difficulties of the climate and terrain. Stefansson goes so far as to make the radical, essentially geopolitical and colonial, argument for the settlement of the Canadian Arctic, a project he sees as vital to long-term human survival. When Noel brings Stefansson's position aboard, he makes plain how his own writing concerns the familiarization of marginal geography.

"The world is owned by man," Noel writes near the end of *Through Tibet* (295). In the context of this remark we can best make sense of his perception of Everest: "I am confident in believing that if ever in future years shelter rest-huts are built in stages up the mountain, the ascent of Mount Everest will be as possible as that of Mont Blanc is at the present day" (239). The mountain is a place to be brought under dominion through the accessibility afforded by technology. The final appendix of *Through Tibet* even describes an elaborate plan for reaching the top of Everest by air. Noel seems to see the difficulty of climbing Everest as a reprimand. He argues that Everest will never truly be climbed until "the ordinary man" (284) does so. He advises: "Send them out equipped with modern scientific appliances and devices. Let them not attack nor assault Everest, but let them *walk up* the mountain and prove its conquest without loss, injury or suffering to themselves. Would not such an accomplishment be a stirring victory? It would be a victory for modern man" (284). Noel's scheme for promoting a fanciful Everyman's version of mountaineering resonates today in the seventy-eight climbers who found the summit of Mount Everest during the 1997 climbing season and as queues of guided amateurs stack up on the summit ridge. Indeed, the professional guide Scott Fischer, before his death on Mount Everest in 1996, boasted,

"We've got the Big E figured out, we've got it totally wired" (quoted in Bryant, 57). Still, Noel's "stirring victory" for tourism sometimes back-fires. For Noel's day the dream of Everyman's mountaineering represents an odd transportation of Western political ideals to an eastern setting. It is a democratization of the mountain, at least for Britishers, in marked con-trast to the isolationism of Tibet and the exclusivity and inaccessibility with which Tibetan notions of the sacred veiled Mount Everest. In light of Noel's hard distinction between Tibetans and "modern man" (147), we can only see this interest in technological "victory" as an intended display of national and racial superiority, a symbolic construct consistent with the many representations that Europeans have made to themselves of their imagined right to empire.

Film, as it is presented in *Through Tibet,* should be understood as a promi-nent part of this technological familiarization. Although a part of the expedition in many ways, sharing its daily experiences and goals, as the official cameraman Noel held a unique position, secondary to the events of exploration in his reportorial or commentatorial role. "I am not myself a mountain climber," Noel points out in *Through Tibet* (249). "My care was to get the picture of the climb," he adds (250).

In his 1927 guidebook to mountain photography, *The Art and Sport of Alpine Photography,* Arthur Gardner described photography as a "pleas-ant if less exciting alternative" to actual mountaineering (19) and even as a "rival sport to that of the climber" (20). Today's Internet cyberclimb sites seem to attest to Gardner's opinion of the potential of photographic tech-nology. This principle is present in an early form in *Through Tibet.* Noel too repeatedly discusses the camera as a kind of translocational device, as a kind of prosthetic substitute for actual physical movement. The camera can proceed even when climbers cannot, even to the summit of Everest, which Noel can bring into the focus of his lens three miles away from the North Col, even if he cannot climb to it himself. Noel, after all, was the one who proposed that the 1922 Everest expedition construct a pipeline to carry oxygen up the mountain instead of carrying heavy cylinders. He has an eagerness for what was then a keen topic among British moun-taineers and adventurers — reaching the top of Everest by airplane and thereby using technology to avoid the punishing, and perhaps impossible, task of climbing its ridges. More specifically, he shows a consistent concern in *Through Tibet* for the *distance* of his photographic subjects — how Everest appears on the approach march through Tibet, the record distance of his two-mile picture of Mallory and Irvine at twenty-six thousand feet, even the photographs-by-proxy of Everest that Dr. Kellas, the man Mallory in many ways considered his mentor, hired the native Nepalese to take.[14] Above all, Noel writes of the camera as the means of mountaineering achievement. Although in telling how he and his porters carried cameras to twenty-three thousand feet, he reminds his readers: "That is the altitude record for any motion-picture machine" (156), his primary concern is not his own advance up Everest. "The picture I wanted," he writes, "and which I could get if the weather were good, was that of the men breasting the summit of the mountain" (211–12). Noel does not express the desire to achieve the summit, simply the desire for a good shot of someone else doing so.

Noel is very much aware that by its nature photography displaces geography and objects, brings the distant within reach, and uses photographic imagery to speak beyond the limitations of the physical location of the photographer. The written text of *Through Tibet* also negotiates its representation of Mount Everest by way of the characteristics of photographic imagery. Describing his filming of Norton and Somervell from Eagle's Nest Point, Noel writes that his three-thousand-yard shot of the climbers "was a prize — the longest distance photograph ever obtained in the world. This record was to be broken later by my second picture of Mallory and Irvine's climb, when I got them at 26,400 feet at 2 miles range" (253).

Noel frequently speaks of his photographs as "representations" of what he sees, his film as a "record," and his presence on the expedition as a "photographic journey" (157). But *Through Tibet* complicates that straightforwardly realist premise by dwelling on the capacity of photography for displacement, a deferral by image or image-making tool. In *Through Tibet* the camera works like the fantastic oxygen pipe, only in reverse; it brings what is higher up on the mountain down, within perceptional reach. But events intervened in Noel's success, Mallory and Irvine never *visibly* reached the summit, and Noel never got his shot. Noel applauds Howard Somervell's Kodak snapshot of the summit from an elevation of twenty-eight thousand feet, cheerfully calling it "one of the most remarkable photographs that have ever been taken in the world" (256).[15] Although the 1922 and 1924 expeditions may have failed to reach the summit — and this was generally the assumption after the disappearance of Mallory and Irvine in 1924 — by way of this snapshot the 1924 expedition was, according to the logic of *Through Tibet,* a photographic first ascent.

The preoccupation with camera work in *Through Tibet* surfaces in Noel's tendency to talk about the expedition as a filmic event almost as much as a physical endeavor. This tendency has a range of implications. Most fundamentally, it points to the fact that Noel's narrative conceives of the spatial boundaries encountered by mountaineering exploration in terms of contemporary and evolving technology. In this sense Dr. Kellas's early "photography-by-proxy" of Mount Everest, which Noel mentions early in *Through Tibet,* establishes a kind of theoretical basis for the book's discussion of film. Enthusing reverently of an unclimbed Mount Everest early in the narrative, Noel asks: "Who was I to violate with impudent temerity these forbidden solitudes?" (45). Noel technologically refigures the ideology of conquest and possession that is so consistently a part of the rhetoric of mountaineering. Those who control the means of representation control the geography. In *Through Tibet* machines violate spatial boundaries their human operators do not have to. That Noel may want to have things both ways here is not, finally, the point. What is important to recognize, however, is that the equipment doing the functional exploration in Noel's account of things is the equipment of representation and communication. Even more interestingly, it is the equipment of what in 1927 was already the visual mass media that continued to play such a prominent and controversial role in twentieth-century life.

This aspect of Noel's text is most poignantly represented in his account of the day after the disappearance of Mallory and Irvine in 1924. The expedition had devised a code of prearranged signals that would announce success or failure on the summit ridge to those watching from below. Noel explains how he watched through his spotting scope as the support party higher on the mountain placed six blankets on the snow in the shape of a cross — signifying the deaths of Mallory and Irvine. Noel writes: "I remember the moment vividly. I saw this signal through my telescope as I was making the photograph of the scene through my high-powered magnifying lens. An electric battery was operating the camera. I was so agitated to read the message that I could hardly have turned the handle of the camera myself" (265). Here Noel tells the most climactic moment of the expedition in terms of its filming. The camera, the new technological device of exploration, runs without Noel's agency or assistance. A machine covers the distance that humans cannot. Cameras do not eliminate the felt need to explore. They do not bring modern explorers back to the experience of Thoreau's "simple races" who know place in ways not dependent on the physical visit of the explorer; Noel's commitment to technological exploration instead uses the tools of communication to merely extend the assumptions and prerogatives of Western exploration.

Mount Everest frequently generates a long, tenuous cloud that blows horizontally from the upper reaches of the mountain. In his *Through Tibet* account of the 1922 expedition, Noel comments on the beauty of what he calls this "great ever-changing, never-ceasing 'streamer' " (155). Although Noel acknowledges that the wind betokened by this streamer actually represents a dangerous obstacle to mountaineers, he remarks: "Personally I admired the streamer. It added to the pictorial photographic effects of the mountain" (155). This moment in the text further points to how Noel's conception of achievement on Mount Everest diverges from the goal of physically reaching the summit, and it suggests how *Through Tibet* can be read as a text that in a sense is subsidiary to the film work that precedes it and comprises much of its subject matter. Noel's text, in fact, has a sufficient amount to say on the topic of film that it can be said to articulate, in a manner of speaking, its own "film theory."

Noel, an enthusiastic proponent of what he calls "modern scientific appliances and devices" (284) for enhancing the human capacity for exploration,[16] constructs *Through Tibet* as a platform to argue for filmmaking as a medium that inevitably, and in his view, rightly, filters and alters its subject matter. Despite his announced role as photohistorian, Noel also declares quite straightforwardly in *Through Tibet* that "the picture would have to be far more than a day-to-day pictorial chronicle," going on to explain that "such chronicles, in themselves unimpeachably truthful, do not always convey true impressions" (209). To crank out a film version of the expedition that attempts to faithfully mimic events according to "realist" assumptions of clock time, empirical observation, causal sequence, and even dominant characterization would, for Noel, simply be to "dabble fatuously in trivialities" (208). The film, in other words, would be no Royal Geographical Society–inspired journal piece.

Instead he explains, first in language that is almost vaguely symbolist in its suggestiveness, his notion of what film's "true impression" should be. "I tried so to compose my pictures as to interpret, if possible, the soulmeaning of these mountains. For me they really lived," he writes (176). Later in the text he claims that the goal of his film work transcends "the spirit of romance and adventure"; it undertakes to capture a " 'something' which would make the spectator feel the immensity of this struggle of man against Nature" (208), that would "convey a series of impressions leading to the one dominant impression" (210). Noel finally defines this impression simply as "an unforgettable impression of power, beauty, grandeur and the insignificance of man" and explains that it is "that climax of sensation that we ourselves experienced among Everest's virgin snowfields" (210).

The poetics of filmmaking that emerges in *Through Tibet* differs markedly from the usual protestations of objective, realist representation that so persistently surfaces in much of modern exploration literature. His poetics plainly partakes of the aesthetic of the sublime. In calling for "effects both subtle and stupendous" (210) in the service of a thematics of transport and authorial inspiration, *Through Tibet* describes the complex relationship between the artist and the mountainscape received from the romantic tradition. Noel's description of the ideal film about Mount Everest would have it be an almost unimaginable amalgam of Ruskin's "Alpine towers," the "unknown omnipotence" of Shelley's "Mont Blanc," Byron's answering Jura and "joyous Alps" in *Childe Harold's Pilgrimage,* and the "mute thanks and secret ecstasy" of Coleridge's "Hymn before Sunrise." But this conjuring of the sublime is descriptive and referential, part of what is actually an abstract film commentary, or "theory," embedded within *Through Tibet.*

Noel's account is somewhat unusual as a modern exploration narrative in that it mentions in any detail a way of representing mountain geography that could be associated with the tradition of the sublime; more typically, as I discussed in the introduction, exploration narratives during the period seem to avoid or undermine rhetoric suggestive of anything transcendent and rely instead on an idiom of empirical observation, even if it is finally shaped by the expression of subjective perception and, finally, historical and political context. But *Through Tibet* is not itself a text operating from the poetics of the sublime. It does not undertake to produce the effect of "transport"; it merely offers an analytical commentary, albeit a somewhat vague one, on the topic of transport. The sublime in Noel is displaced beyond the written word to an after-the-fact reconstruction of intention in films that even in 1927 were already relegated to virtual oblivion.

Noel's apparent evocation of the sublime does prompt a somewhat different line of investigation, however. Far from announcing an aberrant, distorted, or somehow dishonest view of nonfiction filmmaking, Noel's thoughts on his medium suggest the theoretical underpinnings of what was in the 1920s the newly developing documentary film movement in Britain.[17]

Growing up with its medium, film criticism has traced an ongoing dialogue about the "realism" or "arealism" of cinematic images. André Bazin has argued that the invention of cinema was from the beginning guided by the desire for what he calls "a recreation of the world in its own image" (21), and Maya Deren has said that "the photographic image confronts us with the innocent arrogance of an objective fact" (155). But on the other hand, Stan Brakhage has pointed to realism as a mere "invention." Hugo Munsterberg makes the intriguing observation that cinema "tells us the human story by overcoming the forms of the outer world, namely, space, time, and causality, and by adjusting the events to the forms of the inner world, namely, attention, memory, imagination, and emotion" (quoted in Mast and Cohen, 331). Munsterberg's "inner world" can be read, it seems to me, as an ideological complex. Raymond Williams makes this point, I think, when he considers the rise of the cinema in the context of urban and industrial popular culture and the theatrical conventions of "high-brow" culture (15).

During the era of Noel's cinematic work, nowhere in film was the issue and extent of realist assumptions pursued more thoroughly than in the discussion of documentary film. The most substantial theoretical foundation for this genre of film resides in the work of John Grierson, the most important documentary film theorist to emerge in Britain during the 1920s and generally credited with being the founder of the British documentary filmmaking "movement" that developed between the wars. Grierson defined documentary film in general as "all films from natural material . . . where the camera shot on the spot" (quoted in Hood, 101). But plainly, this was strictly the literal component of this thinking. Grierson saw film as the ideal medium to educate the public about the political, economic, and social operations of a modern world that he regarded as increasingly and dangerously complex and difficult. Grierson saw the intervention of the filmmaker as producing this effect through the manipulation of visual and linguistic signs. "You photograph the natural life," he wrote, "but you also, by your juxtaposition of detail, create an interpretation of it" (23). The "troubled or difficult art" of documentary was a matter of "creative shapings" of natural material (quoted in Hood, 106) for socially responsible effect. Primarily a form of communication and persuasion, this view of documentary film equates perception with creation and ultimately appeals to questions of authority and control—the filmic language fashions rather than describes actuality, and the eye and ideology behind the viewfinder finally reveal themselves only in their effect.

Jack Noel's notion of a "dominant impression" of Mount Everest, then, was very much an idea whose time had come in 1927. It was very much in keeping with the methodology that Grierson would begin advocating the next year, and it describes the premise that apparently informs the many exotic "dramatized documentaries" that appeared in the wake of Robert Flaherty's 1921 *Nanook of the North* and later included such films as *Chang* (1927), *Silent Enemy* (1930), and *The Viking* (1931).[18] Furthermore, the way in which *Through Tibet* presumes the translocational function of photography, its capacity to move where the camera operator does not, seems to draw also on the theory of Dziga Vertov and his "Kino-Eye" school of newsreel cinematography in Russia. Vertov had been insisting on this "motive" function since 1918. "The lens of the camera has the power of the moving human eye," Vertov affirmed. "It can and does go everywhere and into everything" (quoted in Rotha, Road, and Griffith, 88). Finally, it is important to recognize that Noel's emphasis on long-distance photography proclaims a growing interest among documentary filmmakers in the kind of deep-focus shots that Flaherty had constructed in *Nanook*. As late as 1918, after all, the official cameramen working on the western front had been forbidden, in the name of security, to use long-focus lenses and had not been permitted within forty yards of aircraft.[19]

Like Mackinder's unpublished narrative and Peck's *Search*, Noel's *Through Tibet* forcefully speaks beyond the very limited, depoliticized range of thematics and subject matter most of us associate with adventure stories. With its geography of perceived margins, its spatially positioned narrative point of view, its concern for "film theory," and its investigation of the interaction of subjective and empirical understanding, *Through Tibet*, in its unique manner, arranges the grammar of exploration to illustrate the historical and ideological environment from which it arises.

Turn a globe to central Asia and you will notice that a small finger, or "panhandle," of Afghanistan extends east to Chinese Turkistan, separating the former Soviet Republic of Tadzhik from Pakistan's Peshawar district and from India's Kashmir region. This territory represents in large part a legacy of almost a century of imperial confrontation and intrigue, or imagined intrigue, between Britain and Russia and later the Soviet Union.

From the 1830s on, British political and military strategists regarded Afghanistan as a potentially significant cusp between Russian- and British-controlled territory. This was one of the many flashpoints at which the two European powers would play what Kipling and others often called the "Great Game" for ascendancy and influence in Asia. The game involved the British in a series of wars with the emirs of Afghanistan and with Sikh tribesmen along the northwestern frontier of India. The Russian Empire, for its part, following its traders and the ambitions of its frontier officers,[20] continued to advance in the second half of the nineteenth century southeast of the Aral Sea toward the Hindu Kush and the Pamir Mountains of central Asia, by some accounts expanding its territory at a rate that would reach a peak of fifty-five square miles a day in the summer of 1902.[21] When Russia established the frontier province of Turkistan in 1865, it gained a tentative hold over native populations of Kapchak and Kirghiz that would embroil it in political, racial, and religious factional conflict in the region for years to come. Russian expansionism also helped created an unstable geographical nexus at which the occupied territories and interests of the Russian, Chinese, and British empires met and sometimes overlapped — always on land previously occupied by indigenous peoples who were often far from willing to give up their hereditary homes. Britain, its wariness of Russian designs on territory still influenced by the memory of the Crimean War (1854–56), was particularly uneasy about the Russian presence in central Asia in the last three decades of the nineteenth century. Through its envoys to the still-independent feudal leaders in Chinese Turkistan, Britain entered into trade and protection agreements designed in part to discourage further Russian expansion.[22]

As British political involvement along the unstable frontier of northwestern India increased, representatives of the empire had better opportunities to add to their knowledge of what was to them a little-known region. Their motives were often strategic in nature. At the instigation of Sir Charles MacGregor, an intelligence division was added to the British Indian Army, and officers were encouraged to travel as a means of gaining geographical and political knowledge of frontier regions. Percy Sykes reported that the army even adopted a "MacGregor Memorial Medal" to recognize exploration that had military value (*History,* 271). Robert Shaw in the 1860s and the military liaisons of the 1873 Forsyth mission to Kashgar in Chinese Turkistan explored Karakorum and the Pamirs and investigated the geographical feasibility of a Russian or Chinese invasion of India from the northwest. In the 1880s Shaw's nephew, Francis Young-husband, who would later play such a prominent role in the Royal Geographical Society and in the exploration of Mount Everest, continued this work by leading a number of important reconnaissance expeditions through Karakorum and the Pamirs. His assignment was to evaluate the extent of the Russian threat through the range's high passes, particularly the possibility of a Russian diversionary attack over a certain Saltoro Pass, which the British then were not even certain actually existed.[23] The Foreign Office underscored this interest in the defensibility of the Indian frontier by stationing political officers at Gilgit and Chitral to monitor situations in the so-called no man's land separating Kashmir from Chinese Turkistan. Tension between the two powers peaked in 1891 when Young-husband was apprehended in a section of the Pamirs held by Russian troops, and in 1895 a British and Russian commission, meeting to resolve the territorial conflict behind this incident, ceded to the emir of Afghanistan the narrow strip of land that we see on our globes today, as a buffer zone between the conquered territories of the two empires.

Although this agreement forestalled immediate confrontation, it did not end British concern for the integrity of its Indian possessions. The independent hill tribes that lived along the Afghan frontier continued to make a life of guerrilla campaigns against the British Army. By 1919 British Indian troops were again fighting an Afghan emir over border disputes. Even more menacing were Russian incursions into China and the regional implications of the Bolshevik Revolution of 1917. When the British intervened on the side of the Whites in the subsequent Russian Civil War the next year, the level of hostility between the two nations regained the intensity of the Crimean War years. John Noel played a small but direct part in this scenario. Already no stranger to frontier political conflict, he served immediately after World War I with the British Norpa Force in northern Persia, guarding the Mesopotamian oil fields from Bolshevik attack. Noel, assigned the task of assessing the possibility of Bolshevik invasion along the southern shore of the Caspian Sea, was sent out on horseback into the Elburz Mountains.[24]

As the British reconnaissance expedition set out for Mount Everest in 1921, Allied forces had barely been out of then-Soviet territory for a year. Even as the 1922 expedition cleared its base camp to go home in defeat, the White Russian "Far East Republic" still survived, propped up by Japanese military intervention. Adding to the political context of the early

British exploratory expeditions in the Himalayas was a marked increase in the momentum of the Indian nationalist movement and a stepping-up of British reaction to it. World War I sparked a major upswing in mostly Muslim anti-British activity, and Indian support for the war effort raised hopes that British concessions on independence would follow. When these concessions failed to develop, the Indian National Congress, active since the 1880s but more effective after the war under the leadership of Gandhi, responded to continued British rule with even stiffer resistance. The tragic Amritsar massacre, which galvanized opposition to British rule, took place on April 13, 1919, in fact barely a month after John Noel stood to address the Royal Geographical Society in London to first propose the 1921 reconnaissance.[25]

Farther to the east along the Indian frontier in the vicinity of Mount Everest, the situation was, if anything, even more complex. Although Tibet and Britain had signed a treaty in Darjeeling in 1893 guaranteeing certain limited British access to Tibet and providing for a British trade market in Gartok, the Tibetans proved reluctant to observe the provisions of the treaty. Finally, in 1903 a military force under Sir Francis Younghusband entered Tibet at the direction of the viceroy of India, Lord Curzon, and after capturing Lhasa forced the treaty on the Tibetan lamas.[26] The events of 1903–4 represent the immediate background to the political climate that nurtured Noel's trips to Mount Everest eighteen years later.

Just as Mount Everest straddles the border between Nepal and Tibet, the political context of Noel's narrative must be understood from two very distinct perspectives, that of the British and the Tibetans. The interplay of these two perspectives was what, first, allowed the expeditions of the 1920s to occur at all and, second, determined their precise historical character.

Although the military incursion of 1903 is usually described in histories as the "diplomatic mission" to Lhasa, the term is far too benign. In reality Younghusband's "mission" was a unilateral military invasion.[27] When the British encountered a Tibetan army of several thousand men armed mostly with muzzle loaders and swords at Guru on the approach to Lhasa, both the true nature of the mission and the devastating effectiveness of modern weaponry became horrifyingly clear. By some accounts almost seven hundred Tibetans died, many of them while slowly walking in retreat from the field of battle with their heads lowered in resignation and defeat. Six British soldiers were wounded. The battle at Guru caused immediate outcry. Henry Savage Landor, an amateur artist then traveling in Tibet, lashed out at "butchering thousands of helpless and defenseless natives in a manner most repulsive to any man who is a man," and the British Parliament condemned the slaughter as "a massacre of unarmed men" (quoted in Richardson, 58).

Although trade relations had certainly been an issue motivating the invasion, it was again the specter of the czar that influenced British action, particularly concern that Russian favor in Tibet would alienate the neighboring neutral states of Nepal, Bhutan, and Sikkim and destabilize India's northeastern frontier. Aggravating this concern was the rumor that the Dalai Lama was negotiating with the czar through a Mongolian lama named Dorjieff and even diplomatic gossip of a secret treaty between the two nations.[28]

But when the British moved through Tibet, they found virtually no evidence of Russian influence, to say nothing of the Russian forts and railroads rumored to exist. As Peter Fleming puts it in his *Bayonets to Lhasa,* Younghusband found that in Lhasa "Russian rifles were considerably scarcer than Huntly and Palmer Biscuits" (267). Moreover, Edmund Chandler, a correspondent for the *Daily Mail* who accompanied the invasion force, reported that the great difficulty that the troops experienced in moving the 150 miles from the Chumbi valley to the Tibetan town of Tuna proved "the absurdity of the idea of a Russian advance on Lhasa" (quoted in Hopkirk, 169).

When the British Alpine Club suggested an attempt on Mount Everest to celebrate its golden jubilee in 1907, the British government refused its request for permission, explaining that it might undermine the empire's relationship with Russia on the eve of the 1907 Anglo-Russian Convention. In his *The Epic of Mount Everest* Younghusband would later downplay the political complexity of British access to Tibet. As he told it, getting to Everest was simply a matter of convincing certain British Indian authorities who felt that "travellers caused trouble" (22). While Younghusband's assessment is not incorrect in substance, it does omit the complexity of the trouble. While treaties were certainly considerations, there was more to the decision to keep British climbers out of Tibet in 1907. That the politically embarrassing Younghusband mission had become to central Asia what Lord Kitchener's infamous concentration camps had been to the South African war was not lost on the Liberal government that came to power in London in 1905. For years after the invasion Britain strenuously sought to avoid even the appearance of involvement in Tibetan affairs. As Peter Hopkirk puts it in his *Trespassers on the Roof of the World,* one way to avoid trouble with Tibet "was not to let anyone in" (197).

After the Chinese were driven out of Tibet in 1913, Britain continued this policy of careful restraint with Tibet, acting, as Fleming puts it, "as a kind of *concierge*" (304), keeping a tactful distance but also controlling Tibet's relationship with the outside world. Britain embargoed arms sales to Tibet during this period, for example, and in turn prevented other nations, notably Japan, from selling to Tibet.[29] Britain solidified this peculiarly remote kind of regency over Tibet in 1914 when it signed with Tibet the Simla Convention, which agreed on a border between Tibet and British territory east of Nepal, along the so-called McMahon Line, and effectively recognized Tibetan independence from China. For Britain, Tibet became in effect a benign blank on the map of the northern Indian frontier.

For Tibetans the "kid-glove" foreign policy adopted by the British toward their nation after 1904 was really the only kind of policy to have. Traditionally a closed society, wary (if not xenophobic) of foreigners, Tibet had resisted all forms of Western encroachment for most of the nineteenth century. In fact, when Younghusband warned Tibetan lamas of the danger of Russian influence, they labeled his concern irrational—they did not allow *any* outsiders to influence them (Richardson, 58). That Britain's restraint actually signified its ongoing attempt to monopolize Tibet's interaction with the outside world was largely irrelevant. But by 1920, from the point of view of the thirteenth Dalai Lama, the time had come for better relations with Britain—if not closer, at least more concrete. In November 1920 the Dalai Lama permitted his old friend Charles Bell, then British political officer in the Chumbi valley, to come to Lhasa for negotiations.[30] The lama had a complex assortment of motives in allowing a Western diplomat to visit Lhasa for the first time in Tibetan history. Since Tibetan independence in 1914 the military had been gaining authority in Lhasa. A faction of "modernized" military men trained in Western methods and often adopting Western dress and even such controversial British customs as polo were causing the lama particular concern. They advocated increasing the Tibetan army from fifteen thousand to twenty thousand to offset the always-present threat of China, which still claimed Tibet as a vassal state. The Dalai Lama became convinced of the need for British arms, munitions, and military training to meet this threat.

But this was a trade-off. Many Tibetans considered the growing influence of the military to be a serious threat to the traditional fabric of their theocratic society. As Bell pursued diplomatic negotiations in 1921, rumors ran through Lhasa that the British were preparing to invade again, this time in support of the Tibetan army against the monasteries. Posters appeared around the city calling for the assassination of Bell and his party.[31] But the Dalai Lama was himself something of a progressive and was willing to allow closer ties with Britain if this would help keep at bay Chinese designs on Tibet.[32] Moreover, he reasoned that a British presence in Lhasa might actually obviate the need for a radical, destabilizing military buildup that seemed likely to incite civil war. In his mind, a few British diplomats might be as effective as a regiment or two of Tibetan troops in discouraging China and might have the additional benefit of undermining the influence of the Tibetan military.

Through the offices of Bell, the Dalai Lama began to get his wish.[33] Ever since the days of open warfare with China in 1912, the lama had wanted a telegraph line from Lhasa to Gyantse (near Bhutan). With British help construction began in 1921, along with the building of a hydroelectric plant at Lhasa and an English school at Gyantse. In addition, officers and men of the Tibetan army were given training by the British, an officer of the Darjeeling police began to organize a Western-style police force in Lhasa, and British arms slowly began to arrive. For the British this growing diplomatic coziness brought another result. The Everest Committee received permission to explore the mountain.

Britain had decided that the Bolshevik Revolution nullified the 1907 convention with Russia that had precluded exploration in Tibet. The Royal Geographical Society and Alpine Club, once they had gained permission from their government for an Everest expedition, persuaded Bell to press their case with the Dalai Lama as well. From the point of view of the Everest Committee, Tibetan permission to climb the mountain was complexly bound up with these political negotiations. Charles Kenneth Howard-Bury, the proposed leader of the first expedition, wrote to Younghusband on July 20, 1920:

> The basis of the whole trouble is the Sec. of State or Lord Curzon's refusal at present to allow half a dozen machine guns and a few thousands of rounds to be sent into Tibet. . . . If you could use your influence as Pres. of the Geographical Society and also with certain officials at the India Office to get the matter settled

favourably, the chief obstacle to the expedition would be removed. (quoted in Unsworth, 26–27)

Amid bargaining for his government's position on arms sales and diplomatic contact, Bell presented his case to the Dalai Lama for an immensely important scientific expedition to Everest. On December 20, 1920, a telegram arrived at the India Office reporting that the give-and-take of negotiation had turned out in the favor of the Everest Committee. After climbing Everest was first publicly proposed in 1906, the British recognized it as an act of fundamental political implication. The messy strings of practical international politics, in fact, made the Foreign Office uneasy about the climbing of the mountain long before men like Mallory, Norton, and Noel met the more objective obstacles of glacier and rock. It would be something of an oversimplification to call the first Everest expeditions part of a "guns-for-mountain" deal, but plainly the context of the first Everest expeditions was military and strategic, from both British and Tibetan perspectives.

From the very beginning of British interest in Mount Everest, that is to say, not long after its "discovery" in the 1850s by the British Trigonometrical Survey of India under Sir Andrew Scott Waugh, climbing the mountain had been bound up with the broader political goals of Britain in central Asia.[34] That Lord Curzon, who as viceroy of India between 1898 and 1905 was perhaps the single most important architect of "Great Game" British expansionism in central Asia (a policy he referred to as "trans-Himalayan"), is not at all coincidental. As an assiduous, or "hawkish," as Peter Hopkirk calls him (162), disciple of the British imperial posture in Asia, Curzon had a tendency to think of Mount Everest as a part of Albion. In a 1905 letter to the mountaineer Douglas Freshfield, Curzon wrote:

It has always seemed to me a reproach that with the second highest mountain in the world [he means at the time Kangchenjunga] for the most part in British territory and with the highest in a neighbouring and friendly state, we, the mountaineers and pioneers par excellence of the universe, make no sustained and scientific attempt to climb to the top of either of them. (quoted in Unsworth, 14)

Likewise, Younghusband's career as military man, explorer, and chairman of the RGS Mount Everest Committee speaks to how climbing Everest overlapped with international political posturing during the period. In his 1926 *The Epic of Mount Everest* he described the society's motives in undertaking the project of an expedition: "It was now laid down from the very first that the attainment of the summit of Mount Everest was the supreme object of the Expedition and all other objects subsidiary to that. Climbing the mountain was no mere sensationalism. It was testing the capacity of man" (25). This remark was typical of the way in which British mountaineers publicly discussed their craft. It seems to announce an apolitical, nonscientific "because it's there" view of mountains that even calls into question the appropriateness of applying the term *exploration* with its associated contexts of imperial conquest and science.[35] But as we have seen already, much about the first Everest expeditions of the 1920s belies the progressive ecumenism of the human spirit that one reads in Younghusband's explanation. The climbing of Everest was nothing if not sensational in its public presentation, and the man whose capacity Younghusband would see tested was not so much a man as he was a Brit. After all, Arthur Robert Hinks, Younghusband's colleague on the Everest Committee, wrote Bailey after the 1924 expedition to pointedly ask the political officer to please render no assistance to proposed Swiss and German expeditions to the mountain.[36]

The Royal Geographical Society also played a role through the years in making sure that non-British climbers would not have particularly easy access to Everest. Although the society was officially a private organization, from its earliest days it enjoyed a close working relationship with the British government. Ian Cameron, in his extremely favorable history of Royal Geographical Society–sponsored exploration, describes a society adept at, as he puts it, "offering advice behind the scenes, using its influence to secure government patronage, using its association with the Navy to obtain ships and crews, oiling the diplomatic wheels by which every expedition has to be set in motion" (18).

It is no wonder that Younghusband observed in 1926 of Tibetan reaction to British Everest climbs: "These wise Tibetans think that merely to climb a mountain cannot be the true object of these huge expeditions coming out from England year after year always commanded by generals and colonels, never reaching the summit, but always prying about round the mountain, and always taking a look into Nepal" (*Epic,* 310). The remark that Younghusband intended as casually and ironically ethnographic contains more literal truth than he openly acknowledged.[37]

The interwar years were a period characterized by an increase in both conspicuous and sub rosa nationalism in exploration, even beyond the broader nationalism that I have asserted dominates the exploration of the entire modern period. In an era when patriotic Germans and Italians would shortly be dying on the north faces in the Alps and unclimbed peaks in South America, and Nazi aviators would claim Antarctic territory by dropping swastika markers on the ice, British exploration writing in general attempted to take a higher ground, in part as a response to what was perceived as the overt nationalism of German exploration writers. Kenneth Mason says of the interwar years in his *Abode of Snow*: "A curious brand of nationalism, quite out of place in the Himalaya, caused some to think that the honour of their country was at stake if they did not climb something larger and higher and more difficult than had been achieved by the climbers of some other country" (280). Like many historians of mountaineering writing in the aftermath of World War II, Mason had a recognizable tendency to see unhealthy nationalism as a predominantly German state of mind. But the political appropriation of mountaineering exploration was far from an exclusively German practice. Despite either the open denials made by many writers, like Mason, or simply the absence of overt political rhetoric in the narratives of most other British mountaineers writing during the 1920s and 1930s, many British mountaineers simply regarded Mount Everest as *their* mountain. The expeditions of the 1920s repeatedly turned down applications from Italian, Russian, and American mountaineers to join, and every attempt was made to make the expeditions as thoroughly British as possible. If anything, the tragedy of the 1924 expedition underscored a perception that can be traced to Curzon. Of future expeditions, Younghusband wrote in 1924, "Attention should be called to the fact that this country should have a priority in view among other things that her countrymen lay at or near the top" (quoted in Unsworth, 159), and the India Office was quick to recognize the political, if symbolic, danger posed by the German and American expeditions rumored to be forming.

John Noel's *Through Tibet*, as I have already pointed out, provides a particularly intriguing illustration of how an exploration narrative can establish a rhetoric laying claim to its geographical object. In the case of Noel, this claim would have been made in a context of British imperial identity and strategic aims that recognized Mount Everest as an appropriate emblem. Technology is the means by which this comes about; "English air," distance photography, and even aircraft assert cultural and ideological dominance and privilege, especially in comparison with obviously "inferior" (for Noel — filthy, superstitious, disgusting) indigenous peoples like the Tibetans. As a "film theory," *Through Tibet* articulates the notion that the film medium not so much documents or represents a foreign place as much as it neutralizes its foreignness. Control of the film medium in *Through Tibet* is tantamount to control of the mountain.

When Noel was making his two Everest films, documentary film was still just coming into its own. British film flourished immediately after World War I, and cinema goers saw a sharp increase both in the numbers of films produced and the number of theaters showing them. But the marked optimism in the British film industry during the early 1920s soon gave way to disaster. The glut of motion pictures left filmmakers with no immediate return on their investment because they frequently could not book theaters sooner than eighteen months. As a result, they made an increasing number of short inexpensive films, even though the demand was actually for longer feature films, and large U.S. distributors gained almost total control of the British film industry. By 1924 the industry was in crisis. November, the month before the first showing of *The Epic of Everest,* became known in British film industry circles as "Black November," during which every studio in Britain was closed. John Noel had inadvertently picked the worst possible moment to introduce his newest film at the Trade Show in December. This was especially unfortunate, first of all, because Noel's photographic record, like all the information coming out of the Everest expeditions, was always conceived of, at least in part, as a money-making venture. The 1922 film was a great, although fleeting, popular and critical success and a modest financial one. After losing £400 the first week it opened in London, *Climbing Mount Everest* began to get good reviews. Although it continued to lose money in some areas — £700 outside the cities in its initial ten-week showing — it took in £10,000 in London during that period. Including the sale of continental rights to the film, *Climbing* finally netted a profit of £500 for the Royal Geographical Society.[38] When Noel and his backers purchased the film rights to the 1924 expedition for the very large sum of £8,000, Noel seems to have been confident of making a sizable return on investment. His venture was a boon for the Everest Committee, not only virtually financing the expedition at one shot but also freeing it from the expense of providing for its own photography, as it had in 1922. Noel and his investors took all the risk; the patrician RGS members, many of whom, like Hinks, deplored publicity, faced no direct financial downside.

In addition, Noel's planned film was likely to have broader promotional effect. The Royal Geographical Society and the Alpine Club were always in serious need of financial support during the 1920s, and the photography and news reports coming out of Tibet served to advertise their exploratory work. Furthermore, a film of a successful or even simply intrepid expedition to Everest would show daring, courageous, and, with good fortune, successful Brits making important achievements on the fringes of their empire; it would send the message of rightful British control of India and proprietary influence in the Trans-Himalaya. And it would point to the central role of the society and the club in seeing that these impressions were made.

The deliberate financial and political functions of Noel's film are broadly representative of the cultural function of documentary film during the modern period. Film historians generally associate documentary film as a movement and genre with the work of Grierson.[39] In addition to his contribution to documentary theory mentioned earlier, as a publicist, producer, and, to a lesser extent, as a filmmaker, Grierson is, in fact, the most conspicuous figure in British documentary film from the late 1920s through World War II. In 1928 Sir Stephen Tallents, secretary of the newly formed Empire Marketing Board, appointed Grierson to head its film unit. The board's mission was economic promotion. Under Grierson the film unit's mission was using the cinema to promote consumption of British Empire products, and the influence of its methods persisted well into the late 1940s.[40] The unit's success led to such government agencies as the General Post Office Film Unit and the wartime Crown Film Unit.

Even before Grierson's work, of course, film had been recognized in Britain as an important tool for shaping political events. Flaherty's *Nanook* was showing in Britain by 1922. The work of Dziga Vertov was widely known among filmmakers, and the work of Sergey Eisenstein had been loudly banned. Under the direction of J. Aubrey Rees and the former prime minister Lord Asquith, the British Empire Film Institute had begun work in 1926, promoting British film production as a financial endeavor and purveying a kind of filmic British nationalism throughout the empire. Working even before the 1927 Cinematographic Act began to protect the British film industry from the control of U.S. investors, the institute sought to promote public enthusiasm for British films and promote film as a means of enhancing the British image in all corners of the world. As one of the institute's first initiatives, it began to assemble a film library, founded on a collection of Ponting's polar films. By 1926, in other words, the cinematic representation of exploration was already clearly recognized for its propaganda value.

This growing British inclination to see film for its capacity to aestheticize political and economic issues in the interest of British prestige continued to pick up speed in the late 1920s and throughout the 1930s.[41] As R. Donald puts it in a 1926 essay entitled "Films and the Empire," the Colonial Office had begun to realize that "trade follows the film" (497). Many officials felt that Hollywood's image of Europeans was not particularly flattering or useful to effective administration of the colonies. As head of the Colonial Films Committee, Sir Hesketh Bell wrote in 1930: "The success of our government of subject races depends almost entirely on the degree of respect we can inspire" (quoted in Curran and Porter, 129). In the belief that it was already too late to recoup the British image in India and the rest of Asia, Bell focused on Africa.[42] This effort culminated in the Bantu Educational Kinema Experiment in the mid-1930s and in Alexander Shaw's 1939 *Men of Africa*, the soundtrack of which claimed on the eve of the World War II that "much can be achieved by money and the initiative of the white man." It is a fitting testimony to the initial circumstances of the showing of *Men of Africa* that a copy of the film and its script are today housed at the Imperial War Museum, London.

In an important sense, however, World War I was what marked the dramatic genesis of British documentary film. Paul Rotha, Sinclair Road, and Richard Griffith, in *Documentary Film* in fact go so far as to insist that the war "began this era of mass persuasion" (57) that signified the twentieth century. The British War Office recognized the importance of portraying the war effort on film early on. Because the War Office had placed a virtual ban on the shooting of military activity by photographers and motion picture cameramen, the first footage coming out of the war, shot mostly by U.S. cameramen like A. K. Dawson and John Allen Everets traveling with German armies, distinctly favored the German view of the war. But film was already becoming the medium of the masses, at home and in battle. A front-line cinema circuit, operated through the British Expedition Forces Canteen, expanded rapidly throughout France, and by the end of the war grim film metaphors had entered common military parlance. Machine guns were commonly called "cinema cameras" by British troops who, instead of being ordered by their officers to open fire, were told to "turn the crank." Trenches were even referred to as "picture house tea rooms."[43]

By 1915, when the widely shown film *Britain Prepares* was first released, with its conspicuous portrayal of British military might, the importance of reaching theater audiences had clearly been recognized. By 1916 the first officially sanctioned British war film using footage actually shot at the front, *The Battle of the Somme*, shocked home audiences with its graphic display of modern warfare, and film was actively being used to promote the war effort.[44] During the 1920s films about the war flourished. The release of such films as *The World's Greatest Story, The Battle of Jutland,* and *Zeebrugge* overlapped with Noel's film work, as well as with the many other exploration and adventure documentary films that appeared during the decade. If the British documentary film is to be traced to Grierson, working mostly in the 1930s, it is important to recognize that Grierson, who had no qualms about thinking of himself as a propagandist, emerged from an era already well versed in the use of film as an effective suasive medium used in the cause of nationalism.[45]

Exploration films have their place in this general overview of British motion picture production. Emerging from such "scenics" as Claude Friese-Greene's 1920 *The Beauty of Britain* and even the faked 1909 Theodore Roosevelt hunting chronicle, *Hunting Big Game in Africa,* as well as heavily influenced by the 1922 success of Flaherty's *Nanook,* exploration films often thrived during the 1920s. "There was no formula," observes Kevin Brownlow in his *The War, the West, and the Wilderness.* "Some of them tried to emulate the feature film, some of them the lantern lecture" (403). Merian C. Cooper and Earnest B. Schoedsack, the U.S. filmmakers parodied in *King Kong,* served up such exotica as *Grass* (1925) and *Chang* (1927), and their work overlapped in Britain with the wildlife films of Cherry and Richard Kearton and such films as Frank Hurley's 1924 New Guinea adventure, *Pearls and Savages,* Rosita Forbes's 1925 *From Red Sea to Blue Nile,* and the 1926 account of the Algarsson–Worsley British Arctic Expedition, *Under Sail in the Frozen North.*

But of all the many exploration and quasi-exploration films produced between the wars, the films of Noel and Ponting probably received the most attention. Ponting's *South* (1919), *Southward on the Quest,* (1922) and *The Great White Silence* (1924) all took aboard the heady mixture of patriotic heroism and dangerous, far-away settings that had earlier captivated British newspaper and magazine readers with written accounts of the exploits of Scott and Shackleton in the Antarctic. A set of Ponting's films representing Scott's valiant death was shown to 100,000 British soldiers in France in 1915. Of Ponting's film account a military chaplain wrote, "The intensity of its appeal is realized by the subdued hush and quiet that pervades the massed audiences of troops," and he called the film version of Scott's heroism "a legacy and heritage of inestimable value in seeing through our present work."[46] Ponting reedited the forty thousand feet of film he had shot during Scott's famous and tragic last expedition in 1912 and released *The Great White Silence* six months before *The Epic of*

Everest in 1924. Impersonal slaughter and annihilation on the western front had made postwar audiences receptive in a new way to Ponting's portrayal of Scott—a story that spoke powerfully of the possibility that risk and even death could still, even in the aftermath of the war, somehow be individualistic and even noble and morally clear.

A great admirer of Ponting's work, Noel also tried to capture not only the spirit of adventure but also the aura of national pride and integrity that often surrounded geographical exploration and its narration during the modern period. His 1922 *Climbing Mount Everest* fell short in both excitement and pathos. But in *The Epic of Everest* Noel had in the deaths of Mallory and Irvine a tragedy redolent with deep national symbolism and the same sense of the purity of the struggle against nature that imbued Ponting's films. Noel's editing of the final climb of the two men makes intentional use of dramatic montage. The film shows Mallory and Irvine at two miles distance, at twenty-six thousand feet on the Northeast Ridge, cuts to what Rachel Low calls an "iris" shot of the summit (288), then cuts back to the ridge, where the climbers have suddenly vanished. The effect is dramatic and powerful. "If you had lived as they had lived and died in the heart of nature," the film's titles pointedly conclude, "would you, yourself, wish for any better grave?"

Almost every issue of the *Geographical Journal* in the early 1920s included articles on Mount Everest. For three years the British press had fanned public enthusiasm about climbing the mountain. The debut of *The Epic of Everest* followed by only two months a memorial service for Mallory and Irvine conducted at St. Paul's Cathedral and attended by members of the royal family and prominent representatives of the Alpine Club and the RGS. A wreath was placed on a model of Mount Everest displayed at the Wembley Exhibition. Public interest in the mountain and particularly in the disappearance of the two climbers was extensive, and popular theories explaining what happened to them and whether they had made the summit abounded. It is fair to suggest that, like Ponting's work, Noel's second motion picture engaged the public imagination through its encomium to heroic British exploration. Noel went on to show the film and his slides to more than one million people in Canada and the United States.

Furthermore, the portrayal of British initiative and courage in *The Epic of Everest* interacted with Britain's postwar reassessment of its relationship with its possessions abroad. With both the internal political instability caused by Indian nationalism and the recent memory of a perceived external military threat, feelings in and concerning British India were, to say the least, charged and expectant during the era of Noel's exploratory work, and they continued to be so through the showing of his films and the publication of his books. When Noel's films came out, bolstering the British image in India and the Trans-Himalaya was not generally regarded as the lost cause that Hesketh Bell claimed it to be in 1930. The ideological cargo carried by Noel's film work can be regarded as a somewhat inadvertent precursor to the more methodical and intentionally purposeful propaganda for colonial rule that grew up soon after. With strategic aims and exploration often overlapping in British thinking about Asia, Noel's films can be seen both as canonizing Mallory and Irvine and the national spirit and as more broadly underwriting the legitimacy of British presence and influence in Asia. *Through Tibet,* a book in large part *about* Noel's expedition films, takes on the same commentary.

For better or for worse, *The Epic of Everest* dramatically backfired both financially and politically. Although Noel's films anticipated the British cinematic rearguard defense of empire, as it turned out they were worse than ineffective. They clearly did not serve the desired purposes of the Everest Committee and British mountaineering in general, and they ironically ended up playing a part in setting those purposes back several years after the 1924 expedition. Noel's camera work, as a matter of fact, caused him a great deal of both financial and professional difficulty, initiated one of the most embarrassing moments in the history of the Royal Geographical Society, and directly and indirectly stalled further exploration of Mount Everest until 1931. It's an odd story.

In 1921 Maj. Frederick Marshman Bailey had succeeded Charles Bell as political officer in Sikkim, a position that allowed him direct control over relations between Tibet and Britain and therefore a position that, for mountaineers interested in attempting Everest, made him one of the most formidable figures in British India. Whereas Bell had helped smooth the diplomatic path for the first three expeditions, Bailey presided with suspicion and even hostility over their aftermath. Bailey had first visited the Himalayas with Younghusband in 1903 and had experienced some rather interesting military and exploratory adventures in the region.[47] The general tendency among British diplomats to try to assume a proprietary role with respect to Tibet may have found its ultimate expression in Bailey. For a variety of idealistic and personal reasons he opposed the British interest in Mount Everest from the beginning, which then was conspicuously associated with Noel and his Royal Geographical Society speech of 1919. Bailey leveled repeated criticisms at the Everest Committee about actions of the 1921 and 1922 expeditions that he considered not in keeping with the British responsibility to Tibet.[48] But when the 1924 expedition returned and Noel began to show the film version of the expedition, Bailey took this as an occasion to really frustrate the progress of British climbing in Tibet.

As it turned out, Noel's resort to a "travelogue" emphasis on Tibetan culture was what caused the trouble. "Some offence has been caused," Bailey wrote to Hinks in late 1924, "by a portion of the Everest film showing a man eating lice" (quoted in Unsworth, 150). Noel offered to edit the offending scene, although he retained a scene showing an old man killing fleas with his teeth. Bailey countered with a new complaint, objecting to Noel's use of Tibetan lamas in the promotion of the film, particularly stressing the inappropriateness of exploiting religious ceremony. In his first communications with Hinks and the committee, Bailey equivocated about whether these objections actually originated with the Tibetans or whether they were a matter of *his* own concern. In fact, Bailey may have been, at least in part, taking it upon himself to speak for the Tibetans. In any case, in 1925 a letter from the government of Tibet eventually corroborated Bailey's objections, referring to the five monks who had been "enticed" (quoted in Unsworth, 151) away from Tibet and announcing a ban on future British expeditions to the country. Pictures of Noel's lamas eventually ran in newspapers in Sikkim and angered both the Tibetan maharaja of Sikkim and the Dalai Lama. The maharaja banned Noel from Sikkim, and the Dalai Lama called for the arrest of the lamas. The Everest Committee increasingly distanced itself from Noel and his film, and within the year Explorer Films was out of business. The committee learned the next year that when in 1924 it had requested permission for another expedition in 1926, Bailey had not even forwarded the request to the Tibetan government. Not until 1932 — when, incidentally, the Tibetans found themselves again in need of closer ties with the British — did the Dalai Lama grant permission for another expedition.

The precise role that Bailey played in this affair is certainly open to question. But regardless of whether he acted faithfully according to the wishes of the Tibetans or actually "framed" Noel on his own initiative, the effect was the same. Noel and his film work, and by extension his narrative writing, were involved in a complicated political and diplomatic incident — maybe intrigue — that ultimately shut down British climbing in Tibet for a full nine years between the wars and did serious damage to

British prestige and credibility in Asia. We should, of course, put the Noel incident in perspective. As Walt Unsworth so nicely puts it, "It was not a great national issue which caused the lamps to burn all night in the India Office" (159). This could be. The lamps might not have burned all night, but they certainly burned well into the evening. There is no mistaking that the Everest expeditions of the 1920s, and their films, did little to shore up the already-shaky foundations of British India, as they were surely in part intended to do. Noel's film was not the only factor involved in this — but by the 1930s it seems to have been this British affront that many people in the region remembered more than others. Not surprisingly, when the British 1933 expedition set off for Everest, it did not include a film crew.

Because John Noel's *Through Tibet to Everest* suggests and invites an examination of these rather involved historical circumstances, it ends up revealing again, although very differently from the narratives of Halford Mackinder or Annie Smith Peck, how expansive individual perceptions of mountain geography can be. In Noel's work the subjective representation of mountain space reaches out to engage the political and economic context of new imperialism, and it does so by way of the democratic leveling function of film, its capacity to reproduce distant landscapes for anyone with the price of a ticket. In "The Work of Art in the Age of Mechanical Reproduction," Walter Benjamin writes that mass-produced and -disseminated media like film do not create what he calls the aura, or "sphere of authenticity" (220) that is the province of true Art. Yet Noel's subjective, edited, and multiplied geography can be seen becoming authentic in the sense that the image, the text, and the reproduction gain political significance through their extraordinary historical circumstances. Benjamin describes how the "presence in time and space" of the work of art is finally never replicable (220). If we take the "work of art" in this case to be Noel's Mount Everest, perhaps the implication is that the individual and imperialist geographies of the earth's highest point mingle to suggest that the mountain never had the innocent unmediated presence of Art, that it could only be fully and affectingly authentic within its historical surroundings.

We have come a long way from the romantic mountains of Wordsworth, Coleridge, and Shelley. We have trespassed mightily on the mountains that were supposed to be pure, unsullied, and sublime, on the sporting playgrounds of men in tweed and puttees. But what were the playing fields of Eton for?

With this account of John Baptist Noel's camera adventures and the context at which they hint, the time has come to close this discussion of how mountaineering participated in the larger current of world affairs that define the age of the new imperialism through the 1930s. World War II marked an effective limit to an era of mountaineering that was at least significantly characterized by the same growing international tension that prevailed in the West to one degree or another from the later years of the nineteenth century. As it did with other types of exploratory activity, the war largely stalled mountaineering in most areas of the world.[49] As Kenneth Mason puts it in *Abode of Snow,* reversing for a moment what is familiar and what is not in the conventional war-exploration metaphor, "The War was like a gigantic avalanche that sweeps everything before it. All were engulfed in the catastrophe" (285).[50] When the catastrophe was finally over, could the trappings and context of nationalism and political symbolism ever be attached so blithely to mountains again? Or was the rock finally clean, the route clear, of the constructed images and associations of conquest? The 1950s marked the beginning of a new and strenuous era of individualism and the "freedom of the hills" in which mountaineering flourished through the 1980s, perhaps still does.

"We have analyzed climbing long enough," writes the climber Chris Jones in the conclusion to his 1976 mountaineering history, *Climbing in North America.* "I am going to throw a rope into my pack and head for the mountains. Care to join me?" (380). This is like the hymn that all climbers I ever knew grew up with, and I'm almost ready to go. Almost.

Epilogue

F6

> What the hell's the matter now? Right now we got to get off
> this mountain, right?
> — Patrick Meyers

REMEMBER WHAT I SAID IN THE INTRODUCTION — THAT this book is not a literary history but that mountaineering literature, and exploration literature more broadly, of course, can be read as embedded in a historical context much broader than the events that they set out to narrate. I would like you to have a chance to see that way of reading in action. Books and history, they can't keep their hands off each other.

In 1897 August Strindberg completed his darkly confessional *Inferno,* a self-portrait of madness and occult obsession that readers continue to appreciate as a significant benchmark of literary modernism. On July 11 of the same year the playwright's nephew, Nils Strindberg, disappeared near Spitsbergen in the Norwegian Arctic while attempting to fly over the North Pole in the balloon *Ornen.*[1] The expedition did not end happily. Not until 1930, when a sealing captain working near the remote island of Kvitoya happened upon a ruined camp and the remains of Strindberg and his two companions, did the mystery of his disappearance begin to unravel. In the debris of the camp the sealers found a log and rolls of exposed film that documented the end of an expedition that had begun with all the optimism of a Jules Verne novel. Forced down upon the ice pack, the three men had endured a desperate winter of exposure and struggle before finally dying inside a makeshift hut.

Readers traditionally have treated texts such as these, one a modernist drama and the other a tragic and fragmentary exploration narrative, quite differently. One is considered "modern literature" and the other evidence in the "history of exploration." Yet in placing them together, perhaps a jarring experience at first, we have a chance to suggest an aspect of the modern period that our customary reading of literature neglects. The period that we measure out with the accretions of naturalism, symbolism, expressionism, dadaism, surrealism, and all the other movements that claim our attention in an urban and fluidly international world — the period that we identify with the monumental works of Joyce, Pound, Proust, and Mann as central artifacts — also represents a distinct epoch in the history of geographical exploration and discovery. Even more significant for those of us who are lovers of reading and literature is the narrative record of these activities. Literally, several hundred authors wrote and published accounts of their explorations during what I have been calling the modern period of mountaineering literature, from the mid-1890s to the beginning of World War II. We recognize some of their names — Mary Kingsley, George Leigh-Mallory, Robert Peary — but a far greater number have now been effectively erased from the institutionalized literary record, although their books and articles were often extremely popular with readers when they first appeared.

Both kinds of writings, of course, Literature and the more culturally marginal literature of exploration, interacted with their times and reflect them for us. The well-respected economist Kenneth Boulding writes that "primitive man lives in a world which has a spatial unknown, a dread frontier populated by the heated imagination. For modern man the world is a closed and completely explored surface" (quoted in Lowenthal, 74). As much as I admire Kenneth Boulding, this remark contains much to quibble with, particularly the self-assured distance from the "primitive" and the implied timing of the closure of the "dread frontier." Maybe *postmodern* humans will live in that closed and explored world that feeds upon itself in parody and redaction. *Modern* humans certainly did not, that is to say, if they were alive in 1899, 1911, 1927, or arguably even now. The odd sense of disjunction that we experience, for example, when we realize that such a horror of the bygone frontier as the 1890 Wounded Knee massacre occurred after the French modernist poet Rimbaud had already given up poetry and when Proust was beginning to write school-boy Symbolism, can help ground our sense of the modern in its most

accurate historical context. By the end of the nineteenth century mountaineering narratives were recognized as chronicles of legitimate exploration, rather than simply of sport or science, records in their own very
different ways of the incompleteness of the modern world.

Mountaineering narratives are rhetorical conquests. They enter public
discourse in part by those terms. Nothing is new in my assertion here that
exploration is inherently a political act. The geographer John L. Allen
observes matter-of-factly in his 1972 essay, "An Analysis of the Exploration Process," that exploration has been and continues to be "an effective
instrument of national policy, with far-reaching commercial, political,
and military consequences" (13). Allen laments, however, that "unfortunately" most studies of exploration focus on "the inherent romance
and adventure, on tedious reconstructions and endless arguments about
routes taken, and on the historical and geographical results" (13). He goes
on to suggest that the solution is to examine the relationship between the
steadily enlarging, yet inherently always limited, subjective experience of
the explorer and what he calls "real" knowledge, that is to say, consensual
geographical knowledge. Yet shaping that body of consensual knowledge
are ideological constraints, among which during the modern period were
the complex network of public behaviors and private motivations that we
describe with the rubric "new imperialism." In terms of mountaineering
this means seeing the distant ridge line as a desacralized, politicized, and
commodified space, a high-altitude *terrae incognitae* that tells us two
things about the world — that it has limits and that those limits are up
for grabs.

If the postcolonial theorist Edward Said's advice is sound — that to understand the world we live in, we should seek out connections between culture and empire, geography and literature — certainly there are some intriguing points at which to begin noticing, for example, how modern
literature locates itself with respect to the politically charged practice of
exploration. Just as Shakespeare showed his awareness of the current state
of geographical understanding in such plays as *The Tempest* and *Two
Gentlemen of Verona*, both Poe and Dickens in the nineteenth century
made significant reference to polar exploration, and Poe to the journey of
Lewis and Clark. Similarly, Ruskin, Tennyson, and Trollope commented
on mountaineering. Ralph Waldo Emerson made passing mention of popular geographical theory, and John Muir wrote of his own Canadian Arc-

tic exploration and climbing on Herald Island. In his 1872 *Roughing It* Mark Twain described an outlandish serialized novel that ended in extravagant and unlikely Arctic adventure.

Modern literature also has made extensive reference to geography and exploration, frequently, however, questioning the validity and applicability of familiar and comforting geographical models of knowledge. Laura Riding, in her 1928 poem "The Map of Places," wrote disturbingly of geography:

Now on naked names feet stand,
No geographies in the hand,
And paper reads anciently,
And ships at sea
Turn round and round.
All is known, all is found.
Death meets itself everywhere.
Holes in maps look through to nowhere. (81)

The often-repeated metaphor of the few remaining "blank spaces" on the map becomes, in Riding's cartography, a kind of manuscript damage, a new development, a kind of erasure. As Riding suggests, modernist geography is frequently philosophically, linguistically, or politically problematized. In his 1902 *Heart of Darkness* Joseph Conrad dramatized the aftermath of exploration and conquest by displacing exploration to its consequences. In D. H. Lawrence's *Women in Love* the character Gerald finds one of the margins of Europe's geographical world, the Amazon, "less exciting" than Europe itself (208), but for Bernard Shaw's Captain Shotover in his 1919 *Heartbreak House,* being "frozen into Arctic ice in darkness" compares favorably to "the soul's prison we call England" (128, 156). In his *The Maximus Poems* Charles Olson draws Columbus's halting metaphors of geographical space into his description of American geography as a process of accumulating history within a specific landscape and experience. For Brendan Behan in *The Hostage,* exploration anticipates nuclear holocaust.

These are fascinating and telling texts, but because they are less concerned with narrating either actual or fictional exploration than they are in thematizing the idea of exploration, their bearing on the kinds of mountaineering narratives that I have been discussing is far from direct. Still, they suggest a useful observation, that we may learn something in looking at all literary texts of mountaineering, both canonical and marginal, and treating them in something of the same light. Do we ever find them suggesting similar historical and political contexts? Let's look.

By far the most remarkable text, in the sense of how it bridges the distinction between canonical modern literature and mountaineering narratives, must be W. H. Auden and Christopher Isherwood's 1937 play, *F6*, a political allegory based on international climbing. Longtime friends, Auden and Isherwood were no climbers, of course. Auden gained attention in 1931 for his book *Poems*, and by 1936 his work had moved ever to the Left, at times, in the view of some, virtually paraphrasing Lenin. Isherwood based his 1939 novel, *Goodbye to Berlin,* on his own experiences in Germany on the eve of World War II. His 1938 *Lions and Shadows* is a novel comparable in theme to Joyce's *Portrait of the Artist as a Young Man.* Auden and Isherwood collaborated on a series of travel pieces and plays, including *F6.* Just as the other texts take their primary meaning not as accounts of exploration but in how exploration can be understood conceptually and experienced aesthetically, as an obvious allegory *F6* would have been perceived by its contemporary audiences as rather transparently "about" the rise of international fascism, not mountaineering per se. The play nonetheless makes explicit the conjunction of mountaineering and imperial politics that I have been discussing. The two-act *F6* was the literary creature of the political anxiety, expectancy, and urgency imposed on Auden and Isherwood, as well as on the British Left in general, by the outbreak of the Spanish Civil War in 1936. Written, repeatedly revised, and first performed between 1936 and 1939, the various versions of *F6* elaborated a shifting emphasis that Edward Mendelson identifies as between "tragedy and farce, between psychology and politics" (xxvii). With the threat of fascism bearing its first horrific fruit in the siege of Madrid in 1936 and the air attack on Guernica in 1937, however, politics easily won.

The plot is a simple one for those with some knowledge of imperial history. The fictional mountain F6, located precisely on the frontier between the two colonies of British and "Ostnian" Sudoland, is the locus of imperial conflict. Act 1, scene 2, of the play opens in the rooms of Sir James Ransom at the Colonial Office. Stage directions indicate that a map of the Sudoland region includes the mountain F6 prominently "ringed with a red circle to emphasize its importance" (Auden and Isherwood, 299). The British colony is in revolt, and although the Sudolandese hate the British, the stakes are too high for the British to withdraw. As the practical Lord Stagmantle reveals, "The truth is that we've got fifty millions invested in the country and we don't intend to budge — not if we have to shoot every nigger from one end of the land to the other" (301). The solution, as Lord Ransom suggests, is to exploit native perceptions rather than yield to them. "The key to the problem," he emphasizes, pointing at F6, "lies there!" (301). Not only is the mountain a landmark of a hostile frontier claimed by both Britain and Ostnia, it remains unclimbed, that is to say, ideologically "unclaimed" by virtue of the persistent Western predicate of the "first" visit. Moreover, as Lord Ransom tells it, the Ostnians have recently been encouraging a volatile native superstition. "The white man who first reaches the summit," he explains, "will be lord over *both* the Sudolands, with his descendants, for a thousand years" (302). The thousand years of the newest Reich, no doubt. At any rate, when a telegram from British Intelligence announces that an Ostnian expedition led by the mysterious climber Blavek has left for Sudoland to attempt F6, Lord Ransom and his mother manage to convince his proverbial obsessive, black sheep brother, the renowned climber Michael Ransom, to mount a British expedition to race the Ostnians for the summit.

The name of Auden and Isherwood's mountain is itself sufficient to suggest the mediation of imperialist assumptions. Although the mountain has many local names, "most of them unpronounceable . . . the survey refers to it simply as F6" (301). The drama's central character, the mountaineer and megalomaniac Michael Ransom, a figure most likely modeled on T. E. Lawrence, views mountains through his passion for personal empowerment, in part that available through a successful climber's fame and prestige, in part from the kind of transcendental moral superiority that Ransom associates with climbing the famous mountain.[2] Yet he rejects the suggestion of the mountain's strategic imperial significance, along, in fact, with the notion that mountains have any *practical* significance at all. While loudly asserting his own innocent disinterest, Ransom proclaims a view of mountaineering reminiscent of Sir Leslie Stephen's notion of the Alps as the "playground of Europe." High over Wastdale in the Lake District, Ransom observes: "Here is no knowledge, no communication, no possession; nothing that a Bishop could justify, a stockbroker purchase or an elderly scientist devote years to explaining" (296).

The play makes clear that in 1937, Ransom's self-deception is not only mendacious but historically atavistic. The *A* in the character Mr. A. surely stands for *average* in the play's depiction of a desolate consumer-based London that draws heavily from Eliot's *The Waste Land*. And this average man laments the ubiquitous intrusion of world events that comes to him over the radio: "All you can hear is politics, politics everywhere: Talk in Westminster, talk in Geneva, talk in the lobbies and talk on the throne; talk about treaties, talk about honour, mad dogs quarrelling over a bone" (298). Not coincidentally, the modern news media is also the means by which Mr. and Mrs. A. follow Ransom's progress on F6. Although the newspapers often refer to Ransom's climb as a "daredevil attempt" (314), the machinations of the Colonial Office make it plain that "weighty political considerations" surround the mountain (310). In a sense that British audiences of the time would have found typical and representative of the fanatical German climbers they read about in the gazettes, Blavek's climbers are soldiers (330). Ransom comes to recognize that "the people in England expect us to get to the top before the Ostnians" (330). For their part, the people, the many Mr. and Mrs. A.'s of Britain, do in fact realize that "there's more than a mountain at stake" (332), so that Mr. and Mrs. A., fetching the newspaper at their front door, enjoin:

MR. A: England's honour is covered with rust.
MRS. A.: Ransom must beat them! He must! He must!
MR. A.: Or England falls. She has had her hour
And now must decline to a second-class power. (332)

The play represents the expedition's greatest influence not as in the colonies but as reverberating in the metropolis. On the mountain Ransom and his companions find a human skull, perhaps that of "some mad European who thought he'd have a shot at F6 on his own" (334), most likely a not-so-oblique reference to the much-publicized 1934 death of the eccentric Maurice Wilson while attempting a solo climb of Mount Everest. Like a high-altitude Prince Hamlet, Ransom reflects on the skull, imagining the mountains as a "Country of the Dead" (334) where dwell mountaineers ranging from Antoine de Ville to, more recently, Edward Whymper, George Mallory, and Andrew Irvine. The presence of the skull transforms the mountain to sacred and memorial English ground. The scene anticipates the worst fears of Mr. and Mrs. A. When Ransom too dies on F6, even Mr. A. eventually realizes that "he has died to satisfy our smug suburban pride" (337).

By the 1990s the last great gasps of imperialist mountaineering exploration seem to have been made in all their high-altitude rasping, at least as far as the West is concerned. Beginning with the first ascent of Mount Everest in 1953 and eventually the unsubstantiated (but increasingly accepted) claim that a Chinese expedition reached the summit in 1950, the nationalist symbolism attached to feats of mountaineering has declined in international significance.[3] It is revealing that by the 1980s, the political landscape of Auden and Isherwood's *F6* would be replaced by a more conventionally apolitical K2. Patrick Meyers's 1982 one-act play, *K2*, which for readers aware of Auden and Isherwood's earlier dramatic work is an inviting analogue and pole for comparison, is set on "a ledge, eight feet wide and four feet deep located on a six hundred foot ice wall at 27,000 feet on K2, the world's second highest mountain" (3) during the late 1970s.

K2 was first produced on Broadway by Mary K. Frank and Cynthia Wood and directed by Terry Schreiber at the Brooks Atkinson Theatre on March 30, 1983. The play was staged on a startlingly vertical set constructed to resemble a sheer ice wall, described by Meyers as "a fifty-five foot crystal masterpiece" (4). The elaborate Broadway stage required that the actors actually master fundamental mountaineering techniques of direct aid and rappeling in order to play their roles.

Instead of locating his imaginative depiction of mountaineering in a context of political events, as had Auden and Isherwood, Meyers made his drama a matter of strenuous, detailed, and clawing survival in which rehydration, frozen feet, and sunscreen factor into the formula for success. "COME ON . . . GOD DAMN YOU, COME ON! COME ON YOU BASTARD!" screams one of Meyers's climbing characters as he exhorts his companion to continue in their quest — not for imperial or symbolic conquest but for desperate individual survival (16). The play dramatizes how the friendship of the climbers is expressed under the stress of a dangerous and exposed climb. Mutual recriminations are punctuated by laconic assertions of affection and vague propositions about how Newtonian physics explains events on the mountain. Meyers's characters are finally individuals isolated on a mountain from the more mundane, low-altitude problems of the mortgages, love lives, and work that they left at home. The unusual set — an artificial climbing wall — used on Broadway worked at cross-purposes to its attempted verisimilitude, emphasizing the artificiality of the isolation of climbing, the transitory escape from the world below. "I mean this is my fucking hobby for Christsake," points out one of the climbers. "It's not my GOD DAMN LIFE!" (32). As things turn out, of course, he is both right and wrong. On the one hand, this 1980s literary depiction demotes mountaineering from its earlier, and relatively short-lived, status as serious exploration and returns it to the arena of sport and recreation that it inhabited under the aegis of Leslie Stephen's *The Playground of Europe* in the second half of the nineteenth century.

On the other hand, this playful recreation does turn out to be a matter of life and death. Meyers's description of his work as played out in "a frozen existential, no-man's land" is remarkably suggestive of the play's emphasis on the private isolated drama of individuals, rather than the broad pageant of geopolitical events suggested by Auden and Isherwood (5).[4] Instead of representing a return to the pure roots of climbing, happily once again untainted by political intrigue and economic scheming, *K2* is perhaps better understood as a very suggestive reflection of the public rhetoric and ideology that flourished during the 1980s. The two decades since its debut have certainly not closed the door on interpreting the decade that began with the hostage crisis in Teheran and the presidency of Ronald Reagan and closed with Irangate and the conviction of Oliver North. The broad themes shaping the decade have already been widely outlined — the impulse to privatize government functions, a reemphasis on the autonomy and license of already-privileged individuals, a free-wheeling sense of economic bonanza bankrolled at public expense, an international policy of bankrupting world communism, the rise to national identity of an alienated and drifting "Generation X." A Meyers character screaming "GOD DAMN YOU, COME ON! COME ON YOU BASTARD!" sounds remarkably like dialogue from *Bonfire of the Vanities* with a mountain view — junk bond traders on a vacation that money could buy them but not buy them out of.

I like to think that the story did not end in 1982 with Meyers's celebration of existential dilemmas on the rock. If *K2* suggests a late twentieth-century context for mountaineering that tends to ignore the climber's immersion in larger contexts while privileging the expensive and short-sighted spirit of individual license that flourished during the 1980s, what are climbing's contexts today, in a new century? Various, I think. Certainly, the reimmersion of mountaineering in an ideology of "pure" personal adventure persists, but the the full weight of the cultural times in which we live still hobbles the gracefulness of this individualistic dance on thin 5.11 handholds and oxygen-free ascents.

Let's agree for a moment with the assertion by Kenneth Boulding that I mentioned at the beginning of this epilogue and say that we have now become "modern," that our spatial world has closed, and that we live on a fully "explored surface." Let's say too that that state of geographical satiation has driven us beyond the modern to the postmodern. I know that *postmodern* is a dodgy and trendy term, "the most over and under-defined" term of all, as the literary critic Linda Hutcheon calls it (3). What does it mean? Taken in a positive sense, as in the work of the French theorist Jean-François Lyotard, postmodernism means cultural fragmentation, a profound skepticism of big answers, totalizing solutions, systems and structures that promote universal answers to the questions asked by a lot of different people. This vision of our alleged postmodern times celebrates that Western standards of culture may someday not be enforced on the entire world, that we don't have to convert and patronize "little brown brothers" at home or abroad, that we might sometime forget why we wanted to convert everybody to be like us. For climbers it could mean a lot of little guys out there roping up for their own reasons, that you don't have to be a member of the English gentry or the American nouveau riche to go on belay, that the days of the proletarian climber that began in the 1930s have triumphed, and that kids around the country can buy a good climbing rope for about the price of a pair of tennis shoes.

Another, less sanguine version of postmodernism, as espoused by Fredric Jameson, suggests that what passes for diversity is really a dangerous and disguised function of late capitalist consumerism and the worst impulses of the societies that nurture it. Jameson argues that focusing on difference diverts us from noticing the machinations of massive state bureaucracies and international corporations that, well behind the scenes of our much-publicized and -advertised individuality, still control our lives. For the climber this means that in our quest for personal meaning and achievement in the mountains, we forget that we buy the privilege of a two-week vacation in the mountains at the price of immersion in a system of risky wage and salary employment largely beyond our control. We purchase our climbing equipment and high-tech clothing in a market-driven, advertising-fueled environment that rejects the old and demands the latest. If we are "serious" climbers, we have to go professional and court corporate sponsorships to finance our expeditions. If we hold other jobs and can afford it, we give our credit card numbers to sign up for prepackaged guided ascents of peaks that only a decade ago we never could have hoped to make on our own. We train in indoor, artificially lighted, and heated rock gyms for a modest annual fee. Teenage sport climbers with 4 percent body fat climb steel-and-plywood towers on primetime television "X games." The French sociologist Jean Baudrillard writes that "everything is destined to reappear as simulation" (32).

Which version of our present mountaineering times is correct? Both, it seems to me. Such are the complex overlapping layers of meaning that characterize this time we spend in the hills.

Examining mountaineering in its historical context as well as in terms of its reception as literature adds a piece to the complicated and still very incompletely understood interaction of private motivations and public acts. As modern exploration writing in the early twentieth century moved through and apart from the idiom of the romantic sublime, the narrative depiction of mountaineering acquired a peculiar double meaning. Michael Ransom reminds his *F6* climbing companions how their exciting adventure originated in the Colonial Office:

> You've thought enough about the ascent of F6 no doubt; about the couloirs and the north buttress and the arete. . . . Have you thought about the descent, too: the descent that goes down and down into the place where Stagmantle and my Brother and all their gang are waiting? Have you thought about the crowds in the streets down there, and the loud-speakers and the posing and the photographing and the hack-written articles you'll be paid thousands to sign? Have you smelt the smell of their ceremonial banquets? (Auden and Isherwood, 329)

The play's thorough immersion in the politics of empire countermands Ransom's distinction between "ascent" and "descent," despite the almost Mosaic simplicity of its moral polarity. The attempt to preserve the purity of mountaineering in the face of sordid imperial intrigue, even on the way up, comes across as a doomed rearguard action, impossible to succeed. Why? Perhaps simply because, as Edward Said suggests, the imagined autonomy of literature beyond context and history is finally "uninteresting" ("Culture," n.p.). Modern mountaineering, as a kind of "text," subsumes rather than precludes its complex and multifaceted historical neighborhood. There is, finally, no cleansing ascent to political refuge, nor is there reason to believe in a disillusioning "down-going" (Nietzsche, 26), when the sanctified mountaineer reluctantly returns to the greed and moral corruption of the valley below. There is only vertical movement, and that movement is inevitably historical, contextual, and, in the modern period, a record of the same larger assumptions that underwrite European and American political and economic conquest in all its variety.

Today, in the newly inaugurated era of a global marketplace and an information age, the historical context in which mountaineering finds itself clearly differs from the nationalism of the new imperialism that oversaw the early decades of the twentieth century. "Adventure is the cheap cologne of the '90s," according to the travel writer Robert Young Pelton (quoted in Anderson, A10). That may be. But if we accept the premise that all human activities occur within, are shaped by, and respond to larger cultural and political currents, it may still be a mistake to forget that mountaineering is no more nor less pure sport than it has ever been.

Notes
Works Cited
Index

Notes

INTRODUCTION

1. In the preface to his *Challenge: An Anthology of the Literature of Mountaineering* (1950), William Robert Irwin remarks that "there is only a small body of poetry which derives from mountaineering itself" (vii). He describes most of this poetry of mountaineering as "intramural" (vii), a clear example that mountaineering literature can be contained by the prescriptions of larger aesthetics. Godley, John Addington Symonds, Michael Roberts, and Geoffrey Winthrop Young are perhaps the most remarkable of the climbing poets, as distinguished from poets like Wordsworth and Shelley, who were poets first and walkers through the Alps second. Irwin implies in *Challenge* that Godley may have fabricated the existence of this article by the dean (376).

2. For Longinus the sublime is a form of rhetorical "amplification." "The effect of elevated language upon an audience," he writes, "is not persuasion but transport" (65).

3. Paul H. Fry observes: "It has become a tradition to end discussions of the sublime with a bow to Wordsworth's great interruptive apostrophe to Imagination in *The Prelude*, Book 6" (205). So naturalized is our conception of mountains as spiritual signifiers that Fry's characterization of this moment in Wordsworth's poem as a kind of digression may even seem odd to some readers. Nicolson writes that "mountain climbers still read reminiscently the passage" (12).

4. "Voices of Madmen: Essays on Mountains and Mountaineering" by Mike Vause is an annotated collection of essays by well-known nineteenth- and twentieth-century mountaineers, including Leslie Stephen, A. F. Mummery, Maurice Herzog, and Doug Scott.

5. J. W. A. Hickson locates sport and philosophy as the foundation of mountaineering in a 1931 essay: "Those who are most attracted by the mountains and constantly return to them, are those who can enjoy the fun and frolic of a sport with the aesthetic delight which is produced by the marvelous forms of the great ranges" (260).

It is interesting that the mountaineer M. M. Strumia inverts the historical sequence in a 1929 essay: "Climbers were first explorers, then sportsmen, then artists; now they are becoming philosophers" (39).

6. From the 1840s Agassiz, Desor, and Forbes conducted foundational investigations in Alpine geology and especially in what would later come to be called glaciology.

7. Said made this point in "Culture and Imperialism," a lecture I heard at the University of Colorado at Boulder, on September 27, 1990. Said urged the West to become more aware of "how our maps overlap with others."

CHAPTER 1. WHERE THE MAP IS STILL BLANK

1. Additionally, while European emigration and settlement characterized the first great era of European imperial expansion from the age of discovery through the early nineteenth century, the second era, which I am designating the era of "new imperialism" (beginning after 1850), was generally less associated with emigration than it was with dominion over preexisting indigenous populations.

2. In addition to Mummery's reputation as a climber, the association of his name with mountaineering results from his invention, the Mummery tent, used so extensively in remote regions such as the Himalayas.

3. Conditioned to read for the sublime as we are, it may be tempting to see Markham's use of the word *delightful* as a lingering remnant of the Burkean rhetoric.

4. This is the Kirong Pass, crossed by an invading Tibetan army during the 1854–56 war with Nepal. Markham's comment here reflects the geopolitical and strategic context of British exploration in central Asia, a topic that I will discuss at length in chapter 5.

5. This figure does not include Maurice Wilson's 1934 fatal solo attempt on the mountain. Key does mention that Eric Shipton found Wilson's body during the 1935 reconnaissance expedition. Usually simply dismissed as an eccentric, Wilson had his own intriguing story to tell. His diary is today housed in the archives of the Alpine Club, London.

6. Conway also wrote an 1893 article for the *Geographical Journal*, "The Crossing of the Hispar Pass," and developed his account of his expedition into a book, the 1894 *Climbing and Exploration in the Karakoram-Himalayas, with Three Hundred Illustrations*. Conway's descriptions of the Karakorum were influential, leading to public speculation in Britain as to whether nearby Mount Everest could be climbed.

7. Trained as a mining engineer, Friedrich Wilhelm Heinrich Alexander von Humboldt is most noted, at least in the Americas, for his 1799–1804 scientific expedition to Central and South America accompanied by the French botanist Aimé Bonpland. Humboldt explored more than six thousand miles of territory and studied botany, meteorology, and geomagnetism. The scientific information that he collected filled thirty volumes.

8. If this sounds vaguely like a concerted attempt to deny the rhetoric of the sublime, it may be so. Jonathan Culler writes in *Structuralist Poetics:* "To write a poem or a novel is immediately to engage with a literary tradition or at the very least with a certain idea of the poem or the novel. The activity is made possible by

the existence of the genre, which the author can write against, certainly, whose conventions he may attempt to subvert, but which is none the less the context within which his activity takes place" (116).

9. R. J. Johnson wrote in his *The Future of Geography:* "As an academic discipline, [geography's] origins and early development reflected nineteenth century interest in the acquisition of information about the great variety of environments, peoples, and places on the Earth's surface, in part to serve the needs of mercantile adventurers, but much of it merely to satisfy the curiosity of the educated, affluent classes" (326).

10. On September 18, 1898, a French force commanded by Jean-Baptiste Marchand confronted a British force under Sir Herbert Kitchener in the Egyptian Sudan town of Fashoda. Both expeditions had been sent to gain control of the Sudan in attempts to consolidate colonial possessions in Africa.

11. For a very readable discussion of this see the first three chapters of Paul Fussell's *Abroad: British Literary Traveling between the Wars.*

12. Although this list is not exhaustive, among the historical works on the topic of exploration and collections of narrative produced by the modern period are M. Cary and E. H. Warmington, *The Ancient Explorers* (1929); Thomas Wright, *The Life of Sir Richard Burton* (1906); *The Cambridge History of the British Empire* (1929); *The Cambridge Modern History* (1902–10); C. Raymond Beazley, *The Dawn of Modern Geography* (1897–1906); Hugh Clifford, *Further India* (1904); D. G. Howarth, *The Life of Charles Montague Doughty* (1928); *Everyman's Classical Atlas* (1907); R. H. Kiernan, *The Unveiling of Arabia* (1937); Foster Rhea Dulles, *Eastward Ho* (1931); Kingsley James, *Vasco de Gama and His Successors, 1460–1580* (1910); George Bruner, *Richard Hakluyt and the English Voyages* (1928); Wilfrid Schoff, *The Periplus of Hanno* (1912); H. F. Tozer, *A History of Ancient Geography* (1897); Sir Percy Sykes, *A History of Exploration* (1934); Fridtjof Nansen, *In Northern Mists* (1911); Clements R. Markham, *The Lands of Silence* (1921); *The Literature of Discovery and Exploration Geography*, a reprint series that included A. P. Newton's *The Great Age of Discovery* (1932); Harry Johnston, *The Nile Quest* (1903); David George Hogarth, *The Penetration of Arabia* (1905); V. T. Harlow and James A. Williamson, *The Pioneer Histories* (1930s); Edgar Prestage, *The Portuguese Pioneers* (1933); Charles F. Rey, *The Romance of the Portuguese in Abyssinia* (1929); Robert Brown, *The Story of Africa and Its Explorers* (1893–95); and Arthur Percival Newton, *Travel and Travellers of the Middle Ages* (1926).

13. The *Geographic* has all along attracted advertisers. During the 1930s the biggest share of its ad space went to travel; the editors rejected ads for alcohol and cigarettes. Ishbel Ross quipped: "Dr. Grosvenor once said that he would take his readers around the world and that he would take them first class. He has done it and, most remarkable of all, he has done it without letting his fireside travelers have a drink, a smoke, or a bicarbonate of soda" (57).

14. These and other clippings are found in the Royal Geographical Society Library's Everest Archives, easily accessible by way of an excellent index.

15. The society began publishing the *Geographical Journal* in 1830. In 1855, when the journal began to include published discussions of the papers presented at meetings of the society, the name was changed to *Proceedings of the Royal Geo-*

graphical Society. It was published monthly until 1878. In that year Markham persuaded the society to update the *Proceedings*. Actually, he had come close to *blackmailing* the membership into doing so. Dissatisfied with the society's journal, Markham had taken over the editorship of a nearly defunct magazine called *Ocean Highways* in 1872 and converted it, in his words, "into a geographical magazine or journal on the plan that I considered should be adopted by the Society's publication" ("Royal Geographical Society," 205). *Ocean Highways* was not only a model to the society but a competitor. After six years the society relented, Markham folded *Ocean Highways*, and the society's *Proceedings* adopted many of Markham's changes. But it was not until 1893, when Markham assumed the presidency, that the society's journal came under the editorial leadership of J. Scott Keltie and fully met Markham's expectations.

16. In Markham's "Royal Geographical Society," a distinct category in his list of papers presented at the society's evening meetings is "Ascent of Mountains" (238). When Douglas Freshfield, who was also at the time president of the Alpine Club, took over as coeditor of *Hints* for the 1893 edition, he included his own essay, "Mountain Travel," a specific sign that mountaineering was beginning to be recognized as a form of exploration. Freshfield made plain that exploration in mountainous regions was contingent on what he called "the rudiments of the mountain craft" (Freshfield and Wharton, 35), skills that in Leslie Stephen's day would for the most part have been considered the specialized techniques of a sportsman. "Without these qualifications," Freshfield and Wharton wrote, "even surveyors will find themselves obliged to leave large and . . . singularly interesting tracts of country ill-mapped and imperfectly explored" (Freshfield and Wharton, 35).

17. The list of basic equipment that the explorer should take along included "sextant, horizon, pocket-sextant, Kater's compass, Ruchon's micrometer, and a sympiesometer; two pocket chronometers, two thermometers, two portable barometers, two aneroids, and two boiling thermometers" (*Hints*, 1854, 2). That edition of *Hints* also advised: "It would also be very desirable to carry a second sextant or circle, an additional horizon, and another prismatic compass, in case of accidents" (2).

18. Just a few of the items listed in Galton's inventory of Victorian writing and drawing materials were "a light board of the very best mahogany to rule and draw upon," "a sheet of blotting-paper cut up and put here and there in the ledgers," a "blank map ruled for latitude and longitude," "two dozen steel pens and holders," "two penknives," and "ink in abundance" (*Hints to Travellers*, 1854, 21).

19. Halford Mackinder, for example, depended greatly on the society in his preparations for Africa (see chapter 3), including picking the expedition's scientific members on RGS recommendation.

20. For further commentary on this see D. K. Fieldhouse's "The New Imperialism: The Hobson–Lenin Thesis Revised," in Nadel and Curtis's *Imperialism and Colonialism*. Fieldhouse's essay informs much of my understanding of theoretical descriptions of twentieth-century imperialism.

21. This refers to the deployment of American and allied forces in Saudi Arabia beginning in 1990 as a response to the Iraqi takeover of Kuwait.

22. See the Fieldhouse essay mentioned in note 20.

23. Lenin replaced Hobson's notion of a reformable "underconsumption" with a more deterministic explanation of how capitalism inevitably leads to imperialist behaviors.

24. The depressed agricultural conditions of the 1890s that gave rise to the populist movement and the demand for inflationary silver coinage also fostered deep interest in expanded foreign markets for U.S. farmers, who had become more productive than ever in the wake of rapid technological advancement and government support of agriculture after the Morrill Act of 1862.

25. After Patrick Porter, the superintendent of the U.S. census, declared the American frontier closed in 1890, the conviction grew that the expansion of domain and settlement that had characterized U.S. history from the beginning of the Republic was meant to continue beyond the continental bounds of the contiguous states. The United States would have to find a new Turnerian "safety valve" for its growing population, as well as markets for its booming agriculture and industry. Furthermore, the claims of social Darwinism, fashionable among many American intellectuals during the last twenty years of the nineteenth century, established what seemed to many Americans to be a scientific and nationalistic mandate for active international involvement in a contentious world arena in which only strong and aggressive nations survived. Idealists and religious writers encouraged Americans to follow Kipling's advice to "take up the white man's burden" and carry the benefits of what Roosevelt liked to call "Anglo-Saxon" culture and Christianity to the non-Western world. This rationale readily met the needs of nationalists committed to territorial and economic expansion. In 1900 Sen. Albert Beveridge, the Indiana Republican who was one of the most outspoken congressional advocates of U.S. expansion since Thomas Hart Benton, said, "We will not retreat . . . we will not repudiate our duty. We will not renounce our part in the mission of our race, trustee, under God, of the civilization of the world" (Beveridge, 704).

26. Military strategists contributed to the growing rhetoric of expansion. A close friend of both Roosevelt's and Lodge's, Rear Adm. Alfred Thayer Mahan, the most outspoken and important advocate of U.S. naval strength at the turn of the century, persistently stressed the need for overseas naval bases and coaling stations to protect U.S. commerce and establish a first-line defensive cordon around North America. In his *The Influence of Sea Power upon the French Revolution,* as well as in many popular articles and public lectures, Mahan argued for a kind of American mercantilism based on naval power.

27. Despite this broad enthusiasm for breaking with the tradition of U.S. isolation from foreign events, many Americans opposed a more active international role for the nation. Led by William Jennings Bryan, E. L. Godkin (editor of the *Nation*), Sen. George F. Hoar, Samuel Gompers, and even Andrew Carnegie, anti-imperialists actively brought their arguments to the forum of public debate from the 1890s to the entry of the United States in the European war in 1917. Anti-imperialists usually claimed that imposing U.S. institutions and values abroad violated the tradition of democratic self-determination that had shaped the independence and customs of the United States. They noted the probable expense of maintaining military presence abroad and warned that growing militarism could threaten democratic government at home.

Despite these serious and loudly voiced objections to a widening international involvement, when it was articulated as a political issue, U.S. expansionism was often so thoroughly and inextricably mixed with other, often conflicting issues, that many Americans never had an opportunity to make a clear-cut choice that did not violate at least some party, class, or vested interest. It would be a mistake to assume that most Americans supported expansionism without reservation, that the United States was a monolithic font of imperialist energy. It would also be simplistic to see U.S. exploration narrative as a straightforward, unambiguous expression of an ambient expansionist impulse. It would be correct, however, to assume that most informed Americans during the modern period recognized expansionism as part of a closely argued public controversy, the substance of congressional and barbershop debate, Chautauqua lectures, and *New York Journal* banner headlines.

28. Perhaps even more menacingly, the *Rivista* article went on to extend its suasive tack to the issue of territorial claims, arguing that two Italian ascents of the Matterhorn from the south and east faces "confirmed Italian rights over the half of the Matterhorn that is lit by the sun" (quoted in Irving, *Romance*, 73).

CHAPTER 2. HALFORD MACKINDER'S AFRICAN PIVOT

1. Sir Frederick Lugard was a major figure in Britain's colonial expansion from 1890 to 1914. While working for the Imperial British East Africa Company, his treaty making laid the groundwork for British political expansion in Uganda. He served as high commissioner for Northern Nigeria and assisted in the unification of Nigeria between 1912 and 1914. His best-known work is his 1922 *The Dual Mandate in British Tropical Africa,* and his Africa diaries make very interesting reading.

2. Mackinder's "A Journey to the Summit of Mount Kenya, British East Africa" appeared in the *Geographical Journal;* "The Ascent of Mount Kenya" ran in *Alpine Journal.* The differences in the titles reflect in a concise way the varying interests of the two organizations, the Royal Geographical Society and the Alpine Club.

3. A letter dated August 23, 1900, from Hausburg to Mackinder offered "any help you may need" in preparing the book, and a letter of July 26, 1904, from E. H. Saunders to Mackinder reminded him that "you kindly promised to send me a copy of the book you intended to publish, dealing with your memorable expedition to Mount Kenya." Both letters are found in the Mackinder Papers, Oxford School of Geography Library.

4. Blouet writes: "Whether or not the failure to publish was a result of a lack of commercial viability or a loss of interest by Mackinder has not, as yet, been ascertained" (*Sir Halford,* 12–13). Additionally, some circumstantial evidence is worth considering. In 1900 Mackinder became estranged from his wife, Bonnie. He also entered politics, standing as a "Liberal Imperialist" (known as a "Limp" in the political banter of the day) at Warwick while continuing to work on his *Britain and the British Seas.* He was, in short, distracted and busy. Having achieved the geographical ends of the expedition and having received, by way of reading his paper at the Royal Geographical Society and its publication in the RGS journal, any accompanying boost in credibility that the climb might have effected, Mackin-

der may have seen the publication of the book as simply superfluous. The only other recompense in publishing would have been monetary, and throughout his life Mackinder showed only an inconsistent interest in financial reward.

5. Lord Elgin, Churchill's superior at the Colonial Office, referred to the trip as an "official progress"(quoted in Brendon, 45).

6. Blouet, for example, makes the intriguing observation that Mackinder's hometown of Gainsborough, which was a developing inland port before a line of the Manchester, Sheffield, and Lincolnshire Railway reached the town in 1849, was thrown into a local depression during the 1850s when its importance as a port was undermined by the rail link to the Humber River port of Grimsby. Blouet acknowledges that no one knows whether this situation had an influence on the young Mackinder. But the capacity of railroads to change geographical and political relations was central to his conception of twentieth-century geopolitics, as described in his famous 1904 paper, "The Geographical Pivot of History." More immediately to the point of this discussion, however, is that when Mackinder planned his 1899 expedition to Mount Kenya, the advancing line of the Uganda Railway made the trip possible in his mind. When he wrote in his journals in Africa and later began to shape them into a narrative, the passage by rail enables the narrative, giving it its clearest sense of linear movement, and controls the narrative's thematic implication in the context of British imperial involvement in East Africa. Regardless of how Lincolnshire railroads might have influenced the growing Mackinder, Blouet's railroad story provides an attractively coincidental way to introduce one of the most complex and theoretically oriented figures in the history of writing about mountaineering exploration.

7. By "new geography" Mackinder essentially meant an amalgamation of physical and historical geography that moved beyond the mere description of terrain to understand the relationship between place and human cultural practice. Mackinder thought of this new geography as more than simply an interdisciplinary combination but as a philosophical basis for twentieth-century life.

8. The assumption of spatial closure in Mackinder's address has frequently been compared to its contemporary appearance in the thinking of the American historian Frederick Jackson Turner, whose 1893 essay, "The Significance of the Frontier in American History," works from the premise of the announced closing of the American frontier in 1890.

9. A 1892 article in *Public Ledger* records a later, broader definition. In a lecture at the Drexel Institute that year Mackinder called geography "a definite and graphic science, the object of which was to study space relations on the earth's surface, together with their cause and effect" (quoted in Blouet, *Halford Mackinder,* 49).

10. Mackinder described this incident by saying, "An arrow fell at my feet when we were traversing a thicket" ("Journey," 458).

11. While in Europe in 1897, for example, Mackinder met with Joseph Partsch, Ferdinand von Richthofen, and Elisee Reclus, all prominent geographers of the day.

12. Nonetheless, it would be a mistake to assume that Mackinder was an armchair (or professor's chair) geographer, lacking completely in the kind of technical training and practical knowledge necessary to carry out an exploration in

remote country. The success of the 1899 expedition clearly demonstrated that this was not the case. In fact, Mackinder's training in the biological sciences, geography, and geology provided exactly the background that he needed to lead the kind of technical and scientific expeditions increasingly encouraged by the geographical societies of the day. Mackinder's involvement at Oxford with the Rifle Volunteers gave him some experience that he could put toward the essentially paramilitary role demanded of an expedition commander.

13. Mackinder's marriage remains difficult to factor into his life and work. Mackinder had married Emilie Catherine (Bonnie) Ginsburg, the daughter of the Surrey clergyman and Old Testament scholar the Reverend David Ginsburg, in 1889. As Brian Blouet writes, "The Mackinder marriage was not a lasting success" (*Halford Mackinder*, 74), but it is almost impossible to say now precisely why. The Mackinders' only child died eleven hours after birth in 1891. Although Bonnie, never completely satisfied with the life of an academic wife in Oxford, moved back to live with her family in Surrey, she did not break completely with Mackinder. She assisted in his campaign for Parliament in 1900 and helped organize the materials from the Kenya expedition. By 1901, however, her health, never strong since their marriage, was deteriorating. In a 1901 letter to John Scott Keltie, secretary of the Royal Geographical Society, Mackinder referred to his wife's "dangerous illness," a condition that Blouet takes to be stress related. Late in 1900 Mackinder and Bonnie had separated permanently. They seem to have reconciled in 1937.

14. Contributing to the turbulence of these years within the society was what Clements Markham called "the females' row" of 1892–93, an extended controversy about the admission of women as members of the RGS. The personal animosity that grew out of this debate resulted in the resignation of a number of members, including Douglas Freshfield, the influential advocate of geographical education. The education faction within the society was significantly reduced in favor of those who promoted the society's role in encouraging and supporting exploration.

15. This is the famous "slug map" that showed a freshwater lake, "Lac d' Uniamesi," a weird gastropod-shaped body of water about eight hundred miles long and three hundred miles wide and so conspicuous that one might wonder how anyone had avoided it for so long. In reality, of course the "Sea of Ujiji" turned out to be a system of lakes rather than a single body of water.

16. Stanley had been sent into the region to locate and rescue Emin Pasha, the British governor general of the southern Sudan who had disappeared somewhere in East Africa after Khartoum and Gen. Charles George "Chinese" Gordon fell to Sudanese rebels under the mystic Mahdi in 1885. Stanley found Emin Pasha near Lake Albert after a six-thousand-mile journey. Emin Pasha was quite well and rather reluctant to be rescued from the heart of the African wilderness.

17. A good overview of the history of European exploration in East Africa appears in J. N. L. Baker's *A History of Geographical Discovery and Exploration*. See also Percy Sykes's *A History of Exploration* and Eric Newby's *Rand McNally World Atlas of Exploration*. I use all these texts as background to this discussion.

18. After nearly dying of thirst, Krapf was understandably preoccupied with his arrival at the river Dana. Certainly, the demands of what he called his "animal wants" for water must have influenced his immediate focus on rivers instead of

mountains. He wrote: "Important result might be attained if Europeans would explore this river more fully, and discover whether it is navigable, and if so, to what distance. In the Mberre-land on the other side of the river, I saw a lofty mountain which I named Mount Albert" (325). Yet behind this remark is the traditional association, engendered by Ptolemy, between the Nile and its legendary mountain source. What appears to be an abrupt transition may in fact serve to signify that association.

19. Mackinder is referring to the 1896 bombardment of Zanzibar by ships of the Royal Navy. When Seyyid Hamed bin Thwain, the sultan of Zanzibar, died on August 25, 1896, Seyyid Khaled bin Barghash, who was not particularly amenable to the British protectorate over Zanzibar, proclaimed himself sultan and barricaded himself with several hundred followers in the royal palace. On the morning of August 27 three British warships under the command of Rear Adm. H. H. Rawson reduced the palace to ruins, killing as many as five hundred of its occupants. When the old wooden corvette *Glasgow*, manned by native sailors, returned the British fire, Rawson sank it in the harbor. Its masts continued to protrude from the water when Mackinder visited three years later.

20. The following works provide an excellent background to the broad imperial context of Mackinder's expedition and inform my discussion: John S. Galbraith, *Mackinnon and East Africa, 1878–95;* John Hatch, *The History of Britain in Africa;* Vincent Harlow, E. M. Chilver, and Alison Smith, *History of East Africa;* Kenneth Ingham, *A History of East Africa;* and George Padmore, *Africa: Britain's Third Empire.*

21. In *Economics and Empire* D. K. Fieldhouse suggests that Lord Salisbury, then the foreign secretary, purposely obstructed the negotiations in 1877 because he felt that granting a concession would involve the British government in administration of the East African mainland.

22. The Deutsche-Ostafrikanische Gesellschaft transferred its claim to a territorial sphere to the Bismarck government in 1890. When Mackinnon's Imperial British East Africa Company faced bankruptcy in 1893 after spending about £450,000 to open East Africa to trade, and after failing to convince the British government of the importance of constructing a rail link between Mombasa on the coast and Uganda, it too gave the government its charter in the interior and in 1895 its territory closer to the coast. Salisbury was right.

With German and British political administration extended to East Africa, more formal partition became inevitable. The two governments divided their spheres of commercial interest in two Anglo-German agreements in 1886 and, because of persistent German trade activity north of the line, again in 1890. Additionally, British territory in East Africa was itself divided between two administrations. When the British protectorate of Uganda was established in 1894, it encompassed the lake region at the headwaters of the White Nile, about five hundred miles inland across the difficult Masai country. So when the British East Africa Company surrendered its influence closer to the coast in 1895, a separate government administration was established there as the British East Africa Protectorate. The boundaries of these two protectorates roughly correspond to those of today's Uganda and Kenya.

In their internal politics the two protectorates developed differences that would become important. Under Frederick Lugard and his successors the British government in Uganda, rather than imposing direct authority, aligned itself with a powerful group of Christian tribal chieftains who dominated the area around the missions in Buganda. British officials followed this pattern throughout the protectorate, governing indirectly by using native governments and leadership hierarchies already in place. In British East Africa, however, this strategy was ineffective. Indigenous cultural differences there left the British without a preexisting native political structure on which to build. The British in this protectorate instead imposed their rule directly or through directly appointed native headmen who often lacked a traditional basis for authority.

23. In *Economics and Empire* Fieldhouse points out that Peters's commercial venture was financed largely by enthusiasts of patriotic, rather than economic, colonialism and that Bismarck established a protectorate in East Africa in 1884 (along with protectorates in Togo, the Cameroons, and Koba Bagas) as evidence of the abstract political principle that German entrepreneurs acting abroad would receive government support, a position undertaken in part to gain the election support of procolonization National Liberals.

24. Lord Salisbury, whose Conservative government during much of the period controlled British colonial expansion, noted that subscribers to the Imperial British East Africa Company were often motivated by philanthropic motives.

25. In *Buganda in Modern History* D. A. Low makes a comparable observation about the events immediately leading up to the Anglo-German agreement of 1890, the dispatching in 1889 of German forces under Carl Peters and British forces under Frederick Jackson to Uganda. Low writes: "By 1890 the scramble for the area of the Great Lakes was leading to a crisis [when Peters and Jackson raced each other for Uganda] that might have created a 'Fashoda' incident eight years before Fashoda" (55).

26. Perhaps the most interesting of these many remarks come on August 15 as the expedition moves through Wangombe's territory. Mackinder compares East Africa's elephants, rhinos, and hippos to English fauna of another age: "The forest, with its familiar plants, took one back to prehistoric England, when the mammoth broke through our thickets" ("Mount Kenya," 322).

27. Perhaps the best single source of information concerning the Uganda Railway is Charles Miller's 1971 *The Lunatic Express,* an engaging and informative history of the early years of the line. Miller subtitles his book *An Entertainment in Imperialism.*

28. A contemporary *Punch* cartoon captioned "John Bull reluctantly accepts Uganda" shows a black infant in a basket left on the doorstep of the waistcoated gentleman (reproduced in Marsh, 122).

29. See chap. 10, "The Partition of Sub-Saharan Africa," in Fieldhouse's *Economics and Empire,* and Mary E. Townsend's "Commercial and Colonial Policies of Imperial Germany" in Nadal and Curtis's *Imperialism and Colonialism.*

30. The Boer War was precisely the kind of military adventure that Mackinder saw as the special province of a maritime power. That it fell dramatically short of being a thoroughgoing success underscored the limitations of British naval power. Furthermore, military recruitment for the war had initiated widespread concern in Britain about the low level of physical fitness of the nation's working, and fighting,

class. This suggested to many that domestic poverty and malnutrition put the nation at risk as much as did an external threat.

31. I discuss the Uganda mutiny in more detail in note 34.

32. Ambler points out that the amount of grain supplied to the Uganda caravans by the trading station of Dagoretti, for example, was 5,000 pounds in 1894 but increased to 33,000 in 1896. In 1897 the protectorate government bought 112,000 pounds of food in a sixteen-day period alone (110).

33. Rachel S. Watt, in her 1920 edition of *In the Heart of Savagedom*, wrote of her experience on the Uganda Railway: "No matter where we went corpses strewed the tracks. Little skeleton babies were found crying by the dead bodies of their mothers" (309).

34. Because it struck in the strategic heart of British East Africa, Uganda, the civil war that began in Buganda in 1897 represented a particular threat to British control of the region. Since the beginning of British influence in Uganda, first the Imperial British East Africa Company and later the protectorate government had ruled through native government. In July 1897, as Mwanga the Kabaka (or ruler) of Buganda revolted against British authority, Trevor Ternan, the British acting commissioner of Uganda, proclaimed that the infant son of Mwanga was the new native ruler, and the child's regents directed military operations against his father. Part of the force that might have been used against Mwanga was a body of Sudanese troops that had been one of the mainstays of British military muscle in the lake region since the days of the company. In 1897, with their pay of cloth bolts several months behind, they were ordered to march under Maj. J. R. L. Macdonald to investigate the rumor of a French advance toward the Nile. Ordered to leave behind their customary retinue of camp followers, three companies of the Sudanese mutinied. After killing three British officers and leading protectorate forces through a series of skirmishes, they dispersed to the north in 1901. In 1899 Uganda was in turmoil.

35. See Robert L. Tignor, *The Colonial Transformation of Kenya*, chap. 2, for an expanded discussion of the British military pacification of the Kenyan highlands and its effect on native populations.

CHAPTER 3. ANNIE SMITH PECK AND THE ECONOMIC APEX

1. The unnamed author of this biographical sketch is most likely Emerson Hough, best known today perhaps to readers of western American regional literature. Hough's first novel, *The Story of a Cowboy* (1897), drew praise from Theodore Roosevelt and was followed by *Heart's Desire* in 1905 and *The Covered Wagon* in 1922.

2. In all fairness, I should note that Pilley was no rank amateur when it comes to mountaineering. She made a point in *Climbing Days* (1935) to distinguish herself from what she called "tourists, those parasites of Alpinism" (126). She traveled the world, climbing in the Rockies and Selkirks of Canada, trekking in the Himalayas, and contemplating a "spur" of Kanchenjunga in 1927. As interesting a place in the literature of mountaineering as her various commentaries occupy, however, she was primarily a traveler rather than an explorer of new terrain, a

climber concerned with the *sport* of climbing rather than its geographical implications. As such she comes into this discussion only marginally. Her husband's rejection in his literary criticism of aesthetic experience as a clear descriptive and communicative strategy may go a long way to explain why he does not occupy a comparable place in mountaineering literature, although he did collaborate with Pilley for the *Alpine Journal*.

3. Patricia Penn makes this assertion about Peck's competition with her brothers in her sketch of Peck in *American Women Writers*, 364.

4. The author of the *Outing* article ("Men and Women") reports that she slept on the summit of Shasta in 1888, which would have repeated the 1875 feat of John Muir, who records in his "A Perilous Night on Shasta's Summit" how he survived a blizzard by lying in the hot mud on the rim of the mountain's volcanic crater in a "frozen-and-broiled condition" until dawn (84).

5. She makes clear the relationship of epidemics and low elevation during her account of her 1903 expedition. After coming down from Illampu only to find that the countryside is beset with plague, she tells her easily discouraged companion, the professor: "Now, you see, you might have stayed at the mountain just as well as not" (*Search*, 55), distinguishing as she does so the mountain as a safe zone apart from the ravages of disease.

6. Outside the pages of *Search*, one of Peck's most direct and persistent opponents was Fanny Bullock Workman, who energetically disputed Peck's (actually rather optimistic) estimate of the twenty-four-thousand-foot height of Huascarán and maintained that Aconcagua, not Huascarán, was the highest peak in South America. After Peck's ascent of Huascarán, Workman had sponsored engineers in their triangulation of Huascarán, and in a 1910 *Scientific American* article Peck responded to Workman, asserting that "there is, however, something to be said in regard to the accuracy of such triangulation," and citing scientific authorities in support of her argument that altitude measurement should not simplistically be regarded as absolute. "No one need feel obliged to accept those figures as final," she concludes (183). Although Workman may have been closer to the truth than Peck, changes in measurement techniques effected in the late 1980s have endorsed Peck's skepticism, which highlights the nature of scientific quantification, which is at best provisional. With this exchange, Peck and Workman engage in the persistent debate between objective measurement and subjective perception that characterizes so much of modern exploration literature.

7. I can locate no published account of an attempt on Grossglockner before 1903.

8. Underhill described how as early as 1927 she had led a number of fairly moderate climbs while climbing with an Italian guide but doing so under a certain constraint. "With Angelo I could lead all I liked, just so long as we were out of sight of his father" (150). When she rejoined her husband, she generously allowed: "For nineteen years, my constant companion on every climb was Robert Underhill. Manless climbing is fun for a while, but this other arrangement is better!" (169), a comment Peck certainly would not have made.

9. In making this distinction between long multiday climbs and shorter alpine ascents, Allen Carpe in 1924 characterized Canada's Mount Logan, clearly the

former, as "*Big Country*" (135). Carpe was an active participant in the first ascent of Logan, one of the longest and most remote climbs in the world, certainly in North America. He died a few years later on the so-called Cosmic Ray Expedition to Mount McKinley, an attempt to set up an electromagnetic wave measurement station high on the mountain.

10. Peck is hardly the only mountaineer interested in business, but she is, as far as I am aware, the one who most overtly encourages commercial ventures. For a contrast see Samuel Turner's *My Climbing Adventures on Four Continents* (1911). Turner traveled to Siberia and New Zealand on business — he wrote that he had to fit his climbing into his business schedule — but he nowhere elaborated the nature of this business and had nothing to say on the subject of commercial opportunity.

11. *Industrial and Commercial South America* falls within what geographers call (now often disparagingly) the "statist tradition" within geography, a rubric that signifies methodologies that emphasize areal differentiation (differentiation by area) and description of the unique characteristics of countries and regions.

12. Verner's thesis was in turn suggestive of the widely circulated and influential arguments advanced by the Englishman Benjamin Kidd in his 1898 book, *The Control of the Tropics.* Kidd maintained that in the 1890s European colonial rivalry no longer concerned itself with places suitable for European habitation. The tropics, in Kidd's view, had only limited value for the kind of permanent relocation that had been important in the colonial development of, say, North America. A European in the tropics, according to Kidd, tended to degenerate physically and "sink slowly to the level" of the "races amongst whom he has made his unnatural home." Consequently, Kidd saw European rivalry in the tropics as fundamentally an economic competition for reciprocal trade. See pages 50–54.

13. Tuan makes this point in his *Landscapes of Fear,* 98.

14. This is Penn's characterization of the reception of the book.

15. In his *U.S. Expansionism* David Healy makes a similar point about this same advertisement. He maintains that the ad demonstrates that the "popular faith that western values were the soundest, and must prevail" became "one of those ultimate sanctions which are used as advertising appeals" (141).

16. Peck does not openly preach cultural or racial chauvinism, but it would not be accurate to say that Peck's stated desire for a "bond of sympathy and union" (xi) between North and South Americans translates into a perfectly egalitarian or relativist view of the two cultures. A number of her parenthetic remarks suggest that at least to some extent she takes aboard the ethnic clichés of her era regarding the Latin south. When one of her Indian porters allows his loaded pack to slide down a snowfield, Peck observes, "Why Ramos did not at once run forward and stop it I cannot see, except for the old reason that they never hurry" (256).

17. John Gallagher and Ronald Robinson point out that this phenomenon also was present in the far more extensive British Empire. By 1913 less than half of the £3.975 billion of British foreign investment remained inside the empire. See their essay in Nadel and Curtis's *Imperialism and Colonialism.*

18. Consider the distance, for example, between her 1901 *Outing* article, "Practical Mountain Climbing," which announced in no uncertain terms an unconventional position on women's dress and behavior, and her 1913 "The South

American Tour" in the *Independent*, in which Peck's feminist politics were almost completely subordinated by the boosterism of her own travel narrative and the arguably patronizing tone of her editor's introduction.

19. See Agnes Murphy, *The Ideology of French Imperialism, 1871–81* (1948). Murphy maintained that Conant's theory borrowed heavily from the work of Paul Leroy-Beaulieu, who was writing as early as 1874.

20. Conant's most important involvement with Asian affairs came in 1901 when Root sent him to Manila to report on economic conditions and make proposals for currency reform. When a new system of coinage recommended by Conant came into use in the Philippines, the new pesos became widely known as "conants," and Conant's portrait eventually appeared on the one peso note (Healy, 207–8).

21. The War of the Pacific was fought over guano. Chilean and British investment in Bolivia's coastal nitrate production prompted the Chilean government to extend its territorial claims and finally push Bolivia and Peru into war in 1879. The victory of Chile resulted in the invasion of Peru and the subsequent annexation of Bolivia's coastal territory.

22. A standard source of information on the history of Bolivia in the nineteenth and twentieth centuries is H. S. Klein's *Parties and Political Change in Bolivia, 1880–1952* (1969).

23. A good overview of Peruvian history is F. B. Pike's *The Modern History of Peru* (1967). A more complete account is Jorge Basadre's seven-volume *Historia de la república del Perú* (1963–64).

24. Peck may have whitewashed Meiggs's career in Peru. While her references to Meiggs are either complimentary or neutral, in fact fraud and corruption characterized much of his work.

25. Peck's mingling of mountaineering exploration and trade promotion is perhaps the most outstanding extant example of this particular conjunction of concerns, but it is not the only example. Although among "types" of exploration, mountaineering figures as less directly linked with economic adventure, mountaineering narratives have a certain minor tradition of mentioning climbing and business in the same breath. A. D. Godley claimed in a 1915 *Alpine Journal* piece that "any business men, then can understand the instinct that prompts to pass-crossing" (Irving, *Mountain Way*, 74). Samuel Turner, in his *My Climbing Adventures in Four Continents*, repeatedly described how his exploratory activities were outgrowths of his business ventures abroad, specifically in Siberia and New Zealand: "I have had to snatch my holidays at the time most convenient to my business" (17).

26. Grace Dodge formed the first "Working Girls Club" in New York City in 1884.

27. See Eleanor Flexner's interesting overview of these organizations in her *Century of Struggle*. Flexner also provides a useful bibliography.

28. Interestingly, Peck did not take aboard the Prohibition argument of many elements within the women's movement. As a matter of fact, Prohibition had its own currency in mountaineering circles. Partly because of nineteenth-century attitudes about alcohol but also partly because of the ambiguous status that mountaineering has maintained as simultaneously a gentlemen's leisure pastime and an

activity with sometimes geopolitical, sometimes spiritual, but always risk-filled significance, a lively debate prevailed concerning strong drink on the crags. In her 1901 *Outing* article Peck observed: "At the International Congress of Alpinism last summer a resolution was passed deprecating the use of alcohol, especially absinthe, in mountaineering, but I fancy it was not designed to condemn the use of wine" ("Practical," 700). In *Search,* as a matter of fact, Peck may have gone well beyond the occasional medicinal use of wine. Advised by a friend to take advantage of the stimulating effects of coca leaves, Peck writes that she "laid in a good supply" (34). She seems to have aligned herself in this regard less with John Muir, Samuel Turner, or George Leigh-Mallory, all of whom spoke against alcohol in the mountains, and more with, say, Geoffrey Winthrop Young, who wrote enthusiastically in *On High Hills* of the benefits of "smoking indulgently" and recuperating after a day of hard climbing with an "unjettisoned residue of . . . butter and alcohol" (quoted in Irving, *Mountain Way,* 493).

CHAPTER 4. JOHN BAPTIST NOEL, A SUMMIT PHOTOGRAPH

1. Sella's photographs appear in books by the duke (Luigi Amedeo di Savoia), *The Ascent of Mount St. Elias* (1900), *Ruwenzori: An Account of the Expedition of . . .* (1908), and *The Karakoram and Western Himalaya* (1912). Also see Sella's own 1900 *Among the Alps: A Narrative of Personal Experiences.* Although other mountain photographers had done earlier work — Ernest Edwards's photographs, for example, illustrated H. B. George's *Oberland and Its Glaciers* as early as 1866 — Sella is clearly the most important figure in early mountain photography. During his career photography came to replace steel and wood engravings and chromolithographs as illustrations in books about mountains and mountaineering. Sella is to photography in the mountains as Herbert Ponting is to photography in the polar regions.

2. An engaging account of the controversy surrounding Cook's probable photographic license appears in David Roberts, *Great Exploration Hoaxes.*

3. The photograph is reproduced in Ian Cameron's *To the Farthest Ends of the Earth,* 174.

4. A more thorough discussion of the political climate of central Asia follows later in this chapter. One of the most useful overviews of the mountaineering history of Mount Everest is Walt Unsworth's *Everest: A Mountaineering History,* a source to which I am very much indebted. In addition, the Special Collections Department of the University of Colorado's Norlin Library houses many important texts dealing with Mount Everest. The Alpine Club Archives and the Everest Archives of the Royal Geographical Society, both located in London, are the foundational sources of material for those of us studying the literature generated by the mountain.

5. Wheeler discovered the route up the East Rongbuk Glacier that would prove to be the access route to the Northeast Ridge followed by the 1922 and 1924 expeditions. An experienced mountaineer himself, Wheeler reached twenty-two thousand feet on Mount Everest in 1921.

6. Unsworth makes this point, p. 74.

7. Unsworth reports that Noel had been the committee's first choice for the 1921 expedition. Because he could not obtain leave from his army post, however, he was unable to participate.

8. Noel had repeatedly seen Herbert Ponting's film presentations of Scott's last expedition to Antarctica at the Philharmonic Hall. He explained the public's reception of *Climbing Mount Everest* to Brownlow like this: "I told the Geographical Society that we should do the same as Ponting. . . . We rented the hall for ten weeks. We had a very fine operator, and we installed two Ross projectors. We had a big lunch at Frascati's Restaurant for the newspapers, and we gave them a private showing. We opened up — and lost £400 the first week. The Geographical Society got very frightened about this. I said, 'Don't bother. The press reports are marvelous, you just wait till people read them. Then they'll come.' We made a small profit the next week. Every week showed an increased profit and on the last of the ten weeks there was a board up outside the hall: 'No Seats.' We couldn't have continued because the hall was booked by somebody else. But it had a smashing run with over £10,000 taken at the door" (Brownlow, 458).

9. Mallory's note to Noel reads:

Dear Noel,
We'll probably start early tomorrow (8th) in order to have clear weather. It won't be too early to start looking for us either crossing the rock band or going up skyline at 8:00 a.m.
Yours ever,
G. Mallory

Noel reproduces the note in *Through Tibet* (plate facing p. 214). This brief text — Noel writes that he "kept that little crumpled note ever since" (213) — serves as a kind of informal litmus test for a reader's interest in mountaineering literature, I think. The context of this note, its laconic, matter-of-fact content, the intent of its conventionalized elements when taken seriously, makes it for me, an admitted fan of mountaineering literature, a powerful and affecting text.

10. An American edition of the book was published the same year by Blue Ribbon Books of New York under the title *The Story of Everest*. The American edition is substantially the same; the major difference is that it is not so extensively illustrated with Noel's photographs as is the British edition. While the illustrations in *Through Tibet* are fairly evenly split between photographs of Tibet and Tibetans and photographs of mountaineering, all the photographs in *The Story of Everest* depict climbing scenes on the mountain. *The Story of Everest* does, however, include two interesting photographs that *Through Tibet* does not: a photograph of Noel operating his motion picture camera from his Eagle's Nest Point, the highest point from which he filmed, and a still from Noel's film showing the crossed blankets being laid out on snow as a distant signal of Mallory and Irvine's deaths. The latter is one of the most strangely moving mountain photographs I have seen.

11. I will discuss this event in more detail later in the chapter.

12. The pope was himself a former mountaineer and had followed the expedition closely. He wrote these lines on the occasion of the anniversary of the birth of St. Bernard.

13. He is writing about a Tibetan funeral ritual. As he describes it, the ceremony consists of dismembering and even virtually decomposing the corpse to reduce it to pieces small enough to be completely eaten by birds.

14. Dr. Alexander Mitchell Kellas was of the generation of influential climbers and explorers, along with Freshfield, Bruce, and Younghusband, who were too old, or on the verge of being too old, for high-altitude climbing when the British expeditions of the 1920s set out. Nevertheless, Kellas was one of the handful of Himalayan climbers who expressed a serious interest in climbing Mount Everest even before World War I. A lecturer in chemistry at Middlesex Hospital, Kellas was chosen to conduct physiological testing on members of the 1921 reconnaissance expedition. He died of heart failure on the approach.

15. This photograph is reproduced in the American edition of the text, *The Story of Everest,* although it does not appear in *Through Tibet.* The caption refers to it as "the highest photograph ever yet taken on a mountain" (plate facing p. 92).

16. Consider, for example, one way in which Noel conducts the now-familiar comparison of mountaineering and polar exploration. In his "Appendix B: Science Versus Nature" at the end of *Through Tibet,* as he surveys the application of technology to mountain climbing, he notes: "Amundsen trekked over the snow to the South Pole with dogs and sledges. Now he flies over the North Pole Continent in an airship with speed, comfort and safety" (283). The reference, of course, is to Roald Amundsen's 1926 flight (with Lincoln Ellsworth and Umberto Nobile) in the dirigible *Norge* over the North Pole from Spitsbergen, Norway, to Alaska. All the "speed, comfort and safety" would dramatically come to an end in 1928 when Amundsen's airplane crashed while he was searching for Nobile, whose dirigible *Italia* had also disappeared.

17. A more detailed discussion of the documentary film movement in Britain appears later in the chapter.

18. Varick Frissell's film *The Viking,* like Noel's Everest films, is a provocative mix of film artifice and historical exploration. During the making of this film on Arctic exploration, the ship commissioned by Frissell to represent a Newfoundland sealer exploded, killing twenty-seven men and all but one of the film crew. The man picked to captain the *Viking* was Bob Bartlett, who had commanded the *Roosevelt* for Robert Peary in 1909; the ensuing rescue mission was carried out with the help of Bernt Balchen, who flew over the South Pole with Richard Byrd. The horrific events of the film expedition were used in the ad for the film's Hollywood premiere: "Twenty-seven men died to open Hughes-Franklin's new Studio Theater" (quoted in Brownlow, 542).

19. See Brownlow's discussion of official World War I photography.

20. Ella and Percy Sykes make this observation in their *Through Deserts and Oases of Central Asia.* Percy Sykes was a veteran of extensive exploration in central Asia between 1893 and 1910 and served as a military surveyor between Baghdad, the Caspian Sea, and the Hindu Kush during World War I. He published a number of historical works, including *A History of Persia* and *A History of Exploration.* The latter work, appearing in 1934, is representative of the many publications reflecting the growing public interest in exploration during the modern period. The historical overview of Turkistan given by the Sykeses in their

Through Deserts and Oases of Central Asia informs my discussion of the political climate of the region.

21. Percy Sykes makes this observation in his *History of Exploration.*

22. One of the most interesting episodes in the complex political history of Turkistan developed in the 1860s when an opportunistic adventurer named Yakub Beg used a revolt in Kashgar against the Chinese as an occasion to carve an independent state out of the disputed territory. Courted by both the Russians and British and sometimes playing the two European powers against each other, Yakub Beg maintained a precarious presence in the area for twelve years.

23. The Himalayan explorer and historian Kenneth Mason makes this point, quoted in Cameron, 164.

24. See Brownlow's account of Noel. Brownlow reports that on this trip Noel brought a Debrie motion picture camera and made a film about the caviar industry. I have not been able to find any record of this film.

25. During a protest of the arrests of two leaders of Congress, British troops fired without warning on ten thousand unarmed men, women, and children. The troops were under the command of Gen. R. E. H. Dyer in the Punjab city of Amritsar. Dyer reportedly kept his men firing into the crowd for ten minutes and expended more than sixteen hundred rounds of ammunition in killing approximately four hundred and wounding approximately twelve hundred civilians.

26. A *Punch* cartoon from November 25, 1903, entitled FORCED FAVORS depicts the British lion with drawn pistol and trade goods trying to talk his way past a Tibetan "llama." "I've come to bring you the blessings of free trade," says the lion. "I'm a protectionist. Don't want 'em," replies the llama. "Well, you've *got* to have 'em!" concludes the lion.

27. Younghusband's mission reportedly included 532 British warrant officers, the Seventh Mountain Battery of the Royal Artillery, a Maxim gun detachment from the Norfolk Regiment, half a company of the Second Sappers, six companies of the Twenty-third Sikh Pioneers, an ammunition detail, and a field hospital. Many books about Lhasa and its capture came out in the year after the invasion. Peter Hopkirk provides a list in his *Trespassers on the Roof of the World* (196). Peter Fleming's 1961 *Bayonets to Lhasa* is, as far as I know, the most complete account of the 1903 invasion.

28. Peter Hopkirk gives a good account of this climate of suspicion in British India. See *Trespassers on the Roof of the World* (159–62).

29. See Hugh Richardson's discussion of this in his 1984 *Tibet and Its History.*

30. The Chumbi valley is a small appendage of Tibet that extends south between Sikkim and Bhutan to the Jelap Pass northeast of Darjeeling. The 1893 treaty between Tibet and Britain, the one enforced by Younghusband's 1903 invasion, established a trade mart at Yatung, six miles inside Tibet in the Chumbi valley. This later became the seat for British political officers in Tibet, who were not allowed to visit Lhasa until Bell did in 1920.

31. For more detailed background on this see Melvyn Goldstein's 1989 *A History of Modern Tibet, 1913–56,* like Richardson's book a valuable source of information on British–Tibetan interaction from the Tibetan point of view, information almost universally absent from histories of Western exploration in the region.

32. All this made the Chinese, in turn, very uncomfortable about their far-flung frontiers. They were worried lest Britain gain the kind of control over Tibet that Russia enjoyed over Mongolia. Among the many steps taken by the Chinese to maintain a foothold in Tibet was to pay Tibet's "war debt" to Britain for the 1903 Younghusband invasion.

33. Bell tells his version of his work in Tibet in two books: *Tibet: Past and Present* and *Portrait of the Dalai Lama*. Bell and the thirteenth Dalai Lama had become friends in 1910 when the lama lived in exile in India (after the 1910 Chinese invasion of Tibet).

34. The usual story about the "discovery" of Mount Everest is that one day in 1852 Radharah Sikhdar, an official of the survey, pushed into Waugh's office, shouting: "Sir! I have discovered the highest mountain in the world!" Unfortunately, the story only flatters our notions of individual achievement in exploration. In actuality, the "discovery" of Everest had been a cooperative effort by many members of the survey over the course of many years.

35. This is, of course, George Mallory's famous take on why people climb mountains. In 1923 Mallory made a three-month tour of the United States, lecturing on the 1922 expedition. He made his "because it's there" comment in response to a question after one of his lectures. In his biography *George Mallory*, David Robertson asserts that some of Mallory's closest friends claimed the remark was merely a spur-of-the-moment dismissal of an all-too-common question (see chap. 9). Unsworth, however, in his history of Mount Everest, shows how Mallory frequently used the term *there* to mean "anything which had a mystical quality" (100).

36. Hinks also mentions that a member of the 1924 expedition may have been planning a private attempt on the mountain.

37. In *Through Tibet* Noel confirms Younghusband's remark that Tibetans suspected that the British were motivated by imperialist designs. "They [the Tibetans] had no conception of the idea of sport, and were certain that the reasons we gave were lies. They decided that what we were really seeking was the magical chair which the Buddhist apostle had left on the mountain" (140).

38. Unsworth reports that this profit was somewhat complicated by legal problems because the Everest Committee accidentally sold the German rights to the film *twice*.

39. For example, Stuart Hood in his "John Grierson and the Documentary Film Movement" in Curran and Porter; Paul Rotha, Sinclair Road, and Richard Griffith, in their *Documentary Film* (prefaced by Grierson), and Rachael Low in her *The History of the British Film*. All these texts, in addition to Richard Meran Barsam's *Nonfiction Film Theory and Criticism* and Kevin Brownlow's *The War, the West, and the Wilderness,* are primary sources for my discussion of film history in this chapter.

40. One of the board's most famous slogans, for example, is "Be British — Buy Empire Bananas."

41. For a thorough discussion of this see Rosaleen Smyth's "Movies and Mandarins: the Official Film and British Colonial Africa" in Curran and Porter.

42. Smyth summarizes Bell's position this way. See Curran and Porter, 129.

43. Kevin Brownlow points this out in his *The War, the West, and the Wilderness,* 46.

44. The perceived realism of *Somme* sometimes worked against its intended design. The film was actually banned in British Columbia in fear that it would hamper recruiting efforts.

45. Grierson called for a departure from "the plain (or fancy) descriptions of natural material to arrangements, re-arrangements, and creative shapings of it" (Hardy, 36). Also see Stuart Hood's essay on Grierson in Curran and Porter. Hood elaborates in this essay on what he calls Grierson's "frank admission that he was always a propagandist" (106).

46. See Brownlow's discussion of Herbert Ponting in *The War, the West, and the Wilderness*.

47. In 1913 Bailey had proved, for example, that the Tsangpo and Brahmaputra Rivers were actually the same river. As a spy in Turkistan during the Bolshevik Revolution he posed as a Russian and was put in charge of finding himself.

48. The Tibetans objected to members of the expedition conducting geological studies and impromptu geographical survey work in areas not stipulated by their Tibetan travel passes.

49. Alaska is an exception. Because they considered Alaska actively threatened by the Japanese, the U.S. military and the American Alpine Club conducted joint operations on Mount McKinley during the summer of 1942. The maneuvers were designed to test equipment and food and provide inexperienced troops with mountain warfare experience. Supported by high-altitude airdrops and establishing a battle line up much of the route, the expedition managed to place seven men on the summit.

50. Mason mentions, for example, his relief on learning that Peter Aufschnaiter, an old acquaintance since the 1929 Kanchenjunga expedition, had been detained by the British. "It was with some satisfaction," Mason writes, "that I learnt early in the war that he and his party had been interned in India and were . . . unlikely to be dropped by parachute into my back garden to be met by pitchfork defiance" (286).

EPILOGUE

1. This expedition is usually referred to as the "Andrée expedition," after its leader, Salomon August Andrée. The original log is reproduced in *Med Örnen Mot Polen* (Stockholm, 1930) and in English translation under the title *Andrée's Story* (Swedish Society, 1930). A reconstructed account of the Andrée expedition appears in George Palmer Putnam's *Andrée: The Record of a Tragic Adventure* (1930). Per Olaf Sundman novelized the events of the expedition in *The Flight of the Eagle*, from which a film version also was made.

2. Edward Mendelson makes the observation about Lawrence in his introduction to his edition of the plays of Auden and Isherwood (xxv).

3. The claim that members of the 214-member expedition reached the summit on May 25, 1960, were widely dismissed when the Chinese produced no summit photographs; they maintained that they arrived at the summit during the night. Shih Chan-chun, the leader of the expedition, also led the successful 1975 Chinese bid for the summit.

4. The preoccupation with the private situation of individuals that the play

dramatizes is perhaps best encapsulated in the exclamation of one of the play's two stranded climbers: "Holy Shit . . . we gotta get off this fuckin' mountain" (9). The small, mundane, and personal elements of mountain experience cannot be over-emphasized as a component of mountaineering narratives. Extravagant emotional responses also have a vital place in the history of the human experience of mountains. The anger and despair that Meyers details in *K2* should not be minimized as a somehow insignificant or illegitimate element of mountaineering. It is, in fact, very real. My point is simply that Meyers constructs a drama that defines the mountain experience in terms of a private existential encounter with the mountain wilderness rather than with a verbal cartography of political delineation.

Works Cited

Abbey, Edward. "The Great American Desert." In *Journey Home: Some Words in Defense of the American Southwest*. New York: Dutton, 1977.

Adams, Cyrus C. "Lieut. Peary's Arctic Work." *Geographical Journal* 2 (new series, 1893): 303–16.

Allen, John L. "An Analysis of the Exploration Process: The Lewis and Clark Expedition of 1804–6." *Geographical Review* 62 (1972): 13–39.

Ambler, Charles H. *Kenyan Communities in the Age of Imperialism: The Central Region in the Late Nineteenth Century*. New Haven, Conn.: Yale University Press, 1988.

Anderson, Dennis. "Travel Guide Finds Dangerous Destinations." *Grand Rapids (Mich.) Press*, November 30, 1997, p. A10, Lakeshore ed.

"Annual General Meeting, 25 June 1945." *Geographical Journal* 105 (1945): 230–32.

Auden, W. H., and Christopher Isherwood. *Plays and Other Dramatic Writings by W. H. Auden, 1928–38*. Edited by Edward Mendelson. Princeton, N.J.: Princeton University Press, 1988.

Back, George, Rear Adm. Collinson, and Francis Galton, eds. *Hints to Travellers*. London: Royal Geographical Society, 1865.

Bailey, J. G., to Halford Mackinder. January 20, 1900. Mackinder Papers, Oxford School of Geography, Oxford.

Baker, Alan R. H., and Mark Billinge, eds. *Period and Place: Research Methods in Historical Geography*. Cambridge: Cambridge University Press, 1982.

Baker, J. N. L. *A History of Geographical Discovery and Exploration*. Boston: Houghton, 1931.

Ball, John, ed. *Peaks, Passes, and Glaciers: A Series of Excursions by Members of the Alpine Club*. London: Longman, Green, Longman, Roberts, 1860.

Barsam, Richard Meran. *Nonfiction Film Theory and Criticism*. New York: Dutton, 1976.

Bartlett, Phil. *The Undiscovered Country*. Glasgow: Ernest Press, 1993.

Baudrillard, Jean. *America*. Translated by Chris Turner. London: Verso, 1988.

Bauer, Paul. "Nanga Parbat, 1938." *Himalayan Journal* 12 (1940): 89–106.

Bazin, André. *What Is Cinema?* Vol. 1. Berkeley: University of California Press, 1971.

Benjamin, Walter. "The Work of Art in the Age of Mechanical Reproduction." In *Illuminations,* edited by Hannah Arendt. New York: Schocken, 1969.

Benuzzi, Felice. *No Picnic on Mount Kenya.* 2d ed. London: William Kimber, 1952.

Bernbaum, Edwin. *Sacred Mountains of the World.* Berkeley: University of California Press, 1997.

Beveridge, Albert. *Congressional Record.* January 9, 1900, p. 704.

Blakeney, T. S. "The *Alpine Journal* and Its Editors, 1863–93." *Alpine Journal* 79 (1974): 166–73.

Blossom, Frederick A. *Told at the Explorers Club.* 1931. New York: Boni, 1935.

Blouet, Brian. *Halford Mackinder: A Biography.* College Station: Texas A&M University Press, 1987.

Blouet, Brian. *Sir Halford Mackinder, 1861–1947: Some New Perspectives.* Oxford: School of Geography, 1975.

Boker, George H. "Dirge for a Soldier." *Technical World Magazine* 19 (1913): 86.

Brakhage, Stan. "Metaphors on Vision." *Film Culture* 30 (1963): n.p.

Brantlinger, Patrick. "Victorians and Africans: The Genealogy of the Myth of the Dark Continent." *Critical Inquiry* 12 (1985): 166–203.

Brendon, Piers. *Winston Churchill: An Authentic Hero.* London: Methuen, 1985.

Brooks, Peter. *Reading for Plot: Design and Intention in Narrative.* New York: Vintage–Random House, 1985.

Brownlow, Kevin. *The War, the West, and the Wilderness.* New York: Knopf, 1979.

Bruce, Charles G. *The Assault on Mount Everest, 1922.* London: Edward Arnold, 1923.

Bruce, James. *Travels to Discover the Source of the Nile.* Edited by C. F. Beckinham. Edinburgh: Edinburgh University Press, 1964.

Bryant, Mark. "Everest a Year Later: The False Summit." *Outside* 22, no. 5 (1997): 57–62, 147–49.

Burke, Edmund. *Philosophical Enquiry into the Origins of Our Ideas of the Sublime and the Beautiful.* Edited by Adam Phillips. New York: Oxford University Press, 1990.

Cain, P. J., and A. G. Hopkins. "Gentlemanly Capitalism and British Expansion Overseas II: New Imperialism, 1850–1945." *Economic History Review* 40 (2d new series, 1987): 1–26.

Cameron, Ian. *To the Farthest Ends of the Earth: 150 Years of World Exploration by the Royal Geographical Society.* New York: Dutton, 1980.

Carpe, Allen. "Mount Logan." *Canadian Alpine Journal* 14 (1924): 134–36.

Carpe, Allen. "The Mount Logan Adventure." *American Alpine Journal* 2 (1933): 69–86.

Churchill, Winston. *My African Journey.* 1908. Reprint, London: Spearman, 1962.

Codrington, Robert. "A Journey from Fort Jameson to Old Chitamba and the Tanganyika Plateau." *Geographical Journal* 15 (1900): 227–34.

Conway, W. Martin. "Exploration in the Mustagh Mountains." *Geographical Journal* 2 (new series, 1893): 291–303.

Cott, Nancy. *The Grounding of Modern Feminism.* New Haven, Conn.: Yale University Press, 1987.

Coupland, R. *The Exploration of East Africa, 1856–90.* London: n.p., 1939.

Crone, G. R. *The Explorers: An Anthology of Discovery.* London: Cassell, 1962.

Culler, Jonathan. *Structuralist Poetics: Structuralism, Linguistics, and the Study of Literature.* Ithaca, N.Y.: Cornell University Press, 1976.

Curran, James, and Vincent Porter. *British Cinema History.* Totowa, N.J.: Barnes and Noble, 1983.

Dalton, A. T. "The First Ascent of Mount Garibaldi." *Canadian Alpine Journal* 1 (1908): 205–10.

Daniels, Stephen. "Arguments for a Humanistic Geography." In *The Future of Geography,* edited by R. J. Johnston. London: Methuen, 1985.

Darwin, Leonard. Unpublished review of manuscript submitted to *Geographical Journal.* Royal Geographical Society Library, London, 1889.

Day, Alan Edwin. *Discovery and Exploration: A Reference Handbook, the Old World.* New York: Saur and Bingley, 1980.

Debenham, Frank. *Discovery and Exploration: An Atlas History of Man's Journeys into the Unknown.* London: Crescent, 1960.

Deren, Maya. "Cinematography: The Creative Use of Reality." *Daedalus* 89 (1960): 150–67.

Donald, R. "Films and the Empire." *Nineteenth Century* 100 (1926): 497–510.

Dunn, R. W. *American Foreign Investment.* New York: n.p., 1926.

Eliot, Charles. *The East Africa Protectorate.* London: Edward Arnold, 1905.

Eliot, T. S. *The Complete Poems and Plays, 1909–50.* New York: Harcourt, 1971.

Facknitz, Mark. "*Through the Dark Continent*: Henry M. Stanley and the Imperialist Narrative." Unpublished essay, 1990.

Fieldhouse, D. K. *Colonialism, 1870–1945: An Introduction.* New York: St. Martin's, 1981.

Fieldhouse, D. K. *Economics and Empire, 1830–1914.* Ithaca, N.Y.: Cornell University Press, 1973.

Fieldhouse, D. K. "The New Imperialism: The Hobson–Lenin Thesis Revised." In *Imperialism and Colonialism,* edited by George H. Nadel and Perry Curtis. New York: Macmillan, 1964.

Fleming, Peter. *Bayonets to Lhasa.* Westport, Conn.: Greenwood, 1961.

Flexner, Eleanor. *Century of Struggle: The Woman's Rights Movement in the United States.* Rev. ed. Cambridge: Belknap–Harvard University Press, 1975.

Freeman, Joseph, and Scott Nearing. *Dollar Diplomacy: A Study in American Imperialism.* 1925. Reprint, New York: Monthly Review, 1966.

French, Patrick. *Younghusband.* New York: HarperCollins, 1994.

Freshfield, Douglas, and W. L. J. Wharton, eds. *Hints to Travellers.* London: Royal Geographical Society, 1893.

Fry, Paul H. "The Possession of the Sublime." *Studies in Romanticism* 26 (1987): 187–206.

Fussell, Paul. *Abroad: British Literary Traveling between the Wars.* New York: Oxford University Press, 1980.

Fussell, Paul, ed. *The Norton Book of Travel*. New York: Norton, 1987.

Galbraith, John. S. *Mackinnon and East Africa, 1878–95: A Study in the "New Imperialism."* Cambridge: Cambridge University Press, 1972.

Gallagher, John, and Ronald Robinson. "The Imperialism of Free Trade." In *Imperialism and Colonialism*, edited by George H. Nadel and Perry Curtis. New York: Macmillan, 1964.

Gardner, Arthur. *The Art and Sport of Alpine Photography*. London: Alpine Club, 1927.

George, H. B. "Monte Rosa Seen from the Simplon." *Alpine Journal* 1 (1863): 207.

Gilpin, William. *Mission of the North American People, Geographical, Social, and Political*. Rev. ed. Philadelphia: Lippincott, 1874.

Goldstein, Melvyn C. *A History of Modern Tibet, 1915–51: The Demise of the Lamaist State*. Berkeley: University of California Press, 1989.

Greenfield, Bruce Robert. "The Rhetoric of Discovery: British and American Exploration Narratives, 1760–1845, and American Renaissance Writing." Ph.D. diss., Columbia University, 1985.

Gregory, Derek. *Regional Transformation and Industrial Revolution*. London: Macmillan, 1982.

Grierson, John. "First Principles of Documentary (1932–34)." In *Nonfiction Film Theory and Criticism*, edited by Richard Meran Barsam. New York: Dutton, 1976.

Grunberger, Richard. *The Twelve-Year Reich: A Social History of Nazi Germany, 1933–45*. New York: Holt, 1971.

Hall, Robert H. "The 'Open Door' into Antarctica: An Explanation of the Hughes Doctrine." *Polar Record* 25 (1989): 137–40.

Harlow, Vincent, E. M. Chilver, and Alison Smith. *History of East Africa*. Vol. 2. Oxford: Clarendon, 1965.

Hatch, John. *The History of Britain in Africa from the Fifteenth Century to the Present*. New York: Praeger, 1969.

Healy, David. *U.S. Expansionism: The Imperialist Urge in the 1890s*. Madison: University of Wisconsin Press, 1970.

Hedin, Sven. "The Scientific Results of Dr. Sven Hedin's Last Journey." *Geographical Journal* 24 (1904): 524–45.

Hickson, J. W. A. "Psychological Aspects of Mountaineering." *American Alpine Journal* 1 (1931): 259–67.

Hinks, Arthur R., to Frederick M. Bailey, February 3, 1924, Everest Archives, Royal Geographical Society Library, London.

Hinks, Arthur R., to John B. Noel, March 18, 1922, Everest Archives, Royal Geographical Society Library, London, 1922.

Hints to Travellers. London: Royal Geographical Society, 1854, 1906.

Hobson, John Atkinson. *Imperialism: A Study*. 1902. Reprint, London: Allen and Unwin, 1938.

Hollingsworth, L. W. *Zanzibar under the Foreign Office, 1890–1913*. London: Macmillan, 1953.

Hood, Stuart. "John Grierson and the Documentary Film Movement." In *British*

Cinema History, edited by James Curran and Vincent Porter. Totowa, N.J.: Barnes and Noble, 1983.

Hopkirk, Peter. *Trespassers on the Roof of the World: The Secret Exploration of Tibet.* Los Angeles: J. P. Tarcher, 1982.

House, William. "K2 — 1938." *American Alpine Journal* 3 (1939): 219–54.

Hutcheon, Linda. *A Poetics of Postmodernism: History, Theory, Fiction.* New York: Routledge, 1988.

Ingham, Kenneth. *A History of East Africa.* Rev. ed. New York: Praeger, 1965.

"Intimate Portraits: Men and Women Who Are Doing Interesting Things." *Everybody's Magazine* 12 (1905): 213.

Irving, R. L. G. *The Romance of Mountaineering.* 1935. London: Dent, 1946.

Irving, R. L. G., ed. *The Mountain Way: An Anthology in Prose and Verse.* New York: Dutton, 1938.

Irwin, William Robert, ed. *Challenge: An Anthology of the Literature of Mountaineering.* New York: Colombia University Press, 1950.

Jenkins, J. R. "A Light Expedition to the Central Caucasus, 1937." *Alpine Journal* 50 (1938): 12–33.

Johnson, R. J. "To the Ends of the Earth." In *The Future of Geography,* edited by R. J. Johnson. London: Methuen, 1985.

Johnston, H. H. "British Interests in Eastern Equatorial Africa." *Scottish Geographical Magazine* 1 (1885): 145–57.

Johnston, H. H. *The Uganda Protectorate.* London: Hutchinson, 1904.

Jones, Chris. *Climbing in North America.* Berkeley: University of California Press, 1976.

Kennan, George. "A Journey through Southeastern Russia." *Bulletin of the American Geographical Society* 15 (1883): 289–318.

Key, Charles E. *The Story of Twentieth-Century Exploration.* New York: Knopf, 1937.

Kidd, Benjamin. *The Control of the Tropics.* New York: Macmillan, 1898.

Knowlton, Elizabeth. "Nanga Parbat, 1932." *American Alpine Journal* 2 (1933): 18–31.

Kolodny, Annette. *The Lay of the Land: Metaphor as Experience and History in American Life and Letters.* Chapel Hill: University of North Carolina Press, 1975.

Krapf, Ludvig. *Travels, Researches, and Missionary Labours . . . in East Africa.* London: Cass, 1968.

Lawrence, D. H. *Women in Love.* New York: Viking, 1920.

Longinus. "On the Sublime." In *The Great Critics: An Anthology of Literary Criticism,* 3d ed., edited by James Harry Smith and Edd Winfield Parks. New York: Norton, 1967.

Longstaff, T. G. "Six Months' Wandering in the Himalaya." *Alpine Journal* 23 (1906): 202–28.

Low, D. A. *Buganda in Modern History.* Berkeley: University of California Press, 1971.

Low, Rachael. *The History of the British Film, 1918–29.* London: Allen and Unwin, 1971.

Lowenthal, David. "Geography, Experience, and Imagination: Towards a Geographical Epistemology." In *Cultural Geography: Selected Readings,* edited by Fred E. Dohrs and Lawrence M. Sommers. New York: Crowell, 1967.

Mackinder, Halford. "The Ascent of Mount Kenya." *Alpine Journal* 20 (1900): 102–10.

Mackinder, Halford. *Britain and the British Seas.* 2d ed. Oxford: Clarendon, 1907.

Mackinder, Halford. *Democratic Ideals and Reality.* 1919. Reprint, New York: Norton, 1962.

Mackinder, Halford. *The First Ascent of Mount Kenya.* Edited by K. Michael Barbour. Athens: Ohio University Press, 1991.

Mackinder, Halford. "The Geographical Pivot of History." *Geographical Journal* 23 (1904): 421–44.

Mackinder, Halford. Journals from the Mount Kenya expedition. MSS Afr.r. 29–30. Eight journals. Rhodes House, Bodleian Library, Oxford University, England. 1899.

Mackinder, Halford. "A Journey to the Summit of Mount Kenya, British East Africa." *Geographical Journal* 15 (1900): 453–86.

Mackinder, Halford. "Mount Kenya: Being the Narrative of a Vacation Journey in Equatorial Africa." Unpublished typescript. Rhodes House, Oxford University, Oxford.

Mackinder, Halford. MS C-100. Mackinder Papers, Oxford School of Geography, Oxford.

Mackinder, Halford. "The Round World and the Winning of the Peace." *Foreign Affairs* 21, no. 4 (1943): 595–605.

Mackinder, Halford. "The Scope and Methods of Geography." *Proceedings of the Royal Geographical Society* 9 (1887): 141–60.

Markham, Clements R. "Address to the Royal Geographical Society." *Geographical Journal* 8 (1896): 1–15.

Markham, Clements R. "The Present Standpoint of Geography." *Geographical Journal* 2 (1893): 481–505.

Markham, Clements R. "Royal Geographical Society." Manuscript, ca. 1904, Royal Geographical Society Library, London.

Marsh, Zoe, ed. *East Africa through Contemporary Records.* Cambridge: Cambridge University Press, 1961.

Mason, Kenneth. *Abode of Snow: A History of Himalayan Exploration and Mountaineering.* New York: Dutton, 1955.

Mast, Gerald, and Marshall Cohen, eds. *Film Theory and Criticism: Introductory Readings.* 3d ed. New York: Oxford University Press, 1985.

"Men and Women of the Outdoor World." *Outing* 42 (1903): 620–25.

Mendelson, Edward, ed. *Plays and Other Dramatic Writings by W. H. Auden, 1928–38.* Princeton, N.J.: Princeton University Press, 1988.

Meyers, Patrick. *K2.* New York: Nelson Doubleday, 1983.

Millard, Bailey. "Where the Map Is a Blank." *Technical World Magazine* 19 (1913): 819–26, 940, 942, 944.

Miller, Charles. *The Lunatic Express: An Entertainment in Imperialism.* New York: Macmillan, 1971.

Moore, Terris. "The Minya Konka Climb." *American Alpine Journal* 2 (1933): 1–17.

Moulton, F. R. "World Gain in Polar Discoveries." *Technical World Magazine* 19 (1913): 180–86.

Muir, John. "A Perilous Night on Shasta's Summit." In *Mountaineering Essays,* edited by Richard F. Fleck. Salt Lake City: Peregrine Smith, 1984.

Nadel, George H., and Perry Curtis. *Imperialism and Colonialism.* New York: Macmillan, 1964.

Nansen, Fridtjof. *The First Crossing of Greenland.* Translated by Hubert Majendie Gepp. London: Longman, 1902.

Newby, Eric. *The Rand McNally World Atlas of Exploration.* New York: Rand McNally, 1975.

Nicolson, Marjorie Hope. *Mountain Gloom and Mountain Glory: The Development of the Aesthetics of the Infinite.* Ithaca, N.Y.: Cornell University Press, 1959.

Nietzsche, Friedrich. *Thus Spake Zarathustra.* Translated by Thomas Common. New York: Modern Library, n.d.

Noel, John Baptist. *Climbing Mount Everest.* 1922. London: National Film and Television Archive, British Film Institute.

Noel, John Baptist. *The Epic of Everest.* 1924. London: National Film and Television Archive, British Film Institute.

Noel, John Baptist. "High on Everest: How Mountaineers Keep Well and Happy and Fit for the Task of Climbing." *Asia* 26 (1926): 1078–83.

Noel, John Baptist. "Photographing 'The Epic of Everest': How the Camera Recorded Man's Battle against the Highest Mountain in the World." *Asia* 27 (1927): 366–73.

Noel, John Baptist. *The Story of Everest.* 1927. New York: Blue Ribbon, 1931.

Noel, John Baptist. *Through Tibet to Everest.* London: Edward Arnold, 1927.

Noel, John Baptist, to Charles Bruce. 1923. Everest Archives, Box 37, Royal Geographical Society Library, London.

Norton, William. *Historical Analysis in Geography.* London: Longman, 1984.

Noyce, Wilfrid. *Scholar Mountaineers: Pioneers of Parnassus.* London: Dobson, 1950.

Oliver, Roland, and G. N. Sanderson. *The Cambridge History of Africa.* Vol. 6: *From 1870 to 1905.* Cambridge: Cambridge University Press, 1985.

Olson, Charles. *The Maximus Poems.* New York: Jargon-Corinth, 1960.

Orwell, George. *Collected Essays.* London: Secker and Warburg, 1961.

Overton, J. D. "A Theory of Exploration." *Journal of Historical Geography* 7 (1981): 53–70.

Owen, W. O. "The Ascent of the Grand Teton." *Outing* 38 (1901): 302–7.

Pacione, Michael, ed. *Historical Geography: Progress and Prospect.* London: Croom Helm, 1987.

Padmore, George. *Africa: Britain's Third Empire.* London: Dobson, 1949.

Parker, Geoffrey. *Western Geopolitical Thought in the Twentieth Century.* New York: St. Martin's, 1985.

Parker, Herschel C., and Belmore Browne. "Expedition to Mount McKinley." *Canadian Alpine Journal* 3 (1911): 57–72.

Patterson, J. H. *Man-Eaters of Tsavo.* London: Macmillan, 1924.

Peck, Annie Smith. *Industrial and Commercial South America*. New York: Dutton, 1922.

Peck, Annie Smith. "Miss Peck Replies to Mrs. Workman." *Scientific American* 102 (1910): 183.

Peck, Annie Smith. "Practical Mountain Climbing." *Outing* 38 (1901): 695–700.

Peck, Annie Smith. *A Search for the Apex of America: High Mountain Climbing in Peru and Bolivia*. New York: Dodd, Mead, 1911.

Peck, Annie Smith. "The South American Tour: Why, When, and Where to Go, What to See, and How Much It Will Cost." *Independent* 74.3363 (1913): 1285–92.

Peck, Annie Smith. "A Woman in the Andes." *Harper's Monthly Magazine* 114 (1906): 3–14.

Penn, Patricia E. "Annie S. Peck." In *American Women Writers,* edited by Lina Mainiero. 4 vols. New York: Unger, 1981.

Perkins, David. *English Romantic Writers*. New York: Harcourt, 1967.

Philby, Harry St. John. *The Empty Quarter: Being a Description of the Great South Desert of Arabia Known as Rub al Khali*. New York: Holt, 1933.

Pike, Frederick B. *The Modern History of Peru*. New York: Praeger, 1967.

Pilley, Dorothy. *Climbing Days*. New York: Harcourt, 1935.

Porteous, Douglas. "Literature and Humanist Geography." *Area* 17 (1985): 117–22.

Pratt, Mary Louise. "Scratches on the Face of the Country; or, What Mr. Burrow Saw in the Land of the Bushmen." *Critical Inquiry* 12 (1985): 119–43.

"The Progress of the World." *American Review of Reviews* 37, no. 2 (1908): 131–54.

"The Real British Empire." *Saturday Review* 109 (1910): 747–48.

Relph, Edward. "An Inquiry into the Relations between Phenomenology and Geography." *Canadian Geographer* 14 (1970): 193–201.

Review of *A Search for the Apex of America*, by Annie Smith Peck. *American Review of Reviews* 44 (1911): 638.

Review of *A Search for the Apex of America*, by Annie Smith Peck. *Book Review Digest* 32 (1911): 368.

Review of *A Search for the Apex of America*, by Annie Smith Peck. *Catholic World* 94 (1911): 398.

Review of *A Search for the Apex of America*, by Annie Smith Peck. *Educational Review* 42 (1911): 428.

Review of *A Search for the Apex of America*, by Annie Smith Peck. *Literary Digest* 43 (1911): 1123.

Review of *Deutsche am Nanga Parbat*, by Fritz Bechtold. *American Alpine Journal* 2 (1935): 398–99.

Review of *Kampf um die Sextner Rotwand*, by Oswald Ebner; *Die Kämpfe in den Felsen der Tofana*, by Guido Burtscher; *Der Krieg an Kärntens Grenze 1915–17*, by Hans Lukas; *Der Krieg in der Wischberggruppe,* by Norbert Nau. *Alpine Journal* 50 (1938): 161–63.

Review of *The Mountain Way*, by R. L. G. Irving. *American Alpine Journal* 3 (1939): 344–55.

Richardson, Hugh E. *Tibet and Its History*. 2d ed. Boulder, Colo.: Shambhala, 1984.

Riding, Laura. "The Map of Places." In *Collected Poems*. London: Cassell, 1938.

Rieves, E. A., ed. *Hints to Travellers*. London: Royal Geographical Society, 1906.

Rieves, E. A., ed. *Hints to Travellers*. London: Royal Geographical Society, 1921.

Roberts, David. *Great Exploration Hoaxes*. San Francisco: Sierra Club, 1982.

Robertson, David. *George Mallory*. Bangkok: Orchid, 1999.

Robertson, Janet. *The Magnificent Mountain Women: Adventures in the Colorado Rockies*. Lincoln: University of Nebraska Press, 1990.

Robinson, Charles Turek. "Peck's Bad Girl." *Yankee* 61 (February 1997): 86–89.

Robinson, Ronald, John Gallagher, and Alice Denny. *Africa and the Victorians: The Climax of Imperialism in the Dark Continent*. New York: St. Martin's, 1961.

Roosevelt, Theodore. *The Works of Theodore Roosevelt*. Edited by Hermann Hagedorn. 24 vols. New York: n.p., 1923–26.

Ross, Ishbel. "Geography, Inc." *Scribner's Magazine* 104 (1938): 23–27, 57.

Roth, Arthur. *Eiger: Wall of Death*. New York: Norton, 1982.

Rotha, Paul, Sinclair Road, and Richard Griffith. *Documentary Film: The Use of the Film Medium to Interpret Creatively and in Social Terms the Life of the People as It Exists in Reality*. 3d ed. New York: Communication Arts, 1963.

Rugoff, Milton, ed. *The Great Travelers: A Collection of Firsthand Narratives of Wayfarers, Wanderers, and Explorers in All Parts of the World from 450 B.C. to the Present*. New York: Simon and Schuster, 1960.

Said, Edward W. "Culture and Imperialism." Lecture, September 27, 1990, University of Colorado, Boulder.

Said, Edward W. *Orientalism*. New York: Pantheon, 1978.

Schreiner, Olive. *Woman and Labor*. New York: Stokes, 1911.

Schumpeter, Joseph Alois. *Imperialism and Social Classes*. Translated by Heinz Norden. New York: Kelly, 1951.

Shackleton, Ernest. *South: The Story of Shackleton's 1914–17 Expedition*. 1919. London: William Heinemann, 1921.

Shakabpa, Tsepon. *Tibet: A Political History*. New Haven, Conn.: Yale University Press, 1967.

Shaw, Alexander. *Men of Africa*. Produced by Basil Wright. Strand, London, 1939.

Shaw, George Bernard. *Heartbreak House*. Harmondsworth, U.K.: Penguin, 1985.

Shipton, Eric. *Upon That Mountain*. London: Hodder and Stoughton, 1947.

Smythe, Frank S. *Kamet Conquered*. London: Hodder and Stoughton, 1947.

Smythe, Frank S. "Kanchenjunga, 1930." *Alpine Journal* 41 (1930): 234–43.

Soja, Edward W. *Postmodern Geographies: The Reassertion of Space in Critical Social Theory*. London: Verso, 1989.

Speare, Charles F. "A Year of Business Recovery." *American Review of Reviews* 38 (1908): 464–67.

Spender, Harold. *In Praise of Switzerland*. New York: Thomas Crowell, 1912.

Stanley, Henry Morton. "Inaugural Address." *Scottish Geographical Magazine* 1 (1885): 1–17.

Stefansson, Vilhjamur. *The Friendly Arctic*. New York: Macmillan, 1943.

Stephen, Leslie. *The Playground of Europe*. Edited by H. E. G. Tyndale. Oxford: Basil Blackwell, 1936.

Stevens, Wallace. *The Necessary Angel: Essays on Reality and the Imagination*. New York: Vintage, 1951.

Stowe, W. W. "The Nineteenth-Century American Travel Narrative." Paper presented at Society for the Study of Narrative Literature Conference, April 1990, New Orleans.

Strumia, M. M. "Moods of the Mountains and Climbers." *American Alpine Journal* 1 (1929): 31–39.

Strutt, Edward. "Valedictory Address." *Alpine Journal* 50 (1938): 1–11.

Stuck, Hudson. *The Ascent of Denali: A Narrative of the First Complete Ascent of the Highest Peak in North America*. 1914. Reprint, Lincoln: University of Nebraska Press, 1989.

Styles, Showell. *On Top of the World: An Illustrated History of Mountaineering and Mountaineers*. New York: Macmillan, 1967.

Swedish Society for Anthropology and Geography, ed. *Andrée's Story: The Complete Record of His Polar Flight, 1897*. New York: Viking, 1930.

Sykes, Percy. *A History of Exploration from the Earliest Times to the Present Day*. 2d ed. London: Routledge, 1935.

Tignor, Robert. *The Colonial Transformation of Kenya: The Kamba, Kikuyu, and Maasai from 1906 to 1939*. Princeton, N.J.: Princeton University Press, 1976.

Tilman, Harold W. "The Ascent of Nanda Devi." *Himalayan Journal* 9 (1937): 21–37.

Tilman, Harold W. *Mount Everest, 1938*. Cambridge: Cambridge University Press, 1948.

Townsend, Mary. "Commercial and Colonial Policies of Imperial Germany." In *Imperialism and Colonialism*, edited by George H. Nadel and Perry Curtis. New York: Macmillan, 1964.

Tuan, Yi-Fu. "Geography, Phenomenology, and the Study of Human Nature." *Canadian Geographer* 15 (1971): 181–92.

Tuan, Yi-Fu. "Geopiety: A Theme in Man's Attachment to Nature and to Place." In *Geographies of the Mind: Essays in Historical Geography in Honor of John Kirkland Wright*, edited by David Lowenthal and Martyn J. Bowden. New York: Oxford University Press, 1976.

Tuan, Yi-Fu. *Landscapes of Fear*. Minneapolis: University of Minnesota Press, 1979.

Turner, Samuel. *My Climbing Adventures in Four Continents*. London: Unwin, 1911.

Ullman, James Ramsey. *The Age of Mountaineering*. Philadelphia: Lippincott, 1964.

Ullman, James Ramsey. *High Conquest: The Story of Mountaineering*. Philadelphia: Lippincott, 1941.

Underhill, Miriam. *Give Me the Hills*. London: Methuen, 1956.

Unsworth, Walt. *Everest: A Mountaineering History*. Boston: Houghton, 1981.

U.S. House. H. Doc. 1, 58th Cong., 3d sess., 1905.

Vause, Laurence Mikel. *On Mountains and Mountaineers.* La Crescenta, Calif.: Mountain N'Air Books, 1993.

Vause, Laurence Mikel. "Voices of Madmen: Essays on Mountains and Mountaineering." Ph.D. diss., Bowling Green State University, Bowling Green, Ohio, 1986.

Verner, S. P. "Effective Occupation of Undeveloped Lands." *Bulletin of the American Geographical Society* 42 (1910): 831–40.

Waddington, Mary King. "In the Dolomites." *Scribner's Magazine* 46 (1900): 88–103.

Walmsley, D. J. "Positivism and Phenomenology in Human Geography." *Canadian Geographer* 18 (1974): 95–107.

Watson, C. M. Unpublished review of manuscript submitted to *Geographical Journal*, Royal Geographical Society, London, 1893.

Watt, Rachel. *In the Heart of Savagedom.* 3d ed. London: n.p., 1920.

Williams, Raymond. "British Film History: New Perspectives." In *British Cinema History,* edited by James Curran and Vincent Porter. Totowa, N.J.: Barnes and Noble, 1983.

Wlecke, Albert O. *Wordsworth and the Sublime.* Berkeley: University of California Press, 1973.

Wordsworth, William. *The Prelude, 1799, 1805, 1850.* Edited by Jonathan Wordsworth, M. H. Abrams, and Stephen Gill. New York: Norton, 1979.

Workman, Fanny Hunter, and William Hunter Workman. *Two Summers in the Ice-Wilds of Eastern Karakoram.* London: T. Fisher Unwin, 1917.

Wright, John K. "Terrae Incognitae: The Place of the Imagination in Geography." *Annals of the Association of American Geographers* 37 (1947): 1–15.

Younghusband, Francis. *The Epic of Mount Everest.* New York: Longmans, Green, 1926.

Younghusband, Francis. "The Expedition to Western Tibet." *Geographical Journal* 25 (1905): 295–96.

Younghusband, Francis. "The Geographical Results of the Tibetan Mission." *Geographical Journal* 25 (1905): 482–98.

Index

Abbey, Edward, 10
Abominable Snowman, 147
Abruzzi, duca d' (Luigi Amedeo), 26, 27, 68, 135
Aconcagua (Peru), 97–98, 133
Adler, Judith, 13
adventure: exploration and mountaineering as, 24, 32, 64, 117, 125, 143, 170, 177, 183, 186
Afghanistan, 156–58
Africa: African people in, 84–85, 88–89, 90–91, 93–94; British image in, 160; British interests in, 55, 70–81, 89, 90–91, 168; Churchill's trip in, 52, 53; early explorations of, 17–20, 24, 33, 34, 67–69, 120–21; and economic issues, 74–76; famine and disease in, 59, 60, 61–62, 85–88, 89–91, 94, 105; filmmaking about, 168; as focus of European exploration, 55; and geographical writing, 43; imperialism in, 14, 67, 70–81, 84, 85, 89, 90–91, 93–94; Mackinder's comparison of England and, 77; Mackinder's views about, 72, 74, 83–85; mountaineering in, 26; and politics, 73–81, 89, 93–94; railroad in, 59, 64–65, 76–81, 88, 90–91, 92; spheres of influence in, 119; as "unnatural home" for Europeans, 72. *See also* Mount Kenya; *specific explorer or nation*
Agassiz, Jean Louis Rodolphe, 12
Alaska, 26
Algarsson–Worsley British Arctic Expedition, 169

Alpine Club, 12, 26, 28, 31, 32, 139, 140, 160, 162, 166–67, 170. *See also* American Alpine Club
Alpine Guide, 11
Alpine Journal: first issues of, 11, 12, 31; Godley's essay in, 8–9; Jenkins's narrative in, 19–20; Longstaff's essay in, 3, 4; Mackinder's writings in, 53; and mountaineering as exploration, 26–27; and nationalization of mountaineering, 49, 50; style of, 31, 32
Alps, 7, 9, 11, 12, 21, 22, 23, 24, 26, 32, 49, 97, 103, 165, 180
American Alpine Club, 112, 122, 133
American Federation of Labor, 130
American Geographical Society Bulletin, 32
American Review of Reviews, 46, 117, 121
Amundsen, Roald, 23
ancient world, 9, 67–68
Andes Mountains, 24, 25, 49, 97, 107. *See also specific mountain*
Antarctica, 20–21, 23, 33, 36–37, 38, 165, 169
Appalachian Mountain Club, 133
Arctic, 20, 22, 23, 24, 36, 122, 132, 136, 149, 169, 175–76, 177–78
Arctic Club of America, 33
Armstrong, Neil, 30
Asia: British interests in, 15, 78–79, 156–63, 167, 168, 171, 172–73; British public's image of, 171; early discussions about mountaineering in, 26; expansion of exploration in, 120–21; "Great Game" for, 157, 163; imperialism in, 15,